Titanic Calls SOS

All material contained herein is
Copyright © Stanisław Bednarz,
Dr Miloš Jesenský & Robert K. Leśniakiewicz
2025 All rights reserved.
***

Translated and published in English with permission.
***

Paperback ISBN: 979-8-9922051-0-7
ePub ISBN: 979-82308388-4-5
***

Written by Stanisław Bednarz,
Dr Miloš Jesenský & Robert K. Leśniakiewicz
Published by Royal Hawaiian Press
Cover art by Tyrone Roshantha
Translated by Rafal Stachowsky
Publishing Assistance: Dorota Reszke
***

For more works by this author, please visit:
WWW.ROYALHAWAIIANPRESS.COM
***

Version Number 1.00

Titanic Calls SOS

Stanisław Bednarz

Miloš Jesenský

Robert Leśniakiewicz

Table Of Contents

This is what it looked like – or instead of an introduction — 5

Chapter 1. 10 versions of the causes of the "Titanic" disaster — 11

Chapter 2. RMS "Titanic" = titanic scam? — 18

Chapter 3. The Mystery of the "Titanic" and the Time — 59

Chapter 4. Torpedoes for the "Titanic" — 64

Chapter 5. RMS "Titanic" vs. the aurora borealis? — 74

Chapter 6. Are the passengers of the "Titanic" lost in time? — 81

Chapter 7. The princess who sank the "Titanic" — 88

Chapter 8. Revenge of the mummy — 103

Chapter 9. Interterrans, Water People, etc. — 108

Chapter 10. Tragedy of the DSV "Titan" — 134

Chapter 11. MS "Jan Heweliusz" – Polish "Titanic" — 143

Chapter 12. MS "Estonia" – The modern "Titanic" of the Baltic Sea — 153

Chapter 13. Slovaks and Czechs on the "Titanic" — 187

Chapter 14. The criminal Operation Hannibal — 207

Chapter 15. The disaster of the "Titanic" of the heavens — 243

Chapter 16. Titanic – Assassination or conspiracy? — 262

Chapter 17. Impossible meetings — 269

Chapter 18. A Leap in Time? — 302

This is what it looked like
– or instead of an introduction

And on that night, the sky was so starry. Early on the night of April 15, 1912, on her maiden voyage between Southampton and New York, the RMS "Titanic" – a British transatlantic liner chafed against an iceberg and sank. At the time of its launch it was the second largest steam passenger ship in the world after the twin "Olympic". The entire hull was divided into 16 separate compartments with a watertight bulkhead closure system. Public opinion considered the ship unsinkable. This opinion was spread by the company that manufactured the watertight bulkheads. The problem was the lifeboats. After all, there were only 20 lifeboats that could accommodate only 1,100 people, which is half the number of people.

The ship surpassed any other vessel in decor and luxury. Promptly, at noon on April 10, 1912, the ship set sail. On the evening of April 14, 1912, the sea temperature was close to zero degrees Celsius and the moon was new.

Iceberg warnings had been received for the past few days. At 11:40 p.m. NDT, sailors from the crow's nest, spotted a black outline – an iceberg – cut off in the starry sky in front of the ship. Approximately 37 seconds elapsed between the sighting of the iceberg and the collision.

From the very beginning, the mechanism of the hull damage was controversial. Initially, the "tear" theory was widely accepted, which stated that the sharp edges of the ice tore the ship's plating.

Currently, the "defective rivets" theory is in effect. During the collision with the iceberg, the plating sheets withstood but, at the same time, the rivets connecting them deteriorated. As a result, gaps formed between the sheets, through which water entered the hull. Initially, no one realized the seriousness of the situation. Captain Edward Smith and the ship's designer immediately went to inspect the ship. When they returned on board, it was determined that the ship would sink in about an hour and a half. It was only forty-five minutes after the collision that the lifeboats were ordered to be prepared and women and children placed in them...

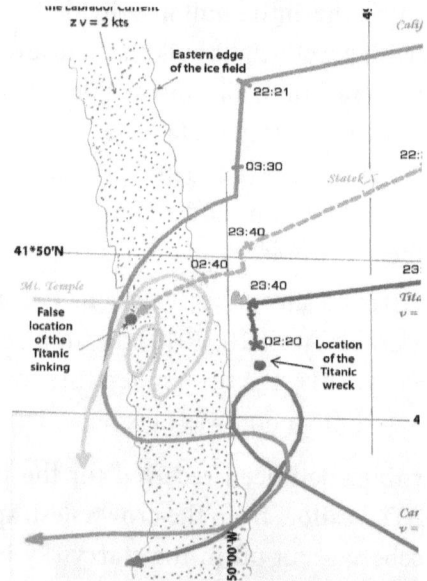

Indicative map of the Titanic tragedy basin
(drawing by the author)

On the captain's orders, Wallace Hartley's orchestra began to play – this was to prevent panic. Only a few people knew about the fact that there was no room in the lifeboats for half the people. Symptoms of panic could only be seen between one and two o'clock in the morning. By then, the unnatural inclination of the ship was already visible to the naked eye. The ship that was closest and responded to the call was the Carpathia, which was 58 nautical miles (about 4 hours) from the Titanic. The last two lifeboats were launched at 02:10 a.m. NDT.

A here's what a certain anonymous person writes on Facebook:

"When the Titanic sank, there were three ships nearby.

The first was called Sampson.

It was only seven miles away and saw the Titanic's distress signals. However, it was engaged in illegal seal hunting. Fearing they might get caught, the crew turned their ship in the opposite direction and fled.

Think about that ship. You will see that many of us are like it – people who only care about themselves, indifferent to the struggles of others. The people on that ship were no different.

The second ship was the Californian.

It was just fourteen miles further away, surrounded by dense ice. The captain saw the Titanic's desperate distress signals but decided that the conditions were unfavorable and it was too dark. Instead of taking action, he chose to sleep, planning to check the situation in the morning. The crew reassured themselves, thinking, "It's probably nothing serious."

That ship reflects the mindset of many people – those who believe that nothing can be done in a crisis but can act when conditions are more favorable.

The last ship was the Carpathia.

In fact, it was sailing in the opposite direction and was about fifty-eight miles away when its crew picked up the Titanic's distress signals. The captain fell to his knees on deck, praying to God for guidance. Then, with full power, they broke through the ice and rushed towards the Titanic.

Thanks to the decision of that ship, 705 Titanic passengers survived.

These ships serve as a metaphor for different attitudes that can be taken in the face of a crisis: avoiding responsibility, indifference, and heroic, selfless actions. The story of the Carpathia shows that those who act selflessly in times of crisis leave a lasting mark in human hearts.

History may not always remember them, but their names will live on in stories passed down from generation to generation.

The RMS Carpathia sank on July 17, 1918, off the coast of Ireland after being torpedoed by the German U-Boat SM U-55. 157 passengers were rescued by HMS Snowdrop the following day."

The ship kept taking on water, reaching a trim of more than 30 degrees. All parts of the upper deck began to slide off, causing people to slide down the planks into the ocean. At 2 a.m., the power generator stopped working – the ship was covered in darkness. At 02:17 a.m., the stern broke away from the forward section in front of the third funnel. The bow part of the ship, which had taken on water, immediately went to the bottom.

The stern floated for a few more moments. It disappeared underwater at 02:20 a.m. NDT on April 15, 1912.

The shipwreck settled to the bottom of the Atlantic, at a depth of about 4,000 meters. It was the first ship collision with an iceberg since 1870.

The last photo of the Titanic after leaving Queenstown, Ireland (Wikipedia)

The survivors, who were rescued in lifeboats, were taken aboard the Carpathia, at 04:00 a.m. NDT. Of the 2,228 passengers and crew, more than 1,500 died. Only about 730 survived the disaster. There was room for more than 1,100 people in the

Titanic's boats, but many of them were partially empty... Only in the later stages of the accident did the boats depart full...

The loss of life also included victims of panic during the escape. Some men tried to break into the lifeboats before the women, among others, line director Bruce Ismay sneaked in secretly. Officers shot 13 such men.

The wreck of the Titanic was found on September 1, 1985 at a depth of 3,802 meters. Between 1987 and 2004, more than 5,500 items were recovered from the wreck. The last person to remember the disaster was Lillian Asplund, an American who was 5 years old at the time of the tragedy, and died on May 6, 2006.

There are alternative theories. One of them is that the sinking was carefully prepared and planned in order to extort a gigantic compensation. In addition, there are a number of theories that place the cause of the ship's sinking in the curse of the transported mummy, mystifications, embezzlements and unsupported factual connections of numbers and events. Every disaster as we know grows with irrational legends. There are always parades of icebergs near Newfoundland in mid–April, this was the case both in 1912 and in 2017, as reported in the press a few days ago. And it is about these alternative theories that this book is about.

And we'll start with...

Chapter 1
10 VERSIONS OF THE CAUSES OF THE "TITANIC" DISASTER

Oleg Gorosov, in the pages of the magazine „Tajny XX wieka" (Secret 20th Century) No. 15/2012, pp.22–23, gave 10 hypotheses about what caused the Titanic tragedy. Here is what he writes.

***

Millionaire Alfred Vanderbilt should have been one of the Titanic's passengers, well, but he for some reason abandoned the trip. In 1915 he was aboard the liner RMS Lusitania, which sank after being torpedoed by the Germans...

April 14 2012 marked the 100th anniversary of the disaster of the famed ocean liner RMS Titanic, during which more than 1,500 people died. Over the past century, a multitude of hypotheses have been published as to the causes of this astounding event: from the obvious to the most unbelievable. I intend to remind the Reader of the most famous of these, and thus:

Hypothesis No. 1 – The Moon is the culprit!

As is well known, the Titanic sank because it ran into an iceberg. But to this day it remains unclear why this concentration of floating ice was in the ship's path. Scientists seismologists from the University of Texas have tried to find the answer to this question. According to them, the cause of the tragedy was the Moon, which approached the Earth on January 4, 1912 at an incredibly short distance. Similar approaches happen once every 1,400 years. As a result, there were very high tides and currents that change the course of the icebergs moving off the coast of Canada, and so on April 14 they may have been on the course of the liner.

Hypothesis No. 2 – In pursuit of the Blue Riband

The first hypothesis does not at all exclude the second possibility of the ship's demise. Titanic's captain – Edward John Smith knew about the ice in front, after all he was warned more than once about this danger from other ships, but he did not change course anyway. Why? It is quite possible that he wanted to win the Blue Riband on his very first voyage – it was the most prestigious award he could get for the fastest way across the Atlantic.

The ships of the RMS Olympic class, one of which was also Titanic, were owned by the White Star Line company, whose competitors were ships of the Cunard Line company. The latter's liner, the RMS Mauretania, held the speed record between Europe and North America from 1907. It developed an average speed of 26 kts/48.1 km/h, Titanic around 25 kts/46.3 km/h. Thus, Captain E. J. Smith had some chance of snatching the Blue Ribbon of the Atlantic from Mauritania. And perhaps that is why, disregarding the danger, he went for such a risk.

Hypothesis No. 3 – Observers failed to notice

But even disregarding the above, the Titanic could have avoided the collision if the observers on the crow's nest had spotted the iceberg lying on their course in time. And to observe it they simply could not, because they did not have binoculars. So it worked out that before the voyage itself, White Star Line management decided to change the senior officer (Chief Officer), to be replaced by Henry Wilde, who was experienced in navigating huge liners. But the transferring senior officer, David Blair, forgot to give Wilde the keys to the safe where the binoculars[1] were kept. Thus, the observers could only rely on their eyes...

Hypothesis No. 4 – "Black" iceberg

In principle, the cause of the disaster could have been such an iceberg, which could not be spotted even by the strongest binoculars. As you know, ice is white and perfectly visible at great distances. However, this iceberg could have been a so-called "black" iceberg – overturned, so that its dark underwater part was visible on the surface. The night was moonless, further reducing visibility, and the weather was windless, so the sailors could not observe the waves crashing against the iceberg, which would have been visible from a greater distance that would have made it possible to perform an evasive maneuver or stop the ship.

Hypothesis No. 5 – "Left" means "right".

And anyway, when observer on the crow's nest sailor Frederick Fleet spotted an iceberg 450 meters away, Titanic still had

---

[1]. In another version of the Legend of the Titanic, binoculars for the watchers from the crow's nest were not on board at all and Captain Smith decided to buy some in New York.

a chance to avoid a collision.[2] Fleet immediately reported the danger to the bridge. The command sounded – "Rudder full RIGHT!", but the ship turned the opposite way – LEFT.[3] There was a crash and the sound of ripping plating. As Second Officer Charles Lightoller later recalled, the helmsman turned the wheel not in the direction he should have. The thing is, the command "full right" actually means turning the ship to the left: the ship turns starboard forward, and the bow goes to the left. Apparently, the panicked helmsman interpreted the command literally...

Hypothesis No. 6 – Builder's fault

Statistically speaking, in the 20 years leading up to the Titanic disaster, collisions with icebergs happened more than once, but only one ship went to the bottom, and even in this one case there were no casualties. So why did the Titanic, which was advertised as unsinkable, not survive a similar collision? It is possible that the full blame for this lies with its designer. In 1994, a piece of the ship's plating was lifted from the ocean floor and subjected to laboratory analysis. It turned out that steel with a large admixture of phosphorus was used to build the ship, making it very brittle at low temperatures. If the hull had been made of high–quality steel, it would have bent when hitting the ice, but not let go. So the damage would have turned out to be minimal.

Hypothesis No. 7 – Another ship sank

Perhaps the Titanic was deliberately set out to meet an iceberg? It turns out that there is such a hypothesis as well! The thing is

---

2. The iceberg was spotted from the Titanic's crow's nest from a distance of about 400 m, while the ship's stopping distance was 777 m or even 7,770 m (sources state it variously!), as measured during sea trials – these chances are unlikely to have been there... – translator's note.

3. And as a result of which it hit the ice spur RIGHT side up – translator's note.

that on September 20, 1911, the RMS Olympic collided with the cruiser USS Hawke[4]. The White Star Line company, which was in financial trouble at the time, decided to improve its position with insurance. But the liner was unharmed in this collision and the compensation was not paid. So the company decided on a scam: the hastily patched up Olympic was renamed Titanic and vice-versa, and as Titanic sailed into the zone of the ice fields in order to obtain there such damage for which the insurance companies would pay fair compensation. It is clear that the management of White Star Line did not take into account the fact that the iceberg would let Titanic sink...

We will return to this topic in the following chapters.

Hypothesis No. 8 – Fire on board

On more than one occasion, a version has appeared that the iceberg was not the cause of the sinking of the ocean liner. Thus, for example, British researcher Ray Boston, who has been investigating disasters for 20 years, came to the conclusion that the real cause of the ship's sinking was a fire. Twelve days before the disaster, coal spontaneously ignited in its CB-5 coal bunker[5]. This fire could not be fully extinguished. But White Star Line's management did not want to interrupt the ship's highly profitable maiden voyage, hoping that the fire would extinguish itself due to lack of oxygen. Otherwise, the coal bunkers in New York would have had to be unloaded and the coal put out with the help of the fire department. Besides, there was a danger that the ship would explode in the middle of the ocean.

Perhaps for this reason, even at the beginning of the voyage, when the Titanic made a stop in the Irish port of Queenstown

---

4. In fact, it was the HMS Hawke – translator's note.
5. The coal on the ship constitutes the fuel supply for the boilers – translator's note.

(today's Cork), a crew member named John Coffie – a stoker – deserted the ship. White Star Line owner John P. Morgan, who was on the passenger list, was also aware of the possibility of an explosion aboard the ship, but 24 hours before the ship's departure he abandoned the voyage, explaining that he was unwell. This would explain why Captain Smith tried to sail to New York as quickly as possible, ignoring reports of icebergs. According to Ray Boston's views, the Titanic broke in two just where the fire occurred – that's where the boiler exploded. And the collision with the iceberg was merely an accidental incident.

Hypothesis No. 9 – German torpedo

Many surviving Titanic passengers claimed to have heard an explosion after the Titanic hit the iceberg. This gave rise to speculation that it was not a boiler explosion, but that a German torpedo hit the ship! Less than two years remained until the start of World War I. At that time, the commander of the German navy, Adm. Alfred von Tirpitz, was sharply expanding the fleet, placing particular emphasis on the construction of submarines calculating that they would be the main weapons in the fight against the British Empire. Thus, the Titanic could have become a shield for the German submarine. Firstly, because on this liner von Tirpitz could test the prowess of his ships, and secondly, by torpedoing the Titanic he finally defined his potential enemy. During the war, the British converted all passenger ships into troop carriers or hospital ships. Thus, for example, the Mauretania mentioned here was used as a war transport ship.

We will also tell about this in the following chapters.

Hypothesis No. 10 – Pharaoh's curse

Well, here's another, unfortunately, completely irrational version of the disaster: Titanic was sunk by an Egyptian mummy!

In the 1880s, during excavations near Cairo, the mummy of the priestess Amen–Otu, who lived during the reign of Pharaoh Amenhotep IV Akhenaten, was found. It was on display in the British Museum until 1912, but an American collector bought it. The priceless artifact was not transported in the cargo hold, but was placed directly on the captain's bridge. The story goes that above the mummy's head was a statue of the god Osiris with the inscription: Rise from the dust and destroy anyone who stands in your way. Perhaps this ancient prophecy brought misery to the Titanic...?

***

Snooping around the Internet, I found some more interesting facts about the Titanic:
- In 1912, a 1st class ticket on the Titanic cost more than US$4,000 or more than US$100,000 in today's money;
- During the construction of the ship there were 246 accidents and 2 deaths;
- There were 4 chimneys on the ship, one of which (the fourth one) was a dummy for greater aesthetics and appearance;
- There were a minimum of a dozen Poles on board the Titanic;
- The water temperature at the time of the sinking was about -2°C;
- The ship took as long as 160 minutes to fully sink;
- The ship's bow hit the ocean floor at 80 km/h[6].

---

6. Source: https://www.facebook.com/reel/563211936626177

Chapter 2
RMS "Titanic" = titanic scam?

Our Japanese friend Mr. Kiyoshi Amamiya sent us the hypothesis of a giant swindle by White Star Line executives this way, and he gives a weighty argumentation proving in favor of the hypothesis.

***

I recently watched a report on TV about the latest data regarding the RMS Titanic disaster. I noted down its main theses in my mind, and so:
1. The Titanic was sunk deliberately
2. But it was not the Titanic that sank, because it was the Olympic
3. Both ships were built according to identical plans
4. But they differed only in the corridors on the sides. There were none on the Titanic
5. There were corridors on the Titanic lying on the ocean floor
6. So the sunken ship does not match the Titanic plan
7. The Olympic was sunk earlier
8. The Company took a huge compensation for the Olympic
9. The Olympic sailed as the Titanic
10. The ship hit the iceberg with its entire length at full travel speed.
11. Survivors who sailed to N.Y. were different from those on the passenger list.

Looking for confirmation, I started searching the Internet. I found one page titled. "The Life and Mystery of 1st Officer William Murdoch." That's where it was laid out in detail, and I'm sending it to you. As you can see, the Conspiracy Theory of History did not miss this tragedy as well. And here are the main theses from the referenced website:

1. Titanic's insurance was increased 5 days before it went to sea;
2. The damage from the collision between RMS Olympic and HMS Hawke was much greater and visible;
3. The Olympic survived more severe damage;
4. The Olympic had a two-stage tilt just like the Titanic;
5. Only a limited number of alterations were needed to launch the ship;
6. Differences in tonnage;
7. "Olympic's accommodations";
8. If uninsured, the inclusion of the ship may have saved the company;
9. Differences on Titanic's name board;
10. Difference in the number of Titanic portholes;
11. Difference in the B deck windows on the Titanic;
12. Difference in the plating joints on the side of the Titanic;
13. Discolored plating on Titanic;
14. The Olympics' wheelhouse was not bent;
15. The ship's name plate was attached with rivets and not welded;
16. There were no publications about the Titanic;
17. The Titanic's bulkheads were intentionally reduced;
18. The Titanic's sea trials were much shorter than Olympic's;
19. The Titanic was not opened to the press and public inspection;
20. J. P. Morgan and 50 other passengers abandoned the *voyage*;

21. Some crew members refused to sail the Titanic;
22. The Titanic's lifeboats bore the designation "RMS Olympic."
23. The Titanic was under full steam, but did not reach top speed;
24. The Titanic did not collide with an iceberg at all;
25. The ice on its deck did not come from an iceberg;
26. Many ships stood around it because of a strike in the coal mines;
27. The bottom valves were opened to hasten the sinking of the ship;
28. On the SS Californian it was thought that it was not a distress call but a rendezvous;
29. The SS Californian had wool sweaters and blankets on board;
30. The survivors on Deck B saw lifeboats lowered from above;
31. Passengers said there was a promenade instead of cabins;
32. The floor linoleum was covered with carpets;
33. The Titanic broke apart in the exact same place that HMS Hawke hit;
34. The rescued crewmen signed a loyalty of silence;
35. Harold Sanderson repeatedly referred to the Titanic as the Olympic;
36. A Titanic crew member on his deathbed admitted the existence of a conspiracy;
37. The number 401 on the carpentry of the Olympic;
38. The name Olympic on the wreck;
39. No. 401: Titanic's propeller is on the Olympic;
40. White paint on the wreck;
41. Marbles in the Conference Room;

REASONING:

Re. 1. Titanic's insurance was raised 5 days before the sailing. As a result of this, J. P. Morgan received $12.5 million US insurance paid out by Lloyd Maritime Insurance. Today, this amounts to $160 million, far more than it would have cost to recover it or if he had sold or scrapped it.

The theory is that the ship was deliberately sunk in order to obtain assurance, which money helped save White Star Line from bankruptcy. However, as already proven (in this section) Titanic was in fact insured for only $2.5 million US dollars.

As if someone countered this, Titanic's insurance was allegedly raised by J. P. Morgan from US$5 million to US$12.5 million five days before the ship left port for the fateful voyage. Some claim that Lloyd's paid out US$12,500,000, but this should be approached with caution, for there is no record of any such thing in Lloyd's records. There is no evidence whatsoever that insurance was raised – let alone to more than double its value, which immediately raises suspicions. [Chairman] Bruce Ismay was questioned by the U.S. Senate Committee in April 1912 and testified that the value of the Titanic was US$7.5 million, a figure verified by The New York Times and The Specrator (at $8 million), while it was insured for $5 million – as reported by the Senate Inquiry, The New York Times and Lloyds. If the Titanic had indeed been insured last minute for $12.5 million – as conspiracy theorists claim – that would have immediately awakened all the alarm bells in the brains of the insurers, especially since in all public records it stood like a bull that the value of the Titanic was US$7.5 million? Quite simply Titanic was insured, and the main reason for this was that White Star Line was currently insuring its ships.

Re. 2 The damage to the Olympic after the collision with HMS Hawke was more apparent. Another key component of the conspiracy theory is the claim that the damage after the collision with HMS Hawke was more significant than believed. However, as it turned out the damage to Olympic after the collision with HMS Hawke did not exceed US$125,000 and this fact has been independently verified.

Mark Chirnside sums it up this way:

Olympic was sufficiently damaged for the voyage to be canceled. Its two largest watertight compartments were flooded, the hull plating was torn, and the starboard propeller was damaged. Photos after the collision show the entire ship all the way to the stern... To my eyes, it is very strange that the damage was more severe than admitted at the time. Hearings conducted after the collision between the Olympic and Hawke included a list of the damage to the Olympic that was compiled by White Star Line and the Royal Navy, and it says this, that the Hawke's bow penetrated 8 ft/2.6 m into the Olympic's hull. (This was written about in a book by Dan van der Vat and Robin Gardiner titled, "The Riddle of the Titanic. "Riddle of the Titanic," 1995, p. 21) I believe it is impossible for the Olympic's keel to have been damaged, as Robin Gardnier speculated in his book titled. "Titanic: The Ship That Never Sank?" And there is no evidence, as I believe the damage was more severe than admitted – however, this is Gardnier's speculation.

Re. 3 RMS Olympic survived too long for a damaged ship. The question is: how could a ship with a damaged keel serve for 24 years (1911–1935) without a complete overhaul?

This line is represented by those who believe that the Olympic's keel was damaged, although there is no evidence of this – as is said in the previous point. This fact that the RMS Olympic sailed for 24 years without a major overhaul is easy to explain, simply the damage was repaired. NB, although named Old Reliable, its 24-year service was not without further incidents, and the ship had several other collisions, including a collision with the Nantucket Lightship LV-117, which caused the lighthouse keeper to fish and sink, resulting in 11 casualties from the lighthouse keeper's crew.

Re. 4 RMS Olympic had a 2-degree heel to starboard, just like Titanic. The damage to the Olympic below the waterline, it was said, was more severe, while the superstructure was dislocated. The damaged keel gave the ship a permanent two-degree tilt to port, and the ship's designers ruled that this could not be corrected without completely rebuilding half the ship. Titanic had a slight but permanent tilt to the port side, as stated by Lawrence Beesley and – several other surviving passengers.

It is true that the tilt to starboard was observed by passengers Lawrence Beesley (in "The Loss of the S.S. Titanic") and Norman Chambers (in "US Inquiry"). Photographs of the Titanic taken as it left Southampton also show a slight tilt to the port side.

However, this is not usual for a modern ship, and could be caused by several factors. In the case of Titanic, it was caused by inaccurate ballasting – too much ballast on the port side and not enough on the starboard side. Using this as evidence in the case of RMS Olympic leads to an extreme conclusion, especially when there is no supporting evidence of some kind. We know from the previous point that if it goes to the damage of the Olympic, nothing is said about the curved keel.

This is confirmed by Titanic researcher Ioannis Georgiu, who adds:

If it is true that a few survivors like Beesley and Chambers spoke of a heeled keel, this was taken out of context referring to the events of April 14. That heel was the result of coal being consumed and the aft bunker being emptied – first CB 6 and then CB 5... That coal bunker was on the starboard side and it was emptied. Certainly the W bunker was emptied and that is what the surviving survivors noticed[7].

Re. 5 Only a limited amount of change was needed to launch the ship. All that was needed to launch the ship was to change all the parts bearing the ship's name – so the plaques bearing the ship's name, the ship's bell, changing the name on the lifebelts and lifeboats, and on all the other plaques and bronze plates bearing the ship's name in the interiors of the Olympic and Titanic.

The above statement shows total ignorance not only about the Olympic and Titanic, but about ships in general and their construction. The fact of the matter is that there were many differences between the two ships that would require considerable work. The list of differences has already been discussed above. Not to mention the difficulty in changing the plating on the bow and stern of both vessels, which bore the names of the ships: these names were not painted on the plates, but were cut into the metal plates and filled in with paint.

Re. 6. Differences in tonnage. RMS Olympic – as recorded – had a tonnage of approx. 45,000 GRT, while Titanic's tonnage was 46,000 GRT. Obviously, adding 1,000 lbs/~490 kg[8] to Titanic made Titanic weigh 46,000 tons, which makes no sense. There is a possibility that it was Olympic that had those 1,000 lbs added to match Titanic.

---

7. The coal bunkers emptied quickly - just remember that Titanic burned 650 tons of coal for every 24 hours, ergo it was 2,600 tons lighter at its destination point.
8. Of course, it was not pounds but tons.

Most records agree that the RMS Olympic in 1911–1912 weighed those 45,324 tons, while its newer sister-ship reached 46,328 tons. Since they had the same dimensions, the differences were simply due to the configuration of interior spaces, such as the Titanic's A Deck promenade, which was blinded by a steel plate with sliding windows to create additional shelter, and the Titanic's B Deck promenade, which was reduced in its dimensions, and the resulting space was used to create additional cabins and public rooms – including two luxury cabins with private promenades. These differences mean that Titanic had a slightly higher gross tonnage.

However, it appears that conspiracy theorists are making a mathematical mistake and labeling this as "sure proof." Their reasoning goes as follows:

You can't add a thousand tons to a 46,000-ton ship and still have a 46,000-ton ship. The vessel that left Southampton on 10.IV.1912 was a mere 45,000-ton ship that had 1,000 GRT added at the last minute to its enclosed areas of Deck B and the public rooms on Deck A.

Their mistake is simple: the Titanic's tonnage at the time was the same as the Olympic at 45,324 GRT, however, the 1,000-ton modifications resulted in a tonnage change to 46,328 GRT. So there is no room for conspiracy here – this tonnage difference is historical, mathematical and logical.

Re. 7. *The Olympic's Room.* There was a new room on the Titanic called the Olympic Room because the ship's owners believed that changing the ship's name was a bad sign, and J. Bruce Ismay and J.P. Morgan thought it would be better if the Olympic name was still somewhere on the ship.

Currently, no evidence has been found that there was an Olympic Room on the Titanic, but that shouldn't surprise anyone. Titanic was what White Star Line called the Olympic Class which referred to three ships: RMS Olympic, RMS Titanic and RMS Britannic.[9]

If there was indeed a room called the Olympic Room on the Titanic, it would seem superstitious that the two ships were connected. If not, then this is a moot point. And there is convincing evidence that the two ships had no connection with each other and their fates were completely different.

Re. 8. If the insurance had not been paid out, the company would have fallen. White Star Line did not have the slightest intention of sinking the ship. The swap was to keep the company in business.

There are those who recognize that Gardiner and others have no evidence of insurance fraud by admitting that the Titanic was insured and that White Star Line planned to sink the ship in an orchestrated mid–Atlantic collision with an iceberg is simply untenable. Some claim that the swap took place out of business and economic necessity for the company. However, the rumor is that White Star Line had financial problems. The issue was the cost of repairing the damage after the collision between the Olympic and the Hawke and the fact that the Olympic was not working for itself and making money, and the fact is that White Star Line's business was not heading for bankruptcy and there was simply no need to do such a swap. Nevertheless, the issue is debatable. Mark Chirnside reports the following:

The company's surplus on the balance sheet of profits and losses rose from US$48,585 in 1910 to US$821,062 on December

---

9. Ex **Giantic**. The name was changed after the **Titanic** disaster so as not to evoke bad associations.

31, 1911. Even if the compensation of this US$750,000 had not been paid, the IMM was still in the red. In 1910, IMM's profits were US$4,849,580 and fell to US$4,509,270 in 1911. As for White Star Line, the "main component of IMM" enjoyed a full year of prosperity, and its profit distribution for the whole of 1910 was 30% after depreciation. In fact, White Star Line's profit and loss account through December 31, 1911 had a surplus of GB£ 1,102,756 – even higher than the IMM.

The cost of switching ships (see point 5 on the number of changes needed for both ships) and the additional ongoing maintenance costs of thousands of people would have been enormous, and most importantly, completely unnecessary.

Re. 9. Differences in Titanic's name plates. Titanic's name board is longer on the ship that embarked on its maiden voyage, compared to the one that was under construction. It was longer because it had to cover the word "Olympic," which took up more space.

These photos are used by supporters of conspiracy theories to show a difference in the length of Titanic's name which suggests that another name was covered up by it.

The answer to this is very simple: the ship's name at the time of its construction and its voyage was in a partially different position and this is because the photo taken at the time of its construction, it was written on the negative of the photo. At the time of its construction, the ship's name is not clear in the photo, so the photographer took the liberty of writing the name on the side of the ship, which was not practiced in those days. We have other night photos of the Titanic with similar retouching that were taken in Cherbourg, which were crafted to look like they were taken at night, when all its lights were illuminated.

Re. 10. Differences in the number of Titanic's portholes. The Titanic had 14 portholes on the bow, while Olympic had as many as 16. The ship photographed as it left Southampton harbor had 16 bow portholes. Thus, it was the RMS Olympic, not the Titanic...

This is one of the crowning arguments in favor of switching ships, but also the easiest to refute. In fact – initially Titanic had 14 portholes on the bow, on the port side of C Deck when she was launched, but in the following months two more were added for better lighting and ventilation. In fact, both ships – RMS Olympic and RMS Titanic – were launched with fourteen portholes in the forward part of the bow, in the forepeak on Deck C, and 15 portholes on the starboard side on the same deck. However, in December 1911, during Titanic's retrofitting, two more were added: on the crew deck and in the washroom, resulting in a total of 16 as seen in the photos from the maiden voyage. It is interesting to note that after the Titanic disaster, the 14 portholes on the Olympic were replaced with 16 during a major overhaul. Thus, after the Titanic sank, the Olympic also had 16 portholes, as can be seen in the photos.

It should be pointed out that only the Titanic's hull was launched, along with the superstructure. After it was launched, it was "filled in", i.e. everything else was added to it. The ships that were then launched were not in a completed state. This circumstance may be one of the reasons why such particular theories hold up so well, despite the obvious answers...

According to Titanic researcher Ioannis Georgiu:

Two additional portholes on the Olympic were added in March 1912, during its brief stopover in Belfast, and shortly before Titanic's first voyage, so that in April 1912 both ships had 16 portholes each on the bow. (This is what I have noticed.)

It should also be suggested – if those who are in favor of swapping ships were so smart as to be able to change all the numbers stenciled on the backs of the wooden panels in all the rooms (relevant to this point) then how would they overlook something like the number of portholes on the ship's hull?

Re. 11. The difference in windows on Deck B on the Titanic. Also at the time of the Titanic's launch, all of the B Deck windows were evenly spaced, whereas during its maiden voyage they were unevenly spaced, exactly as on the RMS Olympic.

This argument is often cited alongside the argument about the different number of portholes on Titanic's port side. And the question is the same. The RMS Titanic was already planned at the time of construction as an improved version of her older sister-ship, the RMS Olympic. The differences in the number of portholes on the B Deck between the time of launching and the first voyage was explained by one of the key differences between the two ships: instead of a promenade as on the Olympic's B Deck, two private verandas and two luxury cabins were made on the Titanic's B Deck, hence the very change in the B Deck's appearance and porthole configuration.

Re. 12. Differences in the port side plating connections. RMS Olympic had vertical connections to her hull of the port side anchor kcy, while RMS Titanic did not have one at the time of construction. Photographs after the Olympic's disaster show that this connection is gone, and that it is indeed Titanic's…

In yet another attempt to find photographic inconsistencies to support the conspiracy theory, a hard-to-see fact was pulled out. Supporters here cite three photos. They are:

I° – a photo of the RMS Olympic at the Harland & Wolff shipyard taken when the ship was at Thompson Graving's dock in 1911, which shows the ship having a vertical joint of the plating plates, right at the jaw tube of the anchor wrench.

II° – in the second photo of the RMS Titanic when it was docked in 1911 and did not have this weld near the wrench, and...

III° – ... in a photo of the Olympic, which was taken in 1912/13, after the Titanic disaster, it is shown that this ship did not have the aforementioned weld. All this has become an argument for the DAR's partisans THAT it was the Titanic, even though the name Olympic is perfectly visible on both sides of the hull.

We must first of all establish that there were differences between the two ships. According to Steve Hall and Bruce Beverindge's book titled. "Titanic or Olympic, which ship sank?" Olympic had a completely different plating at the anchor locks. In fact, there is no problem, and the differences are only due to the different angle of the ship and its lighting.

Re. 13. Titanic's discolored plating. Photographs taken of the Titanic in Southampton shortly before it left on its maiden voyage show a large patch of discolored sheathing, as if it had been freshly painted over with paint that did not match the original color, and in the exact same area of the hull where the RMS Olympic was struck by the HMS Hawke.

Let's look at the two photographs and compare them. I don't see any credible evidence of discoloration there, which would argue for repair work. Any change in color can be explained by changes in lighting conditions and/or imperfections in photographic technique. There is nothing here that would testify in favor of a conspiracy theory.

Re. 14. The wheelhouse on RMS Olympic was not curved. Although the wheelhouse on the RMS Olympic was built to match the curvature of the bow, the photo taken from the top of the high gate appears to show a straight wheelhouse wall, exactly as shown in earlier drawings of the ship.

And this leads us to believe that the Olympics' wheelhouse was straight rather than curved – as we see on the Titanic wreck. However, the problem with this argument is that when the ship was launched, the wheelhouse had not yet been built. What we see in the photos is in fact the straight-built deck of the officers' quarters. [...]

Olympic's wheelhouse in 1912 was built arched at the front, while on Titanic it was straight – as can be seen, for example, in the photo of Captain Smith and Titanic's officers. This can be seen exactly in photos of the shipwreck taken by deep-sea explorers. ("Ghost of the Abyss," Walt Disney Pictures and Walden Media.)

It should be added that after the Titanic disaster, Olympic's wheelhouse was changed to a simple one, as one of the many changes and improvements made during the 1912/13 overhaul.

Re. 15. The ship's name plates were attached with rivets, not welded. Since welding had not yet been invented, it was White Star Line's custom to bend or cut the ship's name of its liners into the plating plates, rather than attaching the plates with rivets. However, both ships: RMS Olympic and RMS Titanic had name plates riveted to the sides... – so what did they cover?

This is one allegation that is not documented anywhere and is not supported by facts. Thus:

I° – First, it should be said that welding was invented and used back in the 19th century, before the two ships were built.

II° – it is true that the outline of each letter was carved into the plating plate and filled in with color – gold or yellow. Such was the standard in White Star Line practice.

However, there is not the slightest evidence that the RMS Olympic and RMS Titanic had name plates riveted to the plating plates. This is demonstrably false information. In fact, the outlines of the letters are visible on parts of the wreck, and the surviving White Star Line passenger tender SS Nomadic, built at the same time as Olympic and Titanic, shows exactly the same process. There were no plaques with the ship's name to be replaced, the name was literally carved into the ship and filled with paint.

Re. 16. Titanic's lack of advertising promotion. Historians have always been baffled by the fact that the Titanic never received the kind of publicity that the Olympic did. "It was such a pretty quiet affair…"

This is true. But this is no revelation to the Reader who has had even a passing interest in the matter. The RMS Olympic was the first to be launched and hailed as the world's largest and most luxurious ship. When the Titanic's first voyage took place, the Olympic had already been sailing for a year. Although Titanic surpassed its sister–ship in length. It wasn't that big a news story, and the public wasn't interested in its maiden voyage too much like the Olympic's voyages. At the time, there was a strike in the coal mines, Olympic was standing by at the repair yard, and Titanic did not have a full complement of passengers. Nothing new was said about it. And only when it collided with an iceberg under unclear circumstances did it get media attention. And since there weren't many photos of the Titanic's launching, they used photos of the twin Olympic in press reports, which caused such strange perturbations in the following years and gave fodder to the partisans of the Conspiracy Theory of (world) History – CTH.

Re. 17. Titanic's watertight bulkheads were intentionally leaky. The unsinkable ship turned out to be submersible… even very submersible. The watertight compartments were open at the top, allowing water to pour over the bulkheads and sink one compartment after another. Did J.P. Morgan and J.B. Ismay know about this?

It is true that Titanic's watertight compartments were not closed from the top for a number of reasons. First: because the collision that would have occurred in the water above the top of the compartment was considered almost impossible. Thus, closing them from the top would have restricted access to other parts of the ship, and this would have limited the luxury of being on board and turned the passenger liner into a casemate battleship. However, it should be added that casemate liners with closed watertight compartments still sank when they capsized. Higher and closed watertight compartments could not save Titanic from sinking, but only slowed down the sinking process itself.

The idea that Ismay or Morgan created a flawed international design is simply absurd for a simple reason: the design of the watertight compartments is identical for both ships – Olympic and Titanic – which, in other words, was introduced years before the collision with HMS Hawke, which could presumably justify the conspiracy theory. Morgan and Ismay could be predictors of the future as much as con artists.

Re. 18. Titanic's sea trials were shorter than Olympic's. The latter's trials in 1910 lasted two days, including several attempts to develop high speeds, while the Titanic's trials lasted only one day, including reportedly not a single one with a speed above half–ahead.

It is true that Titanic's sea trials lasted half as long as Olympic's, but they were shortened for several important reasons.

I° – they were shortened due to bad weather.

II° – was in a hurry due to the fact that it had to sail to Southampton to prepare it for its maiden voyage.

III° – characteristics of the Olympic were known, so there was no point in repeating the tests on the Titanic to obtain them. Titanic was thoroughly inspected every day of its construction, so sea trials were designed to confirm that everything worked as it should.

As Gardiner claims, that the Titanic – currently Olympic – never traveled at more than half the designed speed, because its battered hull might not have been able to withstand full speed – has never been documented anywhere. Of course, Gardiner claims that all documentation indicating the above was falsified in order to extort compensation. However, he failed to explain a trifle, namely: how did the Titanic reach the position where it sank, dragging there at a speed of only 12 kts or 22.22 km/h!?

Re. 19. *Titanic was not open to press and public inspection. While Olympic was open to press and public inspection in Belfast and Southampton, Titanic was not open to any inspections, other than those by the Transport Board (Board of Trade).*

The fact that the Titanic left Belfast and then Southampton in somewhat of a hurry, without any fanfare like Olympic, after one day sea trials, without a stop in Liverpool , without opening it to the public in Belfast and Southampton should not be at all surprising. Given the circumstances, it's perfectly logical. Mark Chirnside explains:

The maiden voyage was postponed for three weeks in October 1911 because shipbuilders were directed to repair the Olympic, and plans were tight until April 12, 1912, and when you add the fact that Titanic's sea trials were postponed due to bad weather, it's not all that surprising... Since the last work was still being done on the ship, it's not surprising that journalists and the curious in Southampton weren't allowed on it.

Also, as stated in point 16, there was less interest in Titanic's maiden voyage than there was for its older sister-ship. But nevertheless, we must point out that prior to the maiden voyage there were tours of the Titanic. E.g., there are photos taken by newspapers aboard the Titanic before it left port. Captain Smith has a photo on the bridge of the ship. We also know that First Officer William Murdoch's wife Ada was on a tour of the Titanic when she toured the ship. So neither the public nor the media were forbidden to tour the Titanic before the first voyage.

Re. 20. J. P. Morgan and 50 other passengers canceled the trip. More than 50 first-class passengers cancelled the last-minute cruise, many of them with social or business ties to J. P. Morgan and Morgan himself, who had placed money with White Star Line, also quit explaining illness. Morgan was found by a reporter two days later in a French resort with his wife and in good health. In addition, Morgan was carrying a dozen bronze statuettes taken from the deck of the Titanic minutes before it left port! Florence Ismay – wife of J. Bruce Ismay, president of White Star Line – also canceled the trip along with their children, and like Morgan claimed to be ill, while in fact she went on a car vacation!

There is no reason to doubt that passengers canceled their departure aboard the Titanic. However, this fits very much into the DAR. In fact, Ismay's wife did not cancel the trip at the last minute. According to Don Lynch and his book „Titanic: An Illustrated History" they did not accompany him on his first voyage, because they instead wanted to spend the holidays on a motor holiday in Wales.

Second: this kind of event was not at all unusual in such cruises, something similar happened during Olympic's maiden voyage. Mark Chirnside claims that:

When the Titanic sailed on its first voyage in April 1912, the number of passengers it had on board was similar to that of the Olympic a year earlier on its maiden voyage. Naturally there were trip cancellations, and the figure of 50 sounds very serious to DAR supporters. If a lot of people canceled because of fears of disaster or insurance scams, they were most likely talking about it after the disaster. There is no record of anyone doing so.

As for J. P. Morgan's "last-minute" cancellation of the trip, on the other hand, researcher Mark Baber, in his "Titanic Encyclopedia," writes about it as an urban legend. Baber compiled a list of Morgan's trips to and from Europe between 1904 and 1912, and only twice (in 1908 and 1910) did he return to New York before June and once (in 1908) in late August.

On these occasions, he always returned from Europe in June and no earlier than April. In an article in the New York Times on Thursday, April 28, 1912, it stands that in March:

J. Pierpont Morgan wrote a cordial letter to the committee announcing that he would be in Venice on April 23 to inaugurate the biennial International Art Exhibition and perform the opening ceremony of the Campanile of St. Mark.

This means that Morgan did not have any reason to return to America on April 10, when he was supposed to be in Venice as early as April 23 (on top of that, given that the one-way trip across the Atlantic took 5 days, he would not have been able to make it on time).

Re. 21. The crew refused to sail on the Titanic. Most of the engine crew had signed off on this fateful voyage starting in Southampton, during a coal shortage, meaning that many of them were on unemployment because their ships were on the ropes. Did they get the idea that the ship they were on was not the Titanic, but its sister ship, the collision–damaged Olympic?

Stories about this fact range from "two firemen, a boiler stoker and a greaser" or "most of the engine crew" to a specific number of 173 crewmen who "preferred to find employment on another ship." Some claim that the reason the crewmen wanted out of the voyage was the ship's boilers, which had already been in use for 12 months on the Olympic before the swap, and during the voyage from Belfast to Southampton they made the decision to flee the ship in Southampton. And while it has been proven that there is a lack of any documentation or even reminders, it should come as no surprise that a large number of crewmen went ashore. And this is for the simple reason that has nothing to do with the CTH, but common sense. The drive from Belfast to Southampton was short, while the North Atlantic Route (from Southampton to New York) is much longer. This can be compared to short–haul and long–haul flights – they require different crews and different cabins. The crew on the voyage from Belfast to Southampton consisted mainly of local seamen (known as runners), who mainly worked on local voyages and on many ships – not just the Titanic. They were not interested in transoceanic sailings that lasted several weeks and were interested in short routes or cabotage.

It is not true that all this was in the midst of the coal strike. In fact, this strike ended 4 days before the sailing (April 6) which resulted in the possibility of hiring sailors for shorter voyages. But for the most part, if indeed "a large part of the engine crew" refused to work on the Titanic due to rumors of a swap, why didn't these crewmen say anything after the disaster? Of course, there is no evidence here of any swapping of ship names.

Re. 22. Lifeboats from the Titanic carried markings from the Olympic. Titanic's lifeboats carried small bronze identification plates with the name "RMS Olympic" engraved on them.

The story goes that after the disaster, 13 lifeboats were recovered and taken to New York, where the plaques were removed by souvenir hunters. During this procedure, workers reportedly found the name "Olympic" "engraved on the gunwales of the lifeboats, where their old name was filled in with putty and painted over." The boats were sent to England and reused, however, boat No. 12 due to the fact that it was considered an unlucky thirteen fished out by the SS Carpathia, making it "unlucky" was not used until World War I, when it was given to the Sea Scouts as a thank you, as many scouts joined the Royal Navy and Home Fleet and lost their lives there. When the Sea Scouts restored the boat, they discovered the name "Olympic" engraved on its gunwale. This lifeboat was destroyed in a collision with the MF Gosport in Portsmouth and taken by the Royal Navy to Haslar for dismantling. For many years, White Star Line's side insignia was used as awards for local Sea Scout groups.

There are two key versions of this story. The first is that there is no document or other evidence to verify it. Assuming that there was an alleged discovery of the name "Olympic" on a boat or boats, on one or two of them, on different continents, and undoubtedly by several people – why didn't they leave a written statement, a drawing, a photo of this much-memorized boat, which would surely have set off all the lights and alarm bells in the minds of serious researchers. Secondly, and most importantly, the names were never engraved on the sides or gunwales of the boat. They were engraved on metal plates bolted to them. And they were never mounted on the gunwales, only on the sides of the lifeboats.

Of course, a bit of mystery hangs over the fate of the Titanic's lifeboats after its disaster. But according to Titanic fate researcher Ioannis Georgiou:

None of Titanic's lifeboats were reused by White Star Line. The statement that Olympic had them is absurd. The lifeboats were in New York in December 1912, while Olympic was in Belfast undergoing a major overhaul that included new davits and new lifeboats that were larger than the previous boats.

Re. 23. Titanic was close to maximum speed, but did not reach maximum speed. The ship was under full steam, but was traveling at 21 kts/38.89 km/h, instead of its theoretical maximum speed of 23 kts/42.6 km/h, despite the fact that the Atlantic was unusually calm the night it sank. This would be consistent with the damage Olympic had.

First, it would be important to point out that Titanic was not technically ready to sail "full speed" at the time of the collision. The speed of Titanic's movement was studied by Mark Chirnside and Samuel Halpern in their article titled "Speed and More Speed. "Speed and More Speed" from which this information was taken. According to Bruce Ismay's testimony before the British Wreck Commission, they intended to increase the speed [of the propellers] on Monday or Tuesday to 78 rpm[10], which he thought – would allow the ship to accelerate to its full speed, if the weather was favorable. Here is his statement:

---

10. rpm = revolutions per minute.

I understand that it was stated that the ship was moving at maximum speed. The ship never moved at maximum speed. Titanic's top speed was at 78 rpm. [The machinery] operated up to 80 rpm. As far as I know, 75 rpm was never exceeded. All the boilers never worked, none of the individual boilers worked. We intended, if there was good weather on Monday afternoon or Tuesday, to accelerate the ship to maximum speed.

Superior stoker Frederick Barrett testified before the BWC that on the day of the disaster, the 3 auxiliary double boilers were started at 08:00 (although they took 12 hours to come to full operation) and he was sure that the five auxiliary single boilers from Boiler Room No. 1 had not been started. He too confirmed that the machines were making 75 rpm, not the possible 80 rpm.

Also, stoker John Thompson said: *I was told that the ship was moving at nearly 23 kts when the collision occurred. Chirnside and Halpern found that: Titanic made 546 mn/~1011 km from Saturday noon to noon on Sunday, which was its best performance, only two miles worse than that achieved by Olympic on its maiden voyage, and sailed using 21 of its 24 twin boilers.*

We must add here that most of Olympic's voyages were made at 21.5 kts/39.82 km/h.

Chirnside and Halpern conclude:

Undoubtedly, Titanic's speed increased gradually during its first voyage, the number of propeller revolutions increased, boilers were brought on line, and preparations were made to further increase the ship's speed. [...] Titanic was well prepared to exceed the speed reached by her sister-ship.

To summarize Gardiner's statements that the Titanic was indeed a damaged Olympic that was trying to maintain its cruising speed, it does not say that the damaged Olympic had a broken keel and was unable to reach half the speed achieved during sea trials.

Re. 24. The Titanic did not collide with an iceberg. An iceberg could not have caused such damage to a ship with a double steel hull like the Titanic, it must have been something else – in this case, an IMM rescue ship that was drifting with its lights off.

This is the point where Gardiner's theory begins to get more and more astonishing. It no longer assumes not only that the Olympic was swapped for the Titanic in order to extract compensation, but also that the Titanic (actually the Olympic) did not collide with an iceberg at all, but with the IMM rescue ship, which was adrift with its lights out. This was part of the scam's financial plan, and the rescue ships were waiting in that very body of water in anticipation of disaster. Gardiner bases his hypothesis on the idea that the alleged iceberg was spotted at too short a distance by sailors from the crow's nest, for it was in fact a blacked-out ship.

This hypothesis has two flaws:

I° – Titanic was not a ship with a double steel hull. In fact, it had a double bottom, because the designers concluded that a double hull meant increased costs and settled for a double bottom. After the Titanic disaster, this all changed. Thus, there is nothing surprising in the fact that the iceberg did sufficient damage to the starboard (not the bottom) of the hull, which caused flooding of the watertight compartments and led to the sinking of the ship.

II° – there are many eyewitness accounts of the iceberg collision, including observer Fredrick Fleet, quartermasters George Rowe and Alfred Olliver and Edith Rosenbaum,

George Rhiems, Albert and Vera Dick and William Sloper. And they weren't the only ones. Survivor Lawrence Beesley wrote about the men sitting in the smoking room seeing the iceberg in his book „The Loss of the SS Titanic":

One of them noticed through the window an iceberg rising above the deck. He called out for them to pay attention to it and they all saw it disappear, so they calmly returned to the game. We asked them about the height of the mountain and someone said one hundred feet, another said sixty, while one of the spectators – an engine engineer going to America with a carburetor model for a car [...] said – "I can judge the height from a distance and I estimate it at eighty to ninety feet."

Re. 25. The ice on board did not come from an iceberg. The ice on board the Titanic, Gardiner explains, came from the rigging of the mystery ship that the Titanic hit.

The above alludes to the thesis in the previous section, and assumes that the Titanic collided with the IMM rescue ship, standing adrift and unlit, instead of an iceberg. One version of this theory states that the passengers' accounts of the large amount of ice on board could not have come from the ship's rigging:

- Seaman William Lucas saw "several tons... on the forward deck on the starboard side" (British investigation – day 3)

- Seaman Edward John Buley also reported "several tons of ice blocks" (British investigation – day 16)

- Seaman Joseph Scarrott: "There was a large amount of ice and snow on the forward deck on the starboard side."

- IV Officer Boxhall: "Some ice on the deck covered an area of three to four feet from the starboard side along the deck." (British Inquiry – Day 13)
- Stoker shift leader Charles Hendrickson noted "a lot of ice... on deck" (British Inquiry – Day 5)
- Observer Reginald Lee: the ice "fell on the deck. He fell on the forward deck" (British investigation – day 4)
- Seaman Thomas Jones testified during the US investigation – day 7 that he went out on deck and saw "some ice" there.
- Lawrence Beesley: "The forward deck was covered with ice that had fallen" in The Loss of the SS Titanic.
- Also, many other passengers such as Lady Duff Gordon and Edith Rosenbaum spoke of ice on board. And there was not a single witness who saw ice in the rigging. Indeed, is there any testimony suggesting ice in the Titanic's rigging? Why would it be there? They just affected the ice field. How much ice could there be in the rigging? Certainly not as much as the testimony of eyewitnesses who saw the amount of ice that fell on board...

Re. 26. Many ships stood adrift near the sinking Titanic because of the coal strike. Ships drifted because of the coal strike with few passengers, and therefore the number of lifeboats did not matter.

It's true that there was such a strike in the coal mines and it had serious repercussions to shipping and the maritime economy. It began in January 1912 and was the first national strike by coal miners in Britain to fight for minimum wage increases. [According to a Mirror article about Southampton titled. "The City That Lost a Generation to the Titanic Disaster" (24.

IV.2012) 17,000 people were out of work that April because of that very strike.

But does that mean we should treat with suspicion that there were many ships in the body of water where the Titanic sank? There are several important points to consider first.

I° – The coal strike ended nine days early on April 6, restoring normalcy to communications.

II° – It was a "national strike" through which bunker shortages primarily affected ships leaving or staying in England.

III° – The term "numerous" is misleading here, and very much so. It is known with certainty that there were only 6 of them in a circle with a radius of 140 mn/~259 km. They were:

- 19 mn – SS Californian from Leyland Line, sailing west from London to Boston
- 50 mn – SS Mount Temple of the Canadian Pacific Steamship Company, freighter, sailing west from London to St. John's, Newfoundland, Canada
- 50 mn – SS Parisian from Allan Line, sailing west from Glasgow to Halifax and Boston
- 58 mn – RMS Carpathia of Cunard Line, sailing east from New York to Mediterranean ports via Gibraltar
- 70 mn – SS Burma from Russian East Asiatic Company sailing east from New York via Rotterdam to Lipawa[11] in Russia
- 140 mn – SS Frankfurt from Norddeutscher Lloyd Line, sailing east from Galveston to Bremen.

---

11. Today in Latvia.

As you can see from this list, of the 6 ships, 3 sailed west and 3 sailed east. Those that sailed east did not sail from England and could not be affected by the coal strike. Thus, they were the three operational ships in the area. So, not many are "numerous," especially considering that Titanic was traveling on the popular North Atlantic Way known for being busy at this time of year.

Re. 27. Bottom valves were opened to speed up the sinking. To sink the Titanic (or Olympics), the plan was to open the bottom valves to slowly flood the inside of the ship's hull and wait for help to arrive.

According to Gardiner, the original plan was to slowly sink the ship by opening the bottom valves and slowly flooding the ship's hull. A collision with an iceberg (Gardiner believes with some IMM rescue ship) spoiled this original plan. One has to admit that this is a strange phenomenon and indicates that after a while someone will try to justify the conspiracy. Realizing that planning a collision in the North Atlantic would be too difficult and improbable, Gardiner comes up with a more deliberate and logical plan.

However, it is definitively illogical. First of all – how did White Star Line bosses imagine that hundreds of crewmen would not notice water pouring through the bottom valves into the hull? In addition, after all, the ship was "practically unsinkable" then how would they explain the "mysterious" flooding to the investigators, who would no doubt look into the matter? For a company that was miraculously able to swap ships by replacing thousands of wooden panels without anyone's knowledge, this seems a rather careless and unlikely plan. But more important than that is, what evidence does Gardiner cite for this plan to sink the Titanic by opening the bottom valves?

None, of course. This is another speculation about a ship swap that never happened.

Re. 28. The SS Californian wasn't expecting a flare, just an encounter with the Titanic. The Californian was sent to meet the Titanic to pick up passengers and crew after it was deliberately sunk.

Something like this was concocted by Gardiner and his partisans to promote the theory that the Californian would be a "rescue ship" that was owned by J.P. Morgan (an important person in the White Star Line), left London in a hurry (it was capable of a top speed of 12 kts and had to be first in position) and mysteriously sailed during a coal strike (when coal would have been most expensive). They also question why, on the night of the collision, the Californian's captain chose to sleep fully clothed on a couch in the navigation cabin and ordered the boilers to be under steam and the machinery to STAND BY. They also claim that the alleged three radio messages were directed to Captain Smith giving him the position, which would mean that the Californian was in position and waiting for him. Captain Smith also – like the Californian's captain – was sleeping fully clothed in the navigation cabin. The Californian had no passengers, although due to the strike at the ports there would be many people who would overpay for tickets just to get to Boston. Gardiner further speculates that the ship struck by the Titanic was one of those that fired flares, and this would explain the idleness of the people on the Californian. [...]

However, there are several big gaps in this theory. First and foremost, the Californian would have been a very poor rescue ship. It had a total of 47 passenger seats and 55 crew. There were more than 2,200 people on the Titanic, and it could have taken 3,000 of them if it had total occupancy. Even if this fact is not enough, other alleged details about the Californian are misinterpreted. The boilers were under steam and the machinery on STAND BY because the ship was trapped by the ice field and could have continued the journey at any time. It is known that the longer they were at sea, the more it cost. The fact that both captains Smith and Lord slept in their clothes is pure speculation and actually irrelevant. And given that the Titanic was about to sink, the conduct of Captain Lord is irrelevant.[12]

Re. 29. The SS Californian was carrying woolen sweaters and blankets. The ship had several thousand wool sweaters and blankets as cargo, as if it was ready for a rescue mission.

The ship was designed to transport cotton, and there is absolutely no evidence that it had a "cargo of several thousand wool sweaters and blankets" at the time. Indeed, there is no Californian cargo manifest from that voyage. In order to prove the CTH's thesis, one would have to produce that manifest (which would neither confirm nor negate the ship–swapping theory anyway).

Re. 30. Survivors of Deck B saw lifeboats being lowered from above. They described, lifeboats being lowered from the top deck, something that would not have been possible on the Titanic, but only just on the Olympic.

According to the book titled "The Ship That Never Sank" (pp. 134–135), Deck B had no cabins extending beyond the hull from which the boats would have been visible. Gardiner argues that when lifeboat No. 12 on the starboard side was being lowered, some Frenchman jumped to it from B Deck. He continues that starboard steward Wheelton met Thomas Andrews on B

---

12. In the early 1980s, Captain Stanley Lord was cleared of all charges by the court and rehabilitated.

Deck, and that the boats were visible from the corridor on B Deck. In both cases, Gardiner raised this claim!

Seaman Frederick Clench, who was in Boat 12, said that the Frenchman jumped into the boat before it was lowered, indicating that he jumped in from the deck (U.S. Investigation, Day 7). It does not mention that he jumped in from B Deck. Several passengers: 2nd Class passengers Lillian Bentham and Emily Rugg recounted that someone jumped from the upper deck, which could have been Deck A. 1st Class steward Edward Wheelton met Thomas Andrews on Deck B, after assisting in launching lifeboat No. 5 to starboard. However, Wheelton went to the storeroom and then went to the starboard boat deck again. After launching lifeboat No. 9, he was ordered by 1st Officer Murdoch to go to Deck A, where he helped launch lifeboat No. 11 (American Investigation, Day 7). Again, there is no mention of there being any lifeboats as seen from Deck B.

The fact remains that if there were such great differences in the construction of the two ships, why were they not noted in the photos and accounts of passengers familiar with the Olympic?

Re. 31. Passengers said there was a promenade there instead of cabins. Eyewitnesses described their wanderings on the decks of the Titanic, but as they said, there were promenades where cabins were supposed to be.

We need to know that nowhere is it mentioned, and there is no testimony about it from any of the surviving passengers. And as above – why isn't it in the photos and accounts from people who knew the Olympic?

Re. 32. The linoleum covering the decks was covered with carpets. J.B. Ismay had all of Titanic's linoleum-covered decks covered with new carpets. Was this to cover for 12 months and did it leave no marks on the linoleum covering?

The idea most likely came from Baker Charles Burgess printed in Walter Lord's "A Night to Remember," who writes thus:

As in Olympic, yes, but much more elaborate. Take such a dining room. On the Olympic, there were no carpets there, but on the Titanic... ah, you were drowning in them up to your knees. Then the furniture: it was too heavy for you to lift. And those panels...

This has led many to believe that there was a carpet in the Titanic's dining room – not like the one on the Olympic, so nicely shown in James Cameron's film "Titanic." It could be that the carpet was tucked away for 12 months and only scratches and marks on the linoleum surface remained?

Researchers Bill Saunder and Parks Stephenson concluded that there was no carpet in the dining room. Evidence of a carpet there is only mentioned by Burgess, without support from other witnesses. In fact, this commentary was written 30 years after the disaster and was probably greatly exaggerated. The case is similar for the Olympics reception area, where there was no huge wall-to-wall carpet. However, his comments about the furniture and panels being better than on the Olympic are not true: the furnishings and panels aboard Titanic were – with the exception of unique rooms such as the Promenade Suites – identical to those on the Olympic. Thus, the statement disputes the mention of the dining room carpet. Also, fragments of linoleum were recovered from the wreck, which proves it more likely. It should also be noted that the Titanic's dining room was huge and was furnished with the most expensive linoleum on board – with a "Persian carpet" pattern – so it doesn't make sense to invest big money in such an investment as carpets in the dining room.

Re. 33. The RMS Titanic broke through at the same spot where the RMS Olympic was struck by the HMS Hawke. This, of course, proves that it was not Titanic but Olympic that sank.

This is complete nonsense. Most agree that Titanic broke almost exactly under the third funnel. HMS Hawke hit the Olympic in the stern. The Titanic's breakthrough was accurately shown by James Cameron in his 1997 film. The damage to the Olympic was caused by the collision with HMS Hawke. It happened exactly in a different place than where the Titanic broke through.

Re. 34. The rescued crewmen signed a loyalty of silence. The rescued crew members were detained during the night and ordered to sign a loyalty of silence under the "Official Secrets Act," mandating that the events that unfolded on the night of April 14/15, 1912 be kept secret forever.

This information seems to have come from Paddy "Pig" known as James Fenton, who later recounted it as follows:

When the rescued crew sailed into port, they were immediately taken to meet two people – one of them was a high official of the company, while the other worked for the government. The one from the government read them the "Official Secrets Act," explaining that if they told anyone about the true causes of the disaster, or even let loose any rumors about it, they would go to jail for at least 20 years and get a "wolf ticket"[13], when they get out of it. Paddy claimed that the order to remain silent for many years undermined the morale and health of the surviving crew members.

However, as stated in paragraph 13 (below) it is almost certain that James Fenton was never aboard the Titanic, as he as-

---

[13]. This was a type of employment ban, known in Nazi Germany as *Berufsverboten*.

serted. Besides, there is no other testimony anywhere that the crew was told to sign a loyalty of silence. It should be added here that the said Act was used only in cases of espionage and secrecy in military affairs. Thus, it is difficult to suppose that it was applied in the case of the Titanic tragedy. However, it is true that the crew, upon their return to England, was instructed during the hearings of the Board of Trade investigation about what to say and what not to say to media representatives. But this is hardly surprising, as this was the official practice not to tell the media on the spur of the moment what would not be known to the investigators.

Re. 35. Harold Sanderson repeatedly refers to the Titanic as the Olympic. This employee of the Harland and Wolff shipyard often refers to the Olympic when talking about the Titanic during the British investigation. Is this because there was an interchange between the two?

Mr. Harold Arthur Sanderson – director of the Oceanic Steam Navigation Company (not the Harland and Wolff shipyard as the CTH says) was 60 years old when the Titanic sank and was interviewed on day 17 of the British Wreck Commissioner's investigation. The statement that he spoke very often about Olympic in the context of Titanic has no basis in fact. There was no occasion on which he could have confused the two names. The closest occasion was when he was asked about the binoculars case:

"19342: Did people tell you if there were binoculars at Olympic?"

"On the trip from Belfast to Southampton."

"19343 At Olympic, as I said?"

"Oh, sorry, yes."

"19344. And there were no binoculars on the Titanic?"

"Yes."

"19345 Oh, sorry, they were on the Oceanic, but on the Titanic they were brought from Belfast?"

"Yes."

Other than this one statement "on the voyage from Belfast to Southampton," there is no statement in which the two ships are confused. Even if he did confuse them, it does not follow that there was any interchange and he was otherwise able to give the correct name of the ship.

Re. 36. A Titanic crewman on his deathbed confessed to swapping ships. Old sailor Paddy "Pig" shortly before his death declared that the Titanic had been swapped for his sister-ship Olympic on a fateful voyage.

The story came from Frank Finch, a retired sailor living in New South Wales, Australia, who wrote a letter to the editor of the Northern Star newspaper, which published it on 31.VII.1996. It was written in response to an article published earlier regarding the "swap theory" – no doubt due to the publication of a book entitled "The Riddle of the Titanic". "The Riddle of the Titanic" in 1996. Frank Finch's letter talks about what his son Dennis remembered from a conversation he had in the early 1970s with old sailor James Fenton also known as Paddy Fenton or Paddy "Pig."

In 1912, Paddy was a 22-year-old sailor aboard the Titanic. He always maintained that it was not an iceberg that sank the Titanic, and that there was a coal bunker fire that had been going on for at least a week, and that the captain and company knew about it. Paddy also said that when the crew boarded the Titanic, there were rumors (sic!) that the company had swapped the two ships and there had been insurance fraud. They sailed in a hurry from Belfast, and he said that the collision with the iceberg did not do that much damage at all, and only the cold water when it reached the burning bunker caused an explosion that did fatal damage. A senior officer (Wilde?) sent him to launch the lifeboats. When the surviving crew members arrived in port, they were met by two heavyweights – one from the company the other from the government, who made them sign a loyalty of silence citing the "Official Secrets Act," explaining that they could be sentenced to at least 20 years in prison and a "wolf ticket" upon their release for telling what happened or spreading rumors. Paddy said that keeping everything a secret cost the crew a lot of health and reflected negatively on them.

Steve Hall and Bruce Beveridge have examined this statement in their book titled. "Titanic Or Olympic: Which Ship Sank?" and concluded that there is no proof of the veracity of Fenton's story and that he himself was not aboard the Titanic, his name is not on the crew list or the list of surviving passengers. Most importantly, no crew member took a paycheck for him and no crew member called James Fenton ever paid for anything. Also, the coal bunker fire did indeed happen on the Titanic, although it was extinguished before the collision, and in no way could this have caused the explosion and all the damage in its aftermath. Not surprisingly, Frank Finch is a dubious witness, even if he was reporting stories known from third parties.

Re. 37. The number "401" on Olympic's wooden structures. Wooden panels from the Class 3 deck now adorn private apartments in Wirral k./Liverpool. The reverse sides of these panels are perfectly marked. The number "400" is perfectly visible on these panels, but the number "401" is perfectly visible on their frames.

Without further information and documentation on these "private dwellings in Wirral" – even a photo – it is very difficult to examine the evidence (if there is any at all) but it must be said that it all sounds like a rumor and an attempt to corroborate this evidence that the number "400" (the serial number of the RMS Olympic) was on all the wooden fittings of this ship.

Re. 38. The name "Olympic" is found on the wreck. The forged letters of the "Titanic" name have corroded and exposed the letters "MP" – part of the word "OlyMPic" that was originally stamped or engraved on the ship's plating.

This particular statement came when Robin Gardiner stated in his book that when the name on the bow of the Titanic wreck was cleaned of rust (allegedly filmed by the crew of Cmdr. Dr. Robert "Bob" Ballard during the 1986 dive into the wreck), the letters "M," "P" and "Y" showed up. However, he neither showed any photo of these letters nor provided any reference to sources. A little later, the following illustration appeared in a document entitled "Titanic – The Shocking Truth" (Figure 15):

Some have analyzed the film transcript, concluding, for example, that the X-shaped field of view seen in the video is caused by camera lighting. One thing they have figured out is that it is a computer-generated hoax and does not match any shot taken from the bow. Not to mention that the name "Titanic" was first filmed on the wreck in 1987, and of course nothing looked like this incriminated photo. The letters of the name are shown here, and in fact are their outlines visible on the hull. Of course, there is no testimony from Ballard, or anyone from his expedition, who saw anything different.

Interestingly, Gardiner personally admitted that the photo was a forgery. In July 2013, he wrote to Alexander Bruce from the ForbiddenKnowledgeTV (*WWW.forbiddenknowledgetv.com*) as follows:

I just learned that you are producing a video entitled "Was the Titanic Deliberately Sunk by J. P. Morgan?" (the original title is "Why They Sank the Titanic") on your web TV. This video was taken by Mr. Andrew Newton in 2000... This photo, the only one in the entire production to which Mr. Newton was entitled, was a later video presumably showing where the ship was renamed. (http://www.forbiddenknowledgetv.com)

The most notorious aspect of this already unintentional already intentional forgery is the desperate need for it. If there was enough evidence that the wreck was indeed the Olympic, why would you fake something like this?

Comparing the two videos – one is an authentic recording showing the name "Titanic" on the wreck, the other is a fake. NB, by coincidence the name "Titanic" was filmed for the first time in 1987 by IFREMER and Titanic Ventures (later RMS TITANIC Inc.), who then cleaned the ship's name from rust on the bow.

Re. 39. The number "401" on the Titanic's propeller was that of the Olympic. The RMS Olympic was equipped with a propeller from the Titanic, it was acknowledged, as an argument defending the DAR's thesis of the swap. The number "401" was carried by the RMS Olympic.

In fact, the Olympic and Titanic had numbers stamped differently on the propeller wings, which, however, does not constitute any argument, as the ship's propeller blades were interchanged and swapped from one ship to another and vice–versa on more than one occasion. But there was also no need to do so. We know that the Titanic had spare propellers that were later, after the disaster, used for various memorials, and there is no reason not to assume that the Olympic did not have the same.

Mark Chirnside concludes:

Olympic was fitted with the starboard propeller shaft from the Titanic. There is no evidence whatsoever that Harland & Wolff used one of Titanic's propellers or propeller blades to build Olympic, and there is no reason to believe that Olympic's spare propeller was not otherwise used.

The number "401" was Titanic's shipyard number and was also placed on the starboard propeller blades.

Re. 40. White paint on the wreck. The hull of the Olympic had been painted white since it was launched to make it look better in photographs. When corrosion and marine animals damaged the upper layers of black paint on the hull of the wreck discovered by Dr. Ballard, it revealed stretches of white paint. This can be seen in detail in the attached photo.

It is true that the hull of the Olympic was covered with white paint from its launching in order to better contrast the image in photographs and films, while the Titanic was not. And we have proof of white paint covering the hull of the wreck. But this is not at all because it was Olympic. It is simply the light gray primer paint that was used on all three Olympic–class ships, including, of course, the Titanic, which showed up in scuffs in good lighting conditions and looked more white than gray.

Re. 41. Marbles in the living room. When James Cameron sent an underwater robot to Bruce Ismay's suite, it filmed the veined marble surrounding the fireplace, which, compared to the photos, corresponds to the reception room at Olympic, photographed in 1911.

According to the documentary "Titanic – Breaking New Ground," James Cameron sent an underwater robot into the living room of the promenade suites on Deck B and filmed a cast-iron fireplace that was surrounded by veined marble, which was still in place. Veined marble is a naturally occurring metamorphic limestone rock and, like snowflakes or fingerprints, no two pieces of it are the same. However, the marbles filmed on the wreck exactly match those in the photos taken on the Olympic in 1911.

It's true that James Cameron sent a robot to lounge in the Millionaire's Suite, or Promenade Suites if you prefer, during a dive in 1995. And in fact, these images were used in his 1997 worldwide blockbuster film "Titanic," while Cameron placed a fictional character named Caledon Hockley in the suite. In the documentary, James Cameron explains:

We went to those rooms, which they called the Millionaire's Suites, and we only went to one that was occupied by J. P. Morgan. We were able to go into that suite and see the marble fireplace still there, and be able to compare our video with old photographs and see the veins on the marble and realize that it was one and the same thing – like fingerprints. And for me it was something surreal to see little white crabs crawling around the fireplace in the apartment that J. P. Morgan occupied.

So Cameron confirms that the marble lining of the fireplace is the same as in the photos taken on Olympic. Has Cameron found proof that the Titanic is in fact the Olympic? No, and for a very simple reason: the fireplace was made of imitation marble. And that's it. Such imitations were made in series and were identical, as one would expect from this.

My 2 cents

So, as shown, the whole hypothesis is worthless, like the vast majority of the wanderings of the conspiracy theory of (world) history creators and supporters. So it is the RMS Titanic and not the Olympic that lies at the bottom of the Atlantic, which was obvious from the very beginning. Not for the conspiracy theory of (world) history followers, of course, because the conspiracy theory of (world) history feeds on urban legends and the maybes of various sensation hunters or just loonies.

Chapter 3

The Mystery of the "Titanic" and the Time

The story of this ship is probably known to all civilized people on Earth. After going to sea from the English port of Southampton on its first passenger voyage[14], the huge ocean liner RMS Titanic headed for the shores of America [15], and on the fifth day of the voyage, April 14, 1912, in the North Atlantic, collided with an iceberg and went down in 2 hours and 20 minutes.[16]

***

"In this imagination–shattering maritime disaster," writes Vladimir Micurov in an article titled „«Titanik»... wspłył czerez 80 let!" in „Kalejdoskop NLO" No. 44[157]/2000 – more than one and a half thousand people died, and just over 700 were rescued.[17] RMS *Titanic* sank in almost four kilometers deep. For a long time it was impossible to get to it. This was accom-

---

14. On April 10, 1912 at 12:00 p.m. GMT.
15. Through the ports of Cherbourg in France (10.IV.) and Queenstown in Ireland (11.IV.), where still doembarked passengers from the Continent and Ireland.
16. On April 15, 1912 at 02:20 a.m. local time (06:20 a.m. GMT) at position N 41°46' and W 050°14'.
17. Exactly 1,502 victims and 705 rescued.

plished thanks to state-of-the-art marine engineering devices, only 73 years after the disaster.

In September 1985, a small underwater work robot called DSV Jason Junior transmitted a TV image from a depth of 3,750 meters of sand and silt-covered huge steel structures lying on the bottom. It was the RMS Titanic.[18]

... In December 1992, Norwegian fishermen were fishing for herring in the North Atlantic. On December 14, the ship's engine malfunctioned. So they stopped fishing and stood in the drift to repair the machine. And suddenly, before their eyes, a huge ship emerged from the sea's depths. By its silhouette (familiar to every sailor), one could easily recognize that it was... RMS Titanic! On its decks, panicked passengers were thrashing about, screaming and begging for help. Some of them jumped from the deck into the icy waters.

Within minutes, the Titanic went underwater again. The Norwegians were unable to approach the site of the disaster, but they radioed the news of this incredible event into the ether in open text. This radiogram was received at the US Navy headquarters and an American ship was sent to the area, which managed to take aboard 13 survivors wearing life jackets with Titanic printed on them. All of these people were alive...

Later, a special statement from the U.S. Navy said that one U.S. ship on December 14, 1992, took part in a rescue operation in the North Atlantic and took 13 people on board.

The name of the ship and the names of those rescued were not disclosed. And then a tight veil of secrecy was lowered over the whole affair. The Pentagon did not provide any more information on the subject. On the other hand, the Norwegian authorities, after consulting with the US authorities, put a gag

[18]. It was an engineering feat by Capt. Dr. **Bob Ballard** and his exploration team.

order on any information about the incident, forbidding the fishermen to say anything about it or tell anyone about what they witnessed.

However, despite the tight curtain of secrecy, there have been leaks. Marine disaster expert Phillip Stearnes stated in an interview with a correspondent of a news agency that the:

I am not going to comment on this report. Perhaps in this case, people were displaced in time and transferred to another dimension. A special research group is currently analyzing and investigating this case. All I can say is that on December 14, 1992, the "Titanic" floated to the surface of the ocean, and there were living people on board!

Stearnes – according to his words – managed to talk to one of the American officers who took part in the rescue operation. He recounted that the survivors taken aboard the ship ranged in age from 21 to 62 and all suffered from memory loss – amnesia. Their personal documents bore dates no later than 1912. The survivors did not give the impression that they were older than their likenesses shown in the documents, as if the 80 years had not passed at all.

However, the RMS Titanic sank for sure in 1912, and its hull – more precisely, its two uneven parts – now lies at the bottom of the ocean, and the problem may relate to the so-called space-time paradox. Such a paradox – the movement of people through time – does indeed exist, and we have plenty of testimony to that effect.

In 1990, a Cuban air force exercise was taking place in the airspace between Cuba and Haiti. One pilot of a jet pursuit aircraft told this story:

As I gained altitude and put the plane on the prescribed course, when all of a sudden – the devil knows from where – a flying balloon with a gondola appeared in front of me.

An aviator forced the balloon to land on the water, from where the balloon's crew was picked up by a Cuban ship.

In the gondola were two men named Garry Logan and Derek Norton. Both of them were shocked and shattered. Garry Logan recounted that they had just participated in a balloon race from Cuba to Puerto Rico; they had taken off a few hours ago, only in... 1954!!!

A source close to the Cuban authorities stated:

The pilots of that balloon confessed that at one point they felt a shudder throughout their bodies, as if an electric discharge had been passed through them. Then everything around them – the sky and the ocean – turned a raspberry color. And then a jet plane forced them to sit on the water...

Indeed, their flight took as long as 36 years!

Kelvin Crow – a specialist from Chicago – confirmed the fact that two aeronauts actually disappeared in the area during a balloon competition in 1954. He believes that these aeronauts fell into some kind of black hole in time. After all, this is the Bermuda Triangle basin...

***

When I did a translation of this article, I couldn't hold back a mocking smile – *yeah! another flummery straight from the "X-Files" and the sick imagination of some Chris Carter disciple, which was picked up by the Russians to have a sensational "stopgap" in the magazine. Too much ado about nothing or a tempest in a teapot. That's what I thought to myself.* And then the sneer disappeared from my lips, because I remembered that there is a whole series of inexplicable events that I had to deal with while carrying out PROJECT TATRA, which I even gave a separate code name – Rip van Winkle. He is the protagonist of a story by American writer Washington Irving, who just fell into such a black hole in time and slept in it for two centuries... Could it be that Washington Irving knew about similar accidents and wanted to give us a signal about them, and could only do so in the form of a fairy tale? After all, the possibility of such time travel exists, but it cannot be realized without the appropriate technical means – and the latter may have UFOs...

As luck would have it, a few days earlier Tomasz Niesporek of the Katowice-based magazine "Sieci" had approached me with similar material. In this material he also writes about the shifting of people in time, which have their reflections in Silesian legends and fairy tales.

The mystery of the disaster and doom of the RMS Titanic has its ufological aspect, which I have written about before. So, would this be one more contribution to this tragedy, which, despite the fact that it is already 110 years old, is still a living memento for our civilization?...

In writing the book "Ghost Trains and Ghosts in Trains," there we cite accounts and urban legends about ghostly rail vehicles and ghostly passengers traveling on them. So there is more to the accounts of ghosts at sea and strange incidents with Time than just fairy tales and stories of senior citizens...

Chapter 4

Torpedoes for the "Titanic"

And here is another interesting article by Alexander Volodiev in "NLO" No. 33(623)/2009, in which he puts forward a thesis about the torpedoing of an English titan by a German U-boat.

***

The fanatics of statistical analysis – the Americans – have calculated that about the sunk on the night of April 14/15, 1912 in the waters of the Atlantic, the miracle of the ship technology of the time, the giant liner RMS. Titanic during the past 20 years, so many publications have appeared and so many films have been made that it surpassed the number of publications about World War II. Why?

4.1. In the four-kilometer deep

And that's because for almost a century of continued silence, one hears some stories about a practically and theoretically impossible to sink colossus, which is not afraid of collision with analogous objects and such ominous actions as bombardment or explosions. This is the first factor heating up interest. But there's also a second one – it's based on the results of deep-sea dives into the giant's wreck, which lies four kilometers deep, that have made it possible to see and study it in detail. Thanks to these technologies, experts in the near future will be able to unequivocally determine the causes of this oceanic tragedy. And so, as English engineer–shipbuilding specialist Donald Wilman believes, the sinking of the Titanic was not led by a collision with an iceberg. The cause – indicated by high-resolution underwater photographs taken – became a torpedo attack. The torpedoes exploded under the boiler room. Isn't this another silly hypothesis? I won't rush the argument – let's look at the arguments Wilman used in turn.

4.2. THE TRAIL LEADS TO THE BANK

We'll start with the fact that just before the ominous voyage, the Royal Bank of Great Britain let loose a series of guaranteed and secured gold and platinum securities valid until 2012. Some of the precious metals had to be transported to the US because of the English preparations for World War I. But how to transport it? Aviation in this case was not suitable for this. The only way out – to rely on a guaranteed means of water transport. The choice fell on the RMS Titanic, and especially because its co-owner and co-shareholder in this huge financial operation was the American banking house G. P. Morgan & Co. The top-secret smuggling of platinum and gold began in a specially prepared, armored and secured room of the liner, as the man who transported the gold and, together with other officers of the liner, moved it bar by bar from the car to the hold – courier to special duties Frank Pretite – told the court two years later after the tragedy, a fact that was categorically denied by George Morgan himself at the time. The latter's memoirs, published in America in 2006, leave no doubt that he feared this journey with a very dangerous cargo. And here is an excerpt from his memoirs:

> *I wasn't the only one who refused to go on this voyage, as well as Lord Hird – director of the Harland and Wolff shipyard in Belfast [19] – Perhaps his decisions were dictated by his eternal preoccupation and overload with work and business. I considered it something mindless to storm the Atlantic with a priceless cargo on board pirated by Germans well aware of our precious cargo and who was carrying it and how it was being carried.*

Of course, the passengers had little idea that they were sitting on a "gold mine" and had become hostages of financiers and politicians. Only the liner's captain Edward Smith, who refused to go behind his ship when its doom became certain, knew of what he was carrying. Sharing Donald Willman's views, American journalist Avraam Holtz explains the firm decision "not to abandon his ship" not only by a deep sense of duty, but also by the fact that if he had survived, it would have become clear that he was prepared for some problems during the voyage and was aware that the ship was surrounded by enemies.

4.3. Hidden coordinates

Holtz points to the source of his argument, a letter to wife dated April 12, 1912, which was published by a whole host of English and American newspapers that appeared at the beginning of the last century and wrote about the possible causes of the huge ship's destruction. Admittedly, the newspapers wrote about the cargo deposited in the transatlantic ship's holds, that there were weapons and war materials, among other things. Holtz writes as follows:

> *Why didn't anyone writing about the disaster pay attention to the clear reference in Captain Smith's letter to his wife about the type of cargo – a flash bringing deadly dullness.*

---

19. This shipyard built the R.M.S. **Titanic** – translator's note.

Well, exactly – why? Well, because the participants in the transatlantic transfer were able to hide the true causes of the mishap and so that the survivors, 705 in number, would not know them, and huge compensation was at stake. The collision with the iceberg allowed them to blame everything on blind luck, coincidence, and this, in turn, allowed them to conceal for a long time the true geographical coordinates of the place where the Titanic sank.[20] The financiers counted well. With testimony that the ship had sunk somewhere near Newfoundland in the "terrible depths," they were confident that no one in their right mind would attempt to get to the wreck and the armored safes inside with the treasure hidden in them.

4.4. Dives to the wreck

Years have passed. Many years. None of the survivors of the disaster are alive anymore. The time is coming to blaze a trail leading to the wreck with valuables. And this is why it is the Americans who are conducting extensive deep-sea Atlantic diving projects. Well, and that's why it no longer made sense to hide anything after the results of the French Ellipse Programmé and British Discovery Chanel expedition to the wreck of the Titanic, which was conducted on the RV Nadir research vessel unloaded to the top of the mast with electronics, fell on people like a bolt from the blue in 1996.[21] According to documents in

---

20. Initially it was reported that the Titanic hit the iceberg at the position: 41°46'N – 050°14'W, but its wreck was found at 41°43'55"N – 049°56'45"W. The lack of exact coordinates is explained by the inaccuracy of counting navigation measurements and the fact that the ship changed the speed of its movement several times, which was not taken into account or only vaguely considered. In addition, the wreck was pushed by underwater currents and lay on the bottom in a completely different place far from the collision site – translator's note.

21. This was not the first dive to the wreck of the Titanic, as the author suggests, for in 1985 the wreck was found and explored by the famous American explorer and scientist Capt. Prof. Dr. **Robert "Bob" Ballard** – translator's note.

Willman's possession, the wreck is at a depth of 3,826 meters, and most interestingly, there are no traces on its hull of a collision – actually a scuffle – with an iceberg in the form of a long and narrow crevice, instead there are six circular holes, which are located in the bow section of the ship, and their edges are curved inwards.[22] Wilman writes:

The ship plunged into the water in just over two hours, initially unnoticeable to the crew. If it had been a collision with an iceberg, the hull would have been quickly filled with it, thanks to the huge influx of outboard water. But this was not observed because the total area of the holes did not exceed 5 m^2. And from this comes the conclusion that the ship succumbed to a torpedo attack. The torpedoes were fired by an unidentified ship, but not a submarine, since these had a rather limited swimming range at the time, and only the best of them could have been ordered to sink a passenger liner in the Atlantic.

In 2002, the Americans again inspected the Titanic's hull, allowing free (cable-free) research probes into the hull, which allowed them to look into the nooks and crannies of the sunken colossus. And interestingly – TV images from inside the hull were not allowed to be broadcast, and only a statement was issued that strange holes were found on the port side under the waterline, resembling holes caused by torpedo warhead explosions. Donald Wilman also recalls that rescued passengers and crew members gave testimony to the fact that they heard a series of strong explosions inside the ship's hull, leading them to believe that two torpedo attacks had occurred. First of all, to be sure, a "control" torpedo firing was carried out, which tor-

---

22. Official reports say the six long and narrow holes may have been created when Titanic's starboard side rubbed against an ice spur below the waterline, which was the cause of its sinking – translator's note.

pedoes were fired by another ship lying adrift and operating under cover of darkness...

The hypothesis of torpedoing of the theoretically unsinkable Titanic is slowly but effectively paving its way among the views of scholars engaged in the study of the ocean depths, for when examining shipwrecks that went down due to collisions with icebergs, holes in the hull plating of at least 25–30 m² were always found. Titanic's hull was damaged in a completely different way – with several small and narrow cracks separated one from the other by large distances. Will an armored safe containing hundreds of gold and platinum bars be lifted from its interior? Probably yes, without looking at the enormous technological difficulties and public pressure.[23]

4.5. My two cents

Actually, I happen to have been interested in the subject for a long time – actually since I was a child since I first saw Jean Negulesco's film "Titanic" (1953). "Titanic" (1953) – the tragedy that took place in the North Atlantic on the memorable night of April 14/15, 1912. Later I watched all contemporary – i.e. post–war – films treating the RMS Titanic disaster up to James Cameron's masterpiece, awarded in 1997 with as many as 11 Oscars. In each of them, the atmosphere of the events unfolding on the ocean changes fundamentally – it is increasingly dark, the characters are ambiguous and thus more human than the steadfast Englishmen of the Edwardian era portrayed by Negulesco.

But that's not my point. I would like to respond to the hypothesis presented here by the Russian author and proclaiming that the RMS Titanic – a theoretically and practically unsink-

---

23. R.M.S. Titanic wreck to be protected as memorial to victims of the disaster – translator's note.

able ship – went down hit by a torpedo salvo from some submarine and was still hit by another torpedo from another U–boat.

I'm afraid that the author of this hypothesis, Donald Wilman, got carried away by fantasy and presented his version of events in an ad hoc and ill–considered manner. Let me start by saying that he assumes that the transatlantic liner was hit by several torpedoes, or at least by one that exploded somewhere amidships. So be it, but...

Torpedo – a type of underwater weapon, a projectile that moves underwater by its own propulsion, used to destroy by means of an embedded explosive charge the enemy's surface or underwater units. This is the encyclopedic definition of this weapon. (à Wikipedia) And further – The first simple torpedoes were merely underwater bombs moving in a straight line. The first torpedo to move by its own propulsion system was the Whitehead torpedo, built in 1866 by Robert Whitehead at the Fiume[24] mechanical factory. From myself, I would add that it was a compressed air torpedo. In the case described here, a vapor–gas torpedo – that is, a screw–propulsion torpedo in which the screw is driven by a turbine powered by steam and combustion gases produced by burning alcohol or kerosene under high pressure with access to water – may have been used. This type of propulsion system was first used in Britain at the turn of the 20th century and remained in use until the end of World War II. It allowed large and heavy heads (several hundred kilograms) to be carried at high speeds (even over 40 knots) over distances of up to several kilometers.[25] Its main shortcoming was a clearly visible frothy track mark on the water formed from the residual propellant gases. This track was a warning to ships under attack and betrayed the position of the submerged submarine.

---

24. Rijeka, Croatia, today.
25. Japan's torpedoes **Long Lances** had a range of up to 40 km!

Well, that's right – in such a case, observers on the bridge, the crow's nest and the Titanic's eye would have to notice frothy traces of fired torpedoes. In addition, in the event of a hit, powerful geysers of foamy water would have appeared at the side of the ship, and the explosion of several hundred kilograms of powerful explosive would have caused a very strong shock to the entire ship. This was not observed. The holes visible in the hull plating of the wreck were caused by the explosion of the boilers.

In addition, let's not forget that at the time of the disaster the surface of the ocean was almost perfectly smooth, the sea was stormy and the slightest wave did not disturb the smoothness of its waters. This and refraction were the reasons for the late sighting of the dark iceberg against the dark sea and sky. If the sea had rippled, the white foam of the waves hitting the ice would have been visible from a great distance. Meanwhile, it was not spotted, and when the sailors on the crow's nest finally saw it against the sky – it was too late. Therefore, the hypothesis that the Titanic was torpedoed is rather unlikely – personally, however, I bet on sabotage. And this sabotage was precisely executed. It could have been a bomb placed in one of the holds of the colossus, which exploded at a specific place and time so that the Titanic sank claiming as many victims as possible, and of course the treasures carried on board at a depth of almost four kilometers.

This kind of sabotage was later repeated successfully on its sister ship RMS Britannic, as early as World War I, specifically on November 21, 1916 at 8:12 a.m. EEST on its sixth voyage in the Aegean Sea HMHS Britannic[26] ran into a mine and sank within 55 minutes. Captain Charles Alfred Bartlett start-

---

26. His/Her Majesty Hospital Ship. The ship was originally called **Gigantic**, but the name was changed after the **Titanic** disaster – translator's note.

ed the engines in an attempt to reach the beach. As the ship's bow slammed into the bottom, the Britannic tilted to starboard and broke away from the bow. The wreck settled to the bottom at 9:07 a.m. Its position was N 37°42'05" – E 024°17'02". The number of casualties was low, due to the sufficient number of lifeboats, proximity to land and the relatively warm waters of the Aegean Sea. At 10 am, the cruiser HMS Scourge arrived at the scene of the disaster and rescued the survivors. There were about 1300 people on board, and 30 died, most as a result of being pulled in by the ship's still-working propellers. The wreck of the Britannica was discovered by Jacques Cousteau in 1975 near the Greek island of Keos (Kos). The wreck is in good condition, resting at a depth of 133 meters. (→ Wikipedia)

In the movie "Britannic" (2000), directed by Brian Trenchard-Smith, it is hypothesized that this was sabotage carried out by German naval intelligence. The goal was – in addition to sinking a huge vessel – to eliminate the transport of weapons and war materials carried aboard the hospital ship, which, by the way, is contrary to all conventions on the conduct of war at sea.

The second issue – who could have cared about sinking the colossus and sending gold and platinum to the bottom with it? This is a good question, especially for historians. Personally, I am of the opinion that someone cared very much that none of the more than 50 millionaires and VIPs traveling aboard it reached the States. Not gold, not platinum, not securities, but people – and specific people: Astor, Guggenheim, Ismay, Butt and other people from the candlestick and financial world were the target of this operation – if it was an operation carried out by people... For me, the list of names of these millionaires is the key to understanding this tragedy, which in fact became an obvious turning point in the history of Europe and the world. A world that two years later was engulfed in the flames of the first terrible war of the 20th century.

And the Titanic itself lies today in almost four kilometers deep and its wreck is slowly but inexorably being eaten away by ferrophages – bacteria of the genus Halomonas titanicae BH1 Mann et al. 2010.

Chapter 5

RMS "Titanic" vs. the aurora borealis?

Almost everything has been written about the RMS Titanic transatlantic disaster, and yet something new is always found. Meteorologist and blogger Marzena Rabczewska on her blog recently gave a very interesting hypothesis about the disaster of this huge ship, and which boils down to the fact that behind the collision and sinking of the Titanic is... the aurora borealis! And here is this peculiar material:

Powerful magnetic storm contributed to Titanic disaster

A geomagnetic storm may have guided a transatlantic liner to an iceberg.

The aurora borealis flashed in the sky over the North Atlantic on April 15, 1912 – The night of the sinking of the RMS Titanic. Recent investigations into the cause of the disaster of the famous transatlantic liner indicate that a powerful geomagnetic storm with aurora borealis may have disrupted navigation and communication systems and hampered rescue efforts, indirectly contributing to the disaster, during which 1,500 people died.

Witnesses who survived the disaster described the colorful lights of the aurora borealis in the region where the Titanic collided with the iceberg, and one observer testified that "the aurora borealis was very strong that night," wrote Mila Zinkova, an independent weather researcher and photographer, in a new study published in the online edition of the magazine Weather.

Auroras are formed during strong solar storms, when the sun ejects streams of electrified gas at high speeds that rush toward Earth. When the charged particles and energy collide with Earth's atmosphere, some travel along magnetic field lines, where they interact with atmospheric gases, glowing green, red, purple and blue, NASA explains. According to NASA, the charged particles are able to interfere with electrical and magnetic signals, contributing to surges.

The solar storm (also known as a geomagnetic storm) was strong enough to produce the aurora borealis and affected compasses and wireless communications on the Titanic and nearby ships. Even a small disturbance could be enough to doom the ship to disaster, Zinkova reported in the study.

The aurora borealis was perfectly visible when the Titanic was sinking. James Bisset, 2nd officer of the RMS Carpathia (the ship that saved the Titanic survivors) wrote in his diary during the fateful night of April 14/15, 1912:

There was no moon, but the aurora borealis shimmered as moonbeams shot out from the northern horizon.

In an entry made five hours later, Bisset noted that he could still see the "green rays" of the aurora borealis as the Carpathia approached the Titanic's lifeboats, Zinkova notes.

Survivors commented that at around 3 a.m. local time they spotted the aurora borealis from the lifeboats.

The light arced across the northern sky, with colorful streamers reaching toward the polar star, wrote Titanic survivor, teacher Lawrence Beesley.

At the same time that the charged particles of the solar storm were generating a pretty show in the sky, the Titanic's compass, on which the captain relied, was able to whirr. A deviation of just 0.5 degrees would have been enough to steer the ship away from safety and set it on a fatal collision course with the iceberg, Zinkova says in the study.

Radio signals that night were also "bizarre," reported operators from the liner RMS Baltic (Baltic was one of the ships that responded to Titanic's distress call, but RMS Carpathia got there first). According to Zinkova, the SOS signals sent by the Titanic to nearby ships were not heard, and responses were not received.

The official report on the Titanic's sinking suggested that amateur radio enthusiasts had caused interference, jamming the radio waves and thus preventing the accurate dissemination of distress signals to other ships nearby, she wrote. – However, at the time they had incomplete knowledge of the effects of geomagnetic storms on the ionosphere and the interference with communications. I believe that the ongoing moderate to severe geomagnetic storm near Aurora had a negative impact on receiving accurate SOS signals from nearby ships, she added.

If the geomagnetic disturbance caused by the solar storm really w as, it could affect all aspects of the tragedy, including the navigational errors that caused the Titanic to collide with the iceberg and the failed SOS communication that delayed the arrival of rescue ships, Zinkova wrote.

Although the Titanic sank more than a century ago, the story of the fateful voyage and its tragic ending continues to intrigue and fascinate. Items recovered from that fateful day command high prices at auctions, such as the April 14 lunch menu sold in 2015 for US$88,000. While the fame of the ship remains, the wreck itself is quickly falling apart. When a team of explorers visited the Titanic in August 2019 after a 14-year hiatus, they discovered that part of the ship's starboard side – where many of the first-class rooms were located – had been destroyed by powerful ocean currents, metal- and salt-eating microbes.[27]

Everything is OK, but are you sure? The hypothesis is very interesting, nevertheless it has its weaknesses, namely.:

- The Titanic's radio operators, Phillips and Bride, maintained communication with Cape Race, almost 600 mn away, at all times and transmitted private telegrams from and to Titanic's passengers there. No problems. When the R/O[28] from the Californian wanting to warn the Titanic about the ice field spoke out on their frequency, then Philips told him to shut up. At such a dictum, Cyril Evans simply turned off the radio and went to sleep... – with known fatal results. The Californian was standing 20 mn/~31.6 km adrift from the sinking Titanic, and therefore the Californian's position lights could not be seen from the deck of the Titanic and vice-versa. It must have been some unidentified ship that stood adrift and then sailed west. To this day, it is not known what kind of vessel it was...[29]

---

27. Source: „Live Science".
28. Radio officer.
29. It turned out that this ship was the SS **Mt. Temple**, which passed there on the fateful evening...

- I don't know where Ms. Zinkova got the information about the aurora blazing in the sky. It was just the opposite – the testimonies of all witnesses claim that the night was dark, moonless, and only in the very black sky did the stars shine. This is obvious, because Titanic was in the center of a high – over 1041 hPa, which gave calm, windless weather from the CAVU. And that's what determined that Titanic went straight for the iceberg – not an overturned growler, not some chunk of ice, but a full-sized iceberg – at 21.5 kts or even 25 kts in Egyptian darkness. The iceberg only appeared to observers at a distance of about 400 m from the ship, as a darker outline against a background of blazing stars.

- What happened next is known: Fleet and Lee sailors hit the bell[30] and notified the officer of the watch – VI Officer Moody on the bridge – that there was an iceberg on the course. I Officer Murdoch immediately assessed the situation and turned the handle of the machine telegraph to WHOLE BACK, at the same time giving the order LEFT TO BURT, intending to avoid the iceberg. Of course, he was aware that the ship would hit an obstacle, since Titanic's stopping distance was more than 7.77 kilometers at top speed... Besides, the very execution of the turn was very difficult – the ship weighed more than 66,000 tons, was moving fast, while its rudder blade was too small to perform such a violent maneuver quickly. The result could only be one – a collision.

- Another issue – the radio call for help. The R/O of the Titanic initially transmitted the CQD MGY signal – come quick danger and the ship's call sign. Only then

---

30. Back then, a simple code was used. 1 bell strike – danger from starboard, 2 strikes – from port side, 3 strikes – ahead of the bow.

was he reminded that another signal – SOS – save our souls – had recently been introduced, and he was already transmitting SOS MGY and the ship's position. Unfortunately – the first position was wrong, only the latter was corrected. Neighboring ships responded to the call, with the exception of the SS Californian. But again – none of them had trouble with communications.

- From what the author reports, it appears that the aurora borealis was not observed until around 03:00 a.m. NDT i.e. at 07:00 a.m. UTC/GMT – so already after the Titanic went down at 02:20 a.m. NDT/06:20 a.m. UTC/GMT.

- Did the aurora borealis have any effect on navigation? Rather not. There was no radio navigation or radiolocation yet, so there is no problem with interference with radio wave propagation. The problem was that the observers on the crow's nest didn't have binoculars – but they should have. And these were brightening binoculars with large diameter objective lenses. They did not have such – they were to be purchased only in New York. Another mistake was the lack of an observer on the eye, i.e. on the bow of the ship, who could sooner see the iceberg against the sky. Starry, but dark, with no aurora borealis fires.

Thus, this hypothesis does not stick to the known facts. Had the sky been brighter and/or perhaps the sickle of the moon (which did not rise until the morning) or the aurora borealis (which showed up after 03:00 NDT) had shone, or had there been even a faint wind that caused ripples, the Titanic would have sailed into the port of destination in New York without any problems. Unfortunately, this did not happen, and all factors created a hellish execution machine that took the lives of more than one and a half thousand people…

ℭ

Chapter 6

Are the passengers of the "Titanic" lost in time?

Ms. Irina Shlionskaya wrote a very interesting article in the pages of „Tajny XX wieka" (Secrets of Twentieth Century) No. 22/2012, pp. 6–7o, about ψ (PSI) phenomena related to the Titanic tragedy. And here is that material.

***

One of Australia's richest men billionaire Clyde Palmer has decided to recreate the Titanic. The liner will be built in China and will be equipped with the instrumentation of the time. Its construction will be completed in 2016.[31]

In April 2012 we celebrated a round anniversary – the 100th anniversary of the sinking of the famous ocean liner RMS Titanic. It would seem that the catastrophe has been described and investigated in all its details and all mysteries have long ceased to be so. But over the course of the last century, newer and newer facts about this ancient tragedy have been coming to the surface all the time. It seems that the ghosts of the people lost in the disaster are still reminiscent of themselves…

---

31. So far, this replica has not been built, but 2 films have already been made about it!

6.1. Prophecy in the Letter

And so a letter from James Arthur Paintine – the personal steward of the Titanic's captain – was recently put up for auction in London. In this letter, which the young man sent to his parents on April 10, 1912, he expressed the thought that the voyage was dangerous and the ship was facing doom...

A 29-year-old James Arthur Paintine, like Captain Edward John Smith, sailed from the beginning on the liner RMS[32] Olympic, an exact copy of the RMS Titanic. Both ships sailed for Cunard Line. In his letter sent to his family residing in Oxford, the captain's steward claims that the Titanic may have crashed , just like the Olympic, which collided with another ship in 1911... (More precisely, with the cruiser HMS Hawke – note.) And so there is a theory proclaiming that the Titanic is nothing more than the Olympic, which was sent doomed opposite to later take compensation for it.

I can say with certainty that the Titanic is nicer than the Olympic, but not at all safer," he wrote.

The letter sent by James Arthur Paintine was protected for a century by his loved ones like a relic passed down from generation to generation. On the 100th anniversary of the sinking of the Titanic, his descendants decided to sell it to the Henry Aldridge & Son Devizes (Auctioneers) auction house. The document was auctioned at an asking price of US$57,000.

---

32. During World War I, it was an HMT (His Majesty Trawler) Olympic and served as a troop transport ship.

6.2. Spectrum of Captain Smith

Also on the occasion of the 100th anniversary of the Titanic's demise, the owners of a two-story house in Staffordshire, according to sources, once owned by the family of Captain Edward John Smith, told of putting it up for sale. The thing is, according to its owners Neal and Louise Bonner, unusual events are taking place there. The specter of Captain Smith himself is said to appear there often!

It is said that when the Titanic collided with an iceberg on the night of April 14–15, 1912, its captain still had a chance to save himself, but he made a manly decision and did not leave the ship until the last moment... This is what the official version of events claims.

Those who survived the disaster claim to have seen Captain Smith standing on the bridge for the last time along with his steward Arthur Paintin. It is clear that both died in the crash...

Smith's house has passed into other hands. The Bonners sold it for £32,000. But the people who acquired it could not find peace in their new home. The residents felt an inexplicable fear and trepidation inside. Twice in the course of several years, for unknown reasons, their kitchen flooded. But most importantly – from time to time they both saw a ghost roaming around the house! The Bonners are absolutely sure that it was the specter of Captain of the Titanic.

Smith wasn't dressed in a captain's uniform or anything like that, but that's what it was, the homeowner claims.

To live in such "unpleasant" apartments the Bonners did not wish to continue and put the house up for sale for £80,000. And, of course, there were many takers who would make money on it if only as a curiosity for tourists. Today's owners such business – as you can see – is not deterred...

6.3. Dead send SOS...

However, this is not the only mystical event associated with the Titanic. Many years after the disaster of this ship, because those passing through the disaster zone repeatedly picked up from the ether calls for help from the liner, which sank in the early 20th century...

First something like this happened on the night of April 14/15, 1924, exactly 12 years after the disaster. At once, several of the ship's onboard radios registered the SOS signal of a ship with the code designation MGY. (It looked in morse like this:

-.././/...../---/...//--/-../-.- ,

however, Titanic's R/O initially used the abbreviation CQD MGY, which looked like this:

-.././/-.-./--.-/-../..//--/-../-

– translator's note.) The MGY designation was just assigned to the RMS Titanic. At the time, no one paid particular attention to it – it was decided that someone had simply pulled a silly prank or mystification. But six years later, the incident repeated itself. After that, the MGY call signal appeared regularly on the air every six years since the fateful date: in 1930, 1936, 1942... – and always on the night of April 14–15. The signals were received by ships within 2,000 miles of the site of the Titanic tragedy.

In the late 1960s, the solution to this mystery was taken up by the CIA. A griffin of secrecy was put on the subject – TOP

SECRET. But the CIA failed to trace the source of these signals, which appeared in the ether every six years.[33]

It is said that the last time a signal from the sinking Titanic was picked up by the crew of the Canadian ship was in April 1996. So it's hard to assume that someone was playing silly jokes on the sailors and the secret service for 72 years!

6.4. Rescue through 80 years

And at the turn of the century or millennium, there were rumors of the miraculous rescue of people from a sunken ship who were thought to be missing. It was also reported that they had moved into... the future!

They say that on December 14, 1992, before the eyes of Norwegian fishermen fishing in the Atlantic, a huge ship suddenly appeared to them from the depths, in which the fishermen recognized the famous Titanic! On its decks, terrified people were thrashing about. They cried out for help, some jumped into the icy water. After a few minutes, the ship hid under the water again. The Norwegians sent a radiogram to US Navy headquarters. A US ship soon arrived on the scene. Thirteen people wearing life jackets with "Titanic" written on them were lifted from the water. All of those rescued manifested memory loss – total amnesia. Some of them were carrying documents that were issued no later than 1912. Their ages matched those of the people pictured in the documents.

Norwegian and U.S. authorities came to an agreement to keep everything secret. The media only reported that survivors were rescued from a sunken ship, but did not state from which ship. What happened next to those rescued – is unknown. Most

---

33. By the way, the matter should be handled not so much by the CIA, but by the National Security Agency – NSA, which was established for, among other things, radio intelligence and radio counterintelligence – translator's note.

likely, they were placed under medical observation and probably in a secret, well-protected medical center.[34]

In 1994, three more victims of the disaster were reportedly fished out of the water in the North Atlantic – including Captain Smith himself and two passengers – someone named Winnie Cootes and a 10-month-old girl in the Titanic's lifebelt. They were all on the lists of those killed in the disaster 82 years ago.

But in all likelihood these are only myths. As for the mysterious radio signals from the deck of the Titanic, they are documented in a multitude of sources. And it is not out of the question that a call for help took place and – of course – it was not sent by ghosts.

6.5. Paradoxes of ether and radio communications

The peculiarities of radio wave propagation in various environments are still not well studied to this day. For example, scientists to this day are working on the mystery of the so-called stopped radioech. It happens that a signal sent into the ether for some time repeats itself, and not once, but several times. There are many stories circulating among radio amateurs about radio messages fixed in the ether, which the addressees received after many years.

And so one frontline radio operator received a radiogram from his friend in the late 1950s. The paradox was that this friend – also a military radioman – had died at the front. The radiogram said that the subdivision had fallen into encirclement and that they had many wounded. The dead radzist asked for artillery support. It is said that after receiving this radio-

---

34. The Italian–French movie "Hibernatus" directed by **Eduardo Molinaro** [1969] with an excellent role by **Luis de Funés** comes to mind here – translator's note.

gram, the frontman no longer engaged in radio amateurism – he gave away all his apparatus and disbanded: in his brain it could not figure out by what miracle he had received a message from that world...

According to the laws of physics, radio waves used in communications either bounce off the ionosphere or pierce it and "escape" into space. Their "return" can only be explained by a collision with some mysterious object that reflects them back to Earth. This is how the hypothesis of an alien interplanetary probe in Earth's orbit, which causes so much trouble for geophysicists, came about.[35] Among others, the brilliant inventor Nikola Tesla claimed that with the help of radio waves it would be possible to make contact with the afterlife...

---

35. It involves mysterious delays in radio signals, which Dr. **Duncan Lunan** interpreted as the intervention of a probe from the Isar (ε–Volarius) star system placed in orbit around Earth 13,000 years ago, or about a mysterious orbital object called the Black Prince, Black Baron, Black or Dark Knight.

Chapter 7

The princess who sank the "Titanic"

Valeriy Nikolaev wrote an engaging article in „Tajny XX wieka" (Secret of the Twentieth Century), No. 20/2015, pp. 20–21, in which he ascertains the causes of this tragedy in the hereafter, and that of the Egyptians!

***

In 1974, archaeologists found that the mummy of Pharaoh Ramesses II was deteriorating. They transported it to France equipped with a normal, modern Egyptian passport, where they wrote "king (deceased)" under the heading "occupation performed."

One of my acquaintances refers to archaeologists with great prejudice, calling them "cemetery hyenas." And he is not alone in this. From time immemorial and in all cultures, grave robbing has been considered one of the most horrible crimes. Cemetery hyenas risked incurring the most severe penalties for violating the tranquility of ancestors' ashes. The heroes of Steven Sommers' avant-garde horror films titled "The Mummy" and "The Mummy Returns" found this out. They discovered an old tomb, from which they released the forces of Evil, which taunted the bodies of the chief priest of Egypt – Imhotep and his lover Ankhesenamun – who was cursed and buried alive for a crime committed. "Well, but after all, it's in the cinema". – you will say. But in real life there are "white" and "black" archaeologists, doggedly digging up strange barrows and uncovering tombs, without looking at the consequences often pay the highest price for their carelessness.

7.1. A FATAL FATE

About 3,000 years ago, the body of the deceased Egyptian princess Amun-Ra was placed in a wooden coffin and buried in a tomb on the banks of the Nile – in Luxor. In 1890, some prospectors, who can be boldly compared to "black" archaeologists, unearthed her remains. They decided to sell their find, the "cemetery hyenas" to four wealthy English tourists who were misguidedly directed to the dig site. The Englishmen liked the colorful sarcophagus so much that they decided to buy it. They cast lots for who would get the treasure. The winner paid several thousand pounds sterling and sent the sarcophagus to the hotel. And then the same Englishman, not knowing why, headed for the desert – and was lost forever in its sands. The second participant in the draw the next day was shot in the hand with a fusion by a serving Egyptian. The limb had to be amputated. The third, having returned to England, found that he had become bankrupt having lost all his shares in the stock market. The fourth became seriously ill, lost his job and ended up selling matches on the street.

It is not known what happened to the one who unearthed the tomb. History is also silent about how the tomb of Princess Amen-Ra ended up in England. There, the artifact changed several owners, with many of them dying under unexplained circumstances. And here is what one of them wrote down in his diary:

When I tried to look into the eyes of the mummy, or more precisely, into the place where they used to be, at one point it began to appear to me that the embalmed body betrayed signs of life – its appearance emanated such hatred that the blood froze in my veins...

And finally this amateur of strong sensations decided to resell the sinister sarcophagus to a certain London businessman who wanted it to complete his collection of Egyptian artifacts. The seller's body was soon found in some alley with a knife in its heart. And in the buyer's case, a black series soon began in his life: three of his relatives died in a traffic accident, while his house burned to the ground (the sarcophagus was not affected at all in the process) The businessman realized that all these events were related to the mummy, on which apparently a curse had been cast, and donated it to the British Museum.

7.2. Butchered at the British Museum

A passerby fell under the wheels of the carriage carrying the sarcophagus with the mummy and received serious injuries. Later, one of the museum's employees who carried this cargo to the warehouse tripped on the stairs, fell and broke his leg. His colleague, who was in good health, soon died within days.

The sarcophagus was placed in the Egyptian branch of the museum. And it was here that the awakened spirit of the princess began to act in its full dimension. This was seen by the night watchmen, who heard it at night as someone in the coffin tapped, called out and cried. These noises drove them out of their senses. And in the morning, employees entering the Egyptian exhibit saw exhibits that were stripped from their places and scattered around the room... When one watchman died while on night duty, his replacement was quickly relieved of his job. And then one of the cleaners sweeping the dust off the sarcophagus allowed herself to shake the dust onto her face from the sarcophagus – and soon her son died of measles.

The museum's management decided not to tempt fate again and moved the sarcophagus to storage. But even so, shortly thereafter, one of the employees became seriously ill, and the one responsible for moving the sarcophagus was found dead behind a work table.

Rumors spread around the capital about an evil spirit haunting the British Museum. A young reporter decided to make money by taking pictures of the awe-inspiring sarcophagus. Having developed the film and made prints, he found that a monstrous face was staring at him from the photo. Shocked by this, the young man shot himself at his home later that evening.

7.3. Evil remains Evil

Then, for some time, museums disposed of the sinister exhibit, and finally it was sold to a private collection. With the buyer immediately began a series of misfortunes. Finally he took the mummy to the attic. The house was once visited by the famous theosophist and occultist Helena Blavatsky. Immediately after entering it she fell into a trance. Returning to herself, she explored the entire house in search of an unusually strong source of Evil and finally entered the attic, where she discovered a sarcophagus. The host asked her:

"Can you banish away this evil spirit?"

"Evil spirits cannot be chased away," replied Blavatsky, "Evil remains Evil forever. Here nothing can be done. I advise you to get rid of this Evil as soon as possible."

But carrying out this advice was not at all easy. The fame of the sinister artifact, meanwhile, had spread throughout the civilized world, and no one wanted to associate with it.

But finally there was such a daredevil, and it turned out to be Lord Canterville – an English aristocrat and well-known collector. He was a very well-read man, and he knew about the fact that a powerful curse had been cast on the sarcophagus, which would strike anyone who dared to disturb the peace of the princess. But the desire to possess the ancient artifact proved stronger than fear. The lord hoped that if he did not open the sarcophagus, the curse would not affect him.

7.4. Three maritime disasters

And indeed, for a while Lord Canterville possessed his treasure without any repercussions. And then he decided to put this sarcophagus on display in New York. He booked himself a cabin aboard the world's finest liner, a passenger transatlantic liner, while the sarcophagus was assigned a place in the cargo and luggage compartment. And everything would have been OK, if not for the fact that the ship in question was called RMS Titanic…

As we know, on the night of April 14/15, 1912, it sank after colliding with an iceberg – according to the official version – and took with it to the depths more than 1500 people. But what about the mummy? We know for sure that she did not sink. There were witnesses who saw Lord Canterville take her with him into the lifeboat, without looking at the protests of the other passengers. And others claim to have spotted this sarcophagus floating on the surface of the ocean among items from the Titanic's hull.[36] As it happened, in 1914 Princess Amun–Ra re-

---

36. Everything would be fine if it weren't for a small detail. On the lists of Titanic 1st, 2nd and 3rd class passengers, I could not find anyone with the surname Can-

minded the world of herself. A wealthy Canadian from Montreal became the new owner of the sarcophagus. He quickly realized how dangerous the artifact was and decided to ship the mummy back to England on a ship named RMS Empress of Ireland. However, on May 29, 1914, shortly after leaving port, this steamer collided with the Norwegian coal carrier SS Storstad. As a result, 1,029 people died. The Canadian himself survived. He realized then that the spirit of the princess would not be appeased until the mummy was returned to its burial place in Luxor. Well, and he decided to return the mummy to the land of Egypt. The ship he boarded with his dangerous cargo left New York on May 1, 1915. After six days it was attacked by a German U-boat. A torpedo fired by it sent the steamer to the bottom along with 1,200 people. The ship was the RMS Lusitania...

The Canadian survived it again, but throughout his life he was tormented by remorse that through his recklessness so many people lost their lives.

Without looking at all the efforts of doctors and scholars, it was not possible to clarify with the owner what happened to the mummy. Most likely, the sarcophagus remained in the hull of the sunken steamer and is now on the seabed somewhere not far from the Irish coast. And God forbid that some treasure hunter would try to bring it to the surface! After all, Princess Amen-Ra's curse remains in effect to this day, until she returns to Luxor.

7.5. My 2 cents

As a rationalist and dialectical materialist, I naturally rule out all sorts of supernatural activities, curses, curses and other such

---

terville/Kanterville or even close to it – see https://en.wikipedia.org/wiki/Passengers_of_the_RMS_Titanic – translator's note.

miracles. There could have been many different reasons for the death of these people and the events described. But...

But there is another, strange and at the same time interesting circumstance, which does not look like a mere coincidence or coincidence. Well, because think Reader – three ships sink for three different reasons: RMS Titanic – a collision, or rather a scuffle with an iceberg; RMS Empress of Ireland – a collision with SS Storstad, and RMS Lusitania – being hit by a torpedo fired from U–20. Now the question:

7.6. What is the common feature of these three disasters?

The answer is – all these ships were stabbed in the forward part of the starboard side! And all of them went down scalloping to the bow and starboard!

And another strange curiosity: in an identical way, after running into a mine, on November 21, 1916, in the position N 37°42′05″ – E 024°17′02″ (Aegean Sea) in 55 minutes went to the bottom of the Titanic's sister-ship – HMHS ex RMS Britannic! More interestingly – the mine exploded in the forward part of the starboard side! Fortunately, almost all crew members and hospital staff were rescued. Coincidence? If so, then very, very strange!

In a similar manner, went down on July 26, 1956, another transatlantic liner – the Italian passenger liner SS Andrea Doria, which sank after a radar collision with the Swedish ship SS Stockholm. And again (another coincidence???) the bow of the Swedish ship slammed into the starboard forepeak of the Italian liner, which went down in position: N 40°30′ – W 069°52′ (50 mn from the Nantucket lighthouse). The Italian ship, fortunately, went down in enough time to save almost all passengers and crew members.

All these disasters give food for thought, as we can talk about the curse of the Titanic rather than some mummy. Just... – where did the curse of the Titanic come from, since it all started with it?

Let me start with the fact that this ship was not christened! No bottle of champagne, wine or even seawater was smashed against its bow! No solemn naming formula was uttered...

His horoscope – according to Czech astrologer Zoša Klinkorová (which I have already written about in the pages of „Nieznany Świat" (Unknown World) in the past) – was also uninteresting and did not bode well for him, as did the horoscopes of the vast majority of his passengers.

Another premise: as the advertising slogan proclaimed, *not even God would be able to sink it* – a blasphemous challenge in itself.

Besides, at least two dangerous artifacts were transported on its decks: the mummy of Princess Amun-Ra and a statue of Satan, according to a popular rumor. Others speak of a statue of Baphomet – the idol of the Knights of the Temple – Templars...

And finally, the last: the crew was uncoordinated, under-equipped, under-attached, its complement incomplete, officers swapped functions, and such a team can make many more mistakes than people who have already sailed with each other. And those mistakes were made!

OK, but this applies to the Titanic, what about the rest of the ships? What do you readers think?

7.7. The Curse of the Titanic

Here, it is worth mentioning two other heroes of the story of the sinking of the RMS Titanic, namely – the RMS Carpathia and the SS Mount Temple. Let's start with the Carpathia. Everyone knows the details of the Titanic disaster, but few are aware of the heroic Carpathia, which rescued 703 Titanic passengers drifting in lifeboats. On April 18, 1912, the RMS Carpathia arrived in the New York harbor with the rescued Titanic survivors. The RMS Carpathia is a transatlantic passenger steamship of the Cunard Line, built in the shipyard in Newcastle on August 6, 1902. It was a typical steamship, used to transport immigrants. The vessel operated on the route from Rijeka to New York and back. The sailings occurred every two weeks, with passengers mainly being Italians, Croats, and Hungarians. The crew consisted of about 70 Croats.

The single-funnel Carpathia was sailing from New York to Rijeka when Captain Arthur Rostron received the SOS signal from the sinking Titanic. He directed the ship to a position 57 nautical miles (105.5 km) away, traveling at a speed that had never been achieved before. Nevertheless, the ship arrived only at 4 a.m. after a 3.5-hour rescue voyage. (The Titanic sank at 02:25). Captain Rostron proved to be a foresighted commanding officer. He immediately organized accommodations for the injured and hypothermic, arranged medical assistance, and prepared the cranes and lifeboats.

The mechanics of the Carpathia shut off the supply of steam and heat to the cabins so that it could be used by the engines to achieve the highest speed possible. Additional observers were posted to ensure that the ship, sailing through the icefield, did not share the fate of the Titanic. The captain ordered the flag to be lowered to half-mast and conducted a service. After rescuing the survivors, he returned to New York. The crew was honored for their bravery with bronze medals, while its officers received silver ones. The captain received a gold medal, which was presented to him by Margaret Molly Brown, a rescued passenger. Additionally, a Congressional Gold Medal was awarded. The ship sank on July 17, 1918, off the coast of Ireland, after being torpedoed by the German U-55. 157 passengers were rescued by HMS Snowdrop (a minesweeper). The wreck of the Carpathia was found in 1999 by writer Clive Cussler.

Josip Car, a Croat, joined the crew of the passenger ship Carpathia in Rijeka. He was a witness to the Titanic disaster. He kept a life jacket – one of the five rescued – and other memorabilia, which he donated to the museum in Rijeka. The exhibition from Rijeka was in Szczecin in 2016. Croatian sailors sailed not only on the Carpathia but also on other Cunard ships – Pannonia, Ultonia, Aurania, Slavonia, Carmania, Ivernia, Saxonia, Laconia, and Franconia.

The fate of the Canadian ship SS Mt. Temple took a different turn, which – as it now turns out – did not provide any assistance to the sinking giant. The Mount Temple set out on its usual voyage on April 3, 1912, at 14:00 from Antwerp towards Saint John in New Brunswick. The ship was under the command of Captain James Henry Moore and carried 1466 passengers, mainly in economy class, and 143 crew members. On the night of April 14 to 15, the radio operator Marconi on the Mount Temple, John Durrant, was just finishing his evening when at around 00:11 ship's time (22:25 EST), he received an SOS signal from the RMS Titanic, which was sinking after hitting an iceberg. The message contained an incorrect SOS position 41°44'N 50°24'W. Durrant relayed the message to the bridge through a steward and confirmed receipt of the signal to Titanic's radio operator, Jack Phillips. However, Phillips had difficulty understanding the transmission from Durrant due to the noise of steam escaping from the Titanic's smokestacks. Durrant made sure not to interfere with the ongoing exchanges between the Titanic and other ships that he assumed were closer to the scene. Ten minutes after receiving the first SOS signal from the Titanic (at 00:21 ship's time, 22:35 EST), a further message arrived from the Titanic with corrected SOS coordinates: The location is 41°46'N 50°14'W. This location was 13 miles (21 km) west of where the Titanic actually sank, as confirmed by the wreck coordinates. (The center of the Titanic wreck field is at 41°43.5'N 49°56.8'W)

When this message was received, Captain Moore was sleeping. Upon waking, he assessed the situation carefully. He had standing orders to avoid icebergs, but after receiving the SOS signal, he decided to initiate a rescue operation. He immediately turned the ship around and headed north-northeast at an estimated speed of 11½ kts (21.3 km/h; 13.2 mph) toward the last reported position of the Titanic at 41°46'N and 50°14'W. He consulted with his chief engineer, John Gillett, to try to extract even more speed from the old vessel. Moore estimated his own approximate position as 41°25'N and 51°14'W, about 61 nautical miles (113 km; 70 miles) south and west of the now-established location of the Titanic wreck (41°43.5'N and 49°56.8'W). Even at full speed, it would take about four hours to cover the distance between his ship and the Titanic.

After setting off, Moore woke and instructed the crew that was not on duty and ordered the unveiling of 20 lifeboats on board. He prepared ropes and ladders, got life belts ready, and set up additional lookout stations to help avoid icebergs reported in the area. Initially, progress was good, but upon discovering that his ship was approaching a large ice field around 03:00 on April 15, the ship slowed down, becoming increasingly surrounded by pack ice. At this time, Mount Temple encountered what was believed to be a schooner with only one green light, which remained unidentified and caused the ship to take evasive action. This green light could have been a rocket or flare fired by survivors of the Titanic or launched by RMS Carpathia racing to the rescue. As the amount of ice increased, Mount Temple moved about 14 nautical miles (26 km; 16 miles) from the last reported position of the Titanic around 03:25 and continued to drift through the ice field until dawn. It reached the last known position of the Titanic around 04:30 and found itself in a heavily packed ice field, but there was no sign of survivors or the wreck. After about half an hour of waiting, Moore headed southeast, searching for a corridor to pass through the pack ice, but eventually changed course back to north-northwest, casting a shadow on the western edge of the ice pack. Somewhere between 6:00 and 06:30, Carpathia, commanded by Captain Arthur Rostron, was sighted to the east of the ship, and SS Californian was spotted to the north, crossing the ice field from east to west. At 6:52, after sunrise, Moore took a vertical measurement of the sun's altitude to determine his location and discovered he was a few miles east of the Titanic's given longitude. Using navigational reasoning, he inferred that the actual accident site was about eight miles (13 km) further east, behind the ice field in front of him.

Mount Temple sent a telegraphic request to Carpathia but received no response. Around 08:30, Californian approached Carpathia as it finished taking on the last survivors. At 08:31, Carpathia reported that it had rescued 20 boats and sent another message at 09:26, informing everyone that there was no longer a need to wait, after which Moore ordered a change of course and continued the journey to New Brunswick. When

Mount Temple docked in Saint John's on April 19, it was called for an American, and later British, inquiry into the sinking.

As soon as Mount Temple arrived in Canada, it became the center of controversy, as two passengers, and allegedly some crew members, stated that the ship was close to the Titanic but failed to come to its aid because they saw distress rockets and even watched the ship sink. The speculation was ignored by American and British investigations, and none of the officers from the Mount Temple testified or made statements to support those claims. Captain Moore testified that no passenger could have witnessed an event such as a rocket explosion above the ship because no passenger was on board at midnight to see it. Over the years, attempts were made to stir further controversy regarding the role of Mount Temple in the sinking of the Titanic, often in a thinly veiled attempt to divert attention away from the guilt and responsibility of the Leyland Californian liner, which was likely closer to the location of the tragedy and whose officers reported seeing several rockets exploding above an unidentified ship they were observing.

The controversies surrounding Mount Temple were further fueled in November 2020 by the "PBS Abandoning the Titanic" program, part of the "Secrets of the Dead" series. Aired in some countries as "Titanic: A Dead Reckoning," it was co-produced and co-written by journalist and Titanic author Senan Molony. The program repeated some old claims about Mount Temple and its role in the disaster, as well as presenting several new ones. Among these claims was the assertion that Mount Temple was much closer to the Titanic when the SOS signal was received, that Mount Temple came within five miles (8.0 km) of the Titanic when Captain Moore decided to retreat after encountering an ice field, trying to avoid risking his own ship, and that Mount Temple resembled the "mysterious ship" that was observed from the Titanic, due to the distance between its four masts, as later noted by the commander of the raider that sank Mount Temple in World War I. The program concluded that Captain Stanley Lord of the SS Californian was unfairly stigmatized for not reaching the Titanic, when in reality it was Captain Moore of the Mount Temple who left the passengers and crew of the doomed liner to their own fate.

This hypothesis, however, is strongly challenged by historians. In January 2021, a well-known group of historians and authors of the Titanic published a polemical document titled: "Abandoning the Titanic," "Abandoning Reality: The Truth About SS Mount Temple." While the new program attempts to discredit Captain Moore of the Mount Temple and blames him for "abandoning" the Titanic and those aboard to their fate, historical records clearly demonstrate otherwise. At a distance of 49.5 nautical miles (91.7 km; 57.0 miles) from the famous danger coordinates of the Titanic and about 60 miles (97 km) from the actual site of the disaster, Mount Temple was simply too far away to be seen from the deck of the Titanic, and for those on board Mount Temple to see the Titanic or its distress rockets. Captain Moore and his crew made a desperate attempt to reach the damaged Titanic but arrived at the western side of the ice field that separated it from the wreck site only after about 2 hours and 40 minutes from the sinking of the Titanic. There was no possibility of reaching the Titanic in time to conduct a rescue operation; they did not "abandon" the Titanic.

The SS Mt. Temple was sunk on December 6, 1916, by the German raider SMS Möwe after a brief exchange of fire. The ship was intercepted and boarded and then blown up 620 nautical miles west of Fastnet. Four crew members died, while the remaining passengers and crew were interned, with American citizens being released to return home[37].

Thus, the matter has not been fully resolved[38].

---

37. The US was neutral at this time.
38. Source – Wikipedia.

Chapter 8

Revenge of the mummy

Being still a teenager, in my grandfather's library I caught one of the issues of the pre-war monthly magazine „Naokoło świata" (Around the World), in which I read a short story by a Polish author entitled. "The Revenge of the Mummy." Years later I tried to find it, but the passage of time and numerous moves caused that issue to be lost somewhere, which is a pity, because the short story was worthy.

It began with the fact that one hot evening on the Nile ship PS Amun Ra two gentlemen met and killed time by telling each other strange and amazing stories. And lo and behold, one of them told the story of the discovery of a mummy of a certain woman who was bringing bad luck upon her owners. All those who had to deal with her at best suffered damage like not to their health, property or something else. I no longer remember exactly how many there were, but her trail across Africa and Europe was marked by corpses and misfortunes. It reminded me of the story of the discovery of the mummy from the tomb of Pharaoh Tutankhamun by archaeologist Howard Carter and Lord Carnarvon or, more precisely, Sir George Edward Stanhope Molyneux Herbert, 5th Earl of Carnarvon. And just as in the case of the curse of Tutankhamun, there were a lot dead bodies[39].

This mummy – which was a mummy of a woman – was distinguished by one thing, and that was its smile. Dark, malicious and sneering at the same time. Well caused people to fear her, and rightly so – because wherever she appeared, death and misfortune also appeared. Well, and of course – as in the case of Tutankhamun – everything looked like pure coincidence: someone there fell under a train, someone there crashed a car, someone there was cut down by a mosquito... in the end, the terrified owner decided to send it to a museum in New York and loaded it on the first better ship sailing in that direction. Luck would have it – or maybe not? – That the ship was the RMS Titanic.

We know the rest.

It makes me wonder: was this a pastiche of William Thomas Stead's story about the curse of the mummy? Krzysztof Załuski writes about it on www.Onet.pl:[40]

Was the Titanic sunk by a cursed mummy? Conspiracy theories about the 1912 disaster

After the crash of the famous liner, such a theory fascinated the world press at the time. The cursed mummy was supposed to belong to the priestess Amun-Ra. The 1912 tragedy caused a rash of all sorts of conspiracy theories to somehow explain to

---

39. Of course, this theme was also attacked by the famous writer Agatha Christie, who confronted her super-detective Hercules Poirot with the curse of the Pharaoh Mer-her-ra in the story "The Mystery of the Egyptian Tomb." In 1993, a film of the same title was made, directed by Peter Barber-Fleming.

40. See: *https://www.onet.pl/styl-zycia/facet-xl/czy-titanic-zatopila-przekleta-mumia-teorie-spiskowe-o-katastrofie-z-1912-r/ldpj62j,30bc1058*, December 4, 2023.

people the sinking of the supposedly unsinkable ship and the death of 1,502 people. 711 were rescued.

Was the Titanic sunk by a cursed mummy? Conspiracy theories about the 1912 disaster.

The Egyptian plague

According to one of the most fantastic theories, this cursed mummy was supposed to have traveled aboard a liner. Legend says that the artifact was the remains of a priestess from the time of Amenhotep IV, named either Amun–Otu, Amun–Ra, or Amenophis. During her lifetime, the priestess was famous as a diviner, so after her death she was rewarded with a magnificent burial: with jewelry, figurines of the gods, and magical amulets. Among them was an image of Osiris, decorated with the inscription: "Awaken from your faint, and your gaze will crush anyone who stands in your way." Others claimed that it was inscribed: "Rise from the dust, and only the look of your eyes will triumph over all intrigues against you." It was a curse. Anyone who approached the sarcophagus was to die an agonizing death.

In fact, the mummy of the priestess Amun–Ra was discovered during excavations near Cairo. This was in the 1880s. Initially, the mummy was exhibited in the British Museum, from where, according to legend, it was bought by an American collector. The millionaire intended to take the valuable artifact to New York. Apparently, the ancient find was not transported in the cargo hold, but was placed directly on the captain's bridge! What does the legend say? That Captain Edward Smith could not resist the temptation and looked into the sarcophagus despite the curse. And then, instead of the overpriced Egyptian priestess, he saw death! The horrible curse came true.

Hardly before the disaster, writer William Thomas Stead wrote a story about a young archaeologist who found the mummy of a cursed woman. In the story, it was the museum in her possession that wanted to transport the ancient treasure by ship to America to get rid of the fatality weighing down on the mummy. On a foreign continent she was to lose her fatal power.

In this remarkable work, the ship was named Titanic, its captain was named E.J. Smith. The drama is completed by the fact that the writer – probably the hero of the story, died in agony during the disaster. The writer, who was on the real Titanic during the fateful voyage, on the last evening before the disaster, reportedly told guests about the curse of a mummy discovered in one of Egypt's tombs. The curse involved repeating the inscription read on the mummy's chest. For this there was a threat of violent death.

It is hardly surprising that people related unusual coincidences and were frightened by the curse of the mummy.

Well, this was the turn of the 19th and 20th century, when ancient Egypt was "in vogue," so such stories were popular. It's worth mentioning that the triumphs included Verdi's opera "Aida" and Bolesław Prus's novel "Pharaoh," in which reality blended with fantasy of the highest order. That's why novels and stories emerged that today we would classify as horrors.

In fact, the mummy of the priestess herself remained in Egypt, and only her sarcophagus was donated to the British Museum in London in 1889. The artifact can still be admired today. The sarcophagus did not leave the museum for the first time until 1990, when it went to other museums around the world for exhibition purposes.

The same is true of another short story by American writer Morgan Robertson entitled "The Wreck of Titan (or "Futility") published in 1898, tells the story of a powerful passenger ship built in England, named Titan, which is considered unsinkable and does not have enough lifeboats. On its third voyage, in April, it hits an iceberg and sinks in the North Atlantic. The similarity to the disaster of the British transatlantic liner Titanic is significant. In 1912, Robertson published a second version of his book, changing the content slightly to make the tragedy described there even more similar to what happened in reality.

Was Robertson a visionary? Wikipedia gives other equally astonishing facts:

In 1905, Robertson wrote a book entitled "The Submarine Destroyer," in which he described a submarine equipped with an instrument called a periscope. The writer later claimed to have worked out its design, but failed to obtain a patent for legal and technical reasons.

In 1914 Robertson wrote a novella, "Beyond the Spectrum," which described the war between Japan and the United States. Like "The Wreck of the Titan," the book "Beyond the Spectrum" contained quite a few parallels to real events in the later history of the World War II conflict.

As I think, there is much to ponder, after all, it's a pure case of precognition triggered by the mass death of more than 1,600 people, which was a massive breach in the fabric of space-time and sensitives must have felt it in some way before, during and after the disaster. It was a stroke of luck that only Robertson managed to put this premonition on paper, and if people had not been so stupidly prejudiced against ψ-phenomena (PSI phenomena), this massacre would not have happened…

Chapter 9

Interterrans, Water People, etc.

Ghosts actually exist. I know, because I myself saw one of them in the morning mist. I watched in disbelief as it shifted before my eyes, as if a monstrous specter banished from hell. Wrapped in an invisible shroud of past tragedy, with the souls of those who died on it floating around...
The sight of it made one feel pride and sorrow at the same time...
Clive Cussler – "Raise the Titanic!"

It was supposed to be the world's greatest ship. Not the biggest, not the fastest – the greatest. Its first and last voyage, despite a sea of written ink and a few forests turned to paper, is shrouded in the mist of Mystery – the kind written with a capital M. And about this Mystery I would like to tell here...

9.1. Maiden voyage

So far, that literary vision of raising the RMS Titanic, which was so vividly described by American writer–mariner Clive Cussler, has not come true – and very well. Instead, another dream of generations of explorers has come true – the DSV Alvin bathyscaphe plunged into the wreck plunged at a depth of more than four kilometers and made a reconnaissance. We know that after slipping under the surface of the water, the Titanic broke into two parts and sank to the bottom becoming a grave for 1513 people. By the way, the same Alvin along with DSV Aluminaut became famous for finding and retrieving an American hydrogen bomb lost by SAC in the Mediterranean Sea near the Spanish town of Palomares in 1961.

The RMS Titanic was a ship that was, in the words of commentators at the time, a floating "Ritz" class hotel, and that was because of the luxuries – obviously for first class passengers. It had a displacement of 66,000 tons, a gross tonnage of 46,328 tons, a length of 270 meters, a width of 28 meters, a height from the keel to the captain's bridge of 32 meters, two steam engines and turbines with a total power of 51,000 horsepower, three propellers, 29 boilers, 11 decks and 2,500 seats for passengers. The whole thing, pushed by the power of steam, which required 600 tons of coal bunkers each day to heat, moved at a traveling speed of 22 knots (kts) – or 40.7 km/h.

The ship embarked on its maiden voyage on April 10, 1912 along the course: Southampton (England) – Cherbourg (France) – Queenstown (Ireland) – New York (USA). After docking passengers in Cherbourg, on Thursday, April 11, the ship dropped its moorings and headed for the shores of Ireland, from where it took the southern course across the Atlantic. Guided by the steady hand of Captain Smith and two officers, Murdoch and Lightoller, the mighty transatlantic set off on its first – and, as it later turned out, also last – voyage to America...

As a curiosity, I will mention that there has been almost something as large as the unfortunate Titanic. It was the SS Great Eastern, designed by Isambard Kingdom Brunel, which was the largest ship ever built in the 19th century when it was completed in 1858. It could carry up to 4000 passengers from England to Australia without refueling, which made it a technical masterpiece of its time. The SS Great Eastern was equipped with sails, paddle wheels, and a screw propeller, marking a turning point in shipbuilding. Its length of 211 meters and double hull were revolutionary features that were later adopted in ship construction. This ship also inspired the writer Jules Verne, who wrote his story "The Floating City" based on a journey on this ship. Its length of 692 feet (211 m) was not surpassed until 1899 by the 705-foot (215 m) 17,274-ton RMS Oceanic, its gross tonnage of 18,915 was only exceeded in 1901 by the 701-foot (214 m) 20,904-ton RMS Celtic and SS Imperator, and its capacity of 4000 passengers was surpassed in 1913. The ship, which had five smokestacks (which were later reduced to four), was remarkable for its time. The ship also had the largest set of paddle wheels[41].

I will not describe what happened on board the Titanic during the voyage – others have done it better than me. I will only focus on the last minutes before the disaster. The 2207 crewmen and 1400 passengers confidently flashed toward what was inevitable. Sailors on the crow's nest spotted a two-topped iceberg on course and...

...on April 14, 1912, at 11:40 p.m. NDT, at a position N 41°46' and W 050°14', speeding at 22 kts, the RMS Titanic hits an iceberg with its starboard side. Two hours later it goes down.

This is what all versions of the disaster report.

A dive by Capt. Dr. Bob Ballard's team in 1985 clarified nothing, and in fact raised even more questions. It was presumed that the Titanic had gone down as a result of the hull being torn by the sharp edge of an iceberg over a length of 60 me-

---

41. Wikipedia.

ters, which in fact would have been enough to send this giant into the arms of Davy Jones... But no, only 6 small holes with outward-turning edges were found in the hull, which rather suggested an explosion inside the hull. So, what? Sabotage?...

Sinking: deliberate and deliberate the RMS Titanic would have been and was a de facto knotty point in history – after all, a sizeable pack of VIPs were on board – including as many as 57 millionaires with J. J. Astor, B. Guggenheim, I. Strauss and G. Wiedener in the top. There was an advisor to U.S. President Taft – A. Butt, the president of White Star Line and builder of the Titanic – Th. Andrews, the main shareholder of the company – J. B. Ismay and "unsinkable" Molly Brown – a millionaire from Montana, about whom our unforgettable sea captain Karol Olgierd Borchardt wrote in his book "Znaczy kapitan". There was also the famous British journalist and writer William I. Stead, at whom we will stop a little longer when discussing the causes of the disaster.

All these people carried with them money, gold, valuables and securities deposited in the captain's safes, with an estimated value of about US$300 million. And it all went down at 02:20 a.m. on April 15, 1912... Insurance companies paid GB£ 14 million to the families of the victims – a sum that was sky-high for the time.

9.2. A MUMMY'S REVENGE AND SICK AMBITIONS

The disaster was tried to be explained in various ways. Of course, the arrogance and sick ambition of White Star Line executives and the bravado of Captain Smith contributed to the transatlantic liner's demise, but not only. If I were a proponent of the conspiracy theory of history, I would focus on those 57 millionaires and other VIPs who traveled aboard it. The deaths of many of them shook their financial empires and certainly significantly changed the course of history. It may have influenced the outbreak and course of the two Great Wars of the 20th century, as well as the subsequent history of the world. I wonder how the fate of the world would have turned out if the Titanic had not chafed against the iceberg on that fateful night...?

Of the unnatural causes – that is, lying outside our world – two can be mentioned. The first was mentioned by William I. Stead – the revenge of the mummy wife of one of the pharaohs, who put a curse on all who disturb her.

Another writer claimed that on the Titanic there was a statue of Satan himself and, to boot, all the instruments for celebrating the black mass... In addition, blasphemous inscriptions such as: This ship will not sink even the Lord God himself!, or There is no God who would be able to sink this ship into the depths of the sea!, which was a blatant challenge to all the forces of darkness and had to end in only one and only fatal way for him... In addition – to make it quite macabre – in one of the watertight compartments, NB the same one that was ripped apart by the ice – was supposed to be the corpse of one of the niters, who was locked up there alive... Coincidence or a deliberate sacrifice for the Prince of Darkness???... Either way – the ship did not reach its destination. It was sunk by Satan himself in persona, who put an iceberg on its course and caused a complete calm, zero wind and the sea smooth as oil – there wasn't even a long Atlantic swell, which is a phenomenon in itself! To make things even more interesting – the sailors on the crow's nest were reliant only on their own eyes – they didn't even have binoculars!!! Captain Smith did not put out an eye post to complement the observers from the bridge and the crow's nest. He didn't see the need, despite warnings about drifting ice... It seemed that

Nature herself had conspired against the transatlantic and the people who traveled on it.

And yet, if Titanic's 1st Officer William Murdoch had given "full reverse" prior to the collision and kept the ship on course for the ice, it would have ended up crashing and crushing the two bow watertight chambers, which would have ended up with the ship's bow trim, which could have been offset by flooding the two stern chambers to bring the ship to an even keel. The remaining 12 chambers would have made it buoyant enough to save all the passengers and crew. Unfortunately, Murdoch gave a "full reverse" and repositioned the rudder "left full rudder" thus exposing the entire starboard side to the impact of the ice. The effects we know – the ship went down in two hours with fifteen hecatombs of casualties.

Dr. Ballard's team determined beyond a shadow of a doubt that the ship did not have a ripped side or bottom section of the hull – as was presumed until the 1980s, but only 6 tears in the side plating plates, slightly below the waterline, whose edges were turned up, but outward! Perhaps this was caused by the explosion of the boilers and the resulting shock wave, which pushed the plates and bent them outward. It is known, the steam trapped at a pressure of 150 atmospheres in the boilers of the transatlantic exploded when the walls of the boilers were cooled by the icy water of the Atlantic. This water was $-2°C$, the air temperature dropped from $+6°C$ to $0°C$, which meant that survivors in the water had virtually no chance of survival. They were dying of cold... Thermal stresses in the walls of the boilers ripped them apart, while steam pressure completed the work of destruction.

What opened the way for the water? Obviously, the impact of the ship against the ice and the ripping of the side plating.

This is obvious. The strangest thing is that neither the crew nor the passengers actually felt hardly anything, yet the pounding of the rock-hard ice with a mass of 66,000 tons would have to be noticeable! Meanwhile, the men felt a slight vibration and heard what seemed like the sound of a distant explosion.

9.3. Could there be a collision with the USO?

And it could have been like this:

The RMS Titanic did not hit an iceberg, but was hit by an Unknown Submarine Object – USO. To understand this, we need to go back to the first pages of Jules Verne's novel "The Undersea Object. "Twenty Thousand Leagues Under the Seas," in which Mr. Verne gives several extremely interesting cases of passenger ships colliding with an unknown submarine object, which he called a "runaway rock." The most famous of these was the incident of the Scotia, which was struck in the predawn hours of April 13, 1867, at a position N 45°37' and W 015°37', by an unknown tool that left a perfectly triangular hole in the cleanly cut sheet of the side plating, slightly below the waterline. This very event is the starting point of Jules Verne's novel. A whole series of incomprehensible maritime disasters falls into place in a logical sequence of events, once we assume that Unknown Submarine Objects are buzzing around in the world ocean. Of course, the matter by no means ended with the Titanic and Scotia, as the most recent such case was the disaster of the Estonian MF Estonia...

The investigation into the Titanic disaster revealed that in the vicinity of that fateful point defined by the coordinates: N 41°46' and W 050°14' there was the ship SS Californian, which at the time stood at N 42°40' and W 050°07' – and for many, many years it was believed that this was the geographically closest naval vessel that could have provided assistance. However, it turned out that...

9.4. ... AT THAT TIME THERE WAS TRAFFIC, LIKE IN ROME!

The following ships were also in the vicinity of the sinking transatlantic: SS Almerian, SS Mount Temple, SS Paula, SS President Lincoln, and a little further away also: RMS Carpathia, SS Frankfurt, RMS Olympic – the sister ship of RMS Titanic, while, in addition, a full array of even smaller fishing vessels. In other words, there was traffic in the vicinity of the sinking giant, like in Rome, or at Krupówki street in Zakopane on New Year's Eve, and yet the Titanic was sinking alone, in an unreal setting of the ice floe and calm, smooth sea. And one could hardly believe it!

One thing became certain – between the sinking Titanic and the Californian, which was standing adrift, there was another ship, which crewmen from both vessels saw, taking it already as Titanic, already as Californian! Indeed, the investigation showed that both ships could not see each other – their distance from each other was too great to see even their top lights! Could it be, then, that the ghost ship seen by the crews of both ships was the culprit of the whole mishap – this mysterious USO? Impossible – and yet history knows of examples of sightings of such mysterious ghost ships in all bodies of water in the world ocean, not even excluding our tiny, but very dangerous and terrible in its wrath of the Baltic, as I know from personal experience...

9.5. VANITY PUNISHED

Speaking of novels, it is worth mentioning that several writers predicted the Titanic tragedy many years before the event. Here we should mention the novel by Morgan Robertson, who described an identical tragedy of a huge passenger liner that went down due to a collision with an iceberg. The book was titled "Futility" as we have already discussed here.

How fitting it was for what played out in the Atlantic a dozen years later!

The memory of this tragedy saved the lives of many a sailor, who, mindful of the Titanic's fate, strained his eyes as his ship approached the foul body of water on April nights.

And speaking of art, it is worth citing the list of movies, which were made inspired by this disaster:

1. "Atlantis" – directed by August Blom (1913, Denmark) – narrative;

2. "Atlantic" – directed by E. A. Dupont (1929, UK) – narrative;

3. "Titanic" – directed by H. Selpin and W. Klinger (1943, III Reich) – narrative and propaganda;

4. "Titanic" – directed by Jean Negulesco (1953, USA) – narrative;

5. "A Night to Remember" – directed by Roy Baker (1958, USA) - narrative;

6. "SOS Titanic" – directed by William Hale (1979, USA) – narrative, for TV;

7. "Rise the Titanic" – directed by Jerry Jameson (1980, USA) based on the novel by Clive Cussler, narrative, adventure;

8. "Titanic: A Question of Murder" – directed by Alan Ravenscroft (1983, USA) – docudrama;

9. "Secrets of Titanic" – directed by G. Hurley, R. Ballard, L. N. Noxon (1987, USA) – documentary;

10. "Titanic" – directed by Stephen Low (1991, USA) – narrative;

11. "Titanic" – directed by Melissa Beltier (1995, France-USA) – docudrama;

12. "Titanic" – directed by Robert Liebermann (1996, USA) – narrative;

13. "Titanic" – directed by James Cameron (1997, USA) – narrative.

14. "Titanic II" – directed by Shane Van Dyke (2010, USA) – techno-thriller.

15. "The Last Moments of Titanic" – directed by Richard Dale (UK, 2012) – documentary.

16. "Out of Control: Titanic" – directed by François Tribolet (2018, France) – documentary.

17. "Ten Mistakes That Caused the Titanic to Sink" – directed by Mike Ibeji (2019, UK) documentary.

18. "Titanic – a Tragic Mistake" – directed by Peter Leninger (2020, UK) – documentary.

19. "Mysteries of the Titanic Wreck" – directed by Thomas Risch (2020, UK, France) documentary.

20. "Titanic on the Waves (Titanic III)" – directed by Nick Lyon (2022, USA) – horror.

21. "Titanic – Secrets from Beyond the Grave," directed by David McCauley (2022, USA) – documentary.

22. "Titanic in Color," directed by Jonathan Mayo (2024, UK) – documentary series.

As can be seen from the attached list, to which I have added a few documentary films made after 2000, none of the themes used as a basis for film scripts has received as many films as the tragedy of April 14, 1912!

Have we all succumbed to the magic of this event and created a kind of inevitable doom syndrome – the Titanic syndrome, which was especially intensified after September 11, 2001?

9.6. Captain Stanley Lord's rehabilitation

As expected, the commission of inquiry investigating the circumstances of the Titanic's demise and the deaths of more than 1,500 people also found Captain Stanley Lord, who on that fateful night was in command of the SS Californian, standing adrift, to be one of the guilty parties in this monstrous disaster. Of course, the commission's ruling resulted in his person being swept up in the mud for failing to render assistance at sea, for they wanted to make him a scapegoat, as someone guilty must! In 1968, Captain Lord asked the Merchant Master's Society of America to reconsider his case and rehabilitate his good name. The MMSA reanalyzed the events and concluded that he was innocent allegations against him! For it was shown n o t h e r t h a t t h e SS Californian was too far north of the sinking Titanic and could not see it! Moreover, it was found conclusively that there was still third ship, which was spotted by the watchkeepers of both vessels at 10:25 p.m. and disappeared from the sight of the sailors of the Californian – in the twenty minutes after the Titanic sank in the Atlantic waters! And in fact, the lights of the ghost ship, which was at a distance of about 6 Mm from the sinking transatlantic, disappeared…

It is a great pity that the "Focus", which considers itself a monthly popular science magazine, in No. 2(26)/1998, uncritically published a version that someone badmouth on someone who, if only because he is dead – can no longer defend himself!... Not nice! If such is the knowledge of various "specialists" and "heads of schools of journalism" – as presented by a certain Wolf Schneider, the editors of "Focus", then I'm not at all surprised that it continues to happen to it various stupid slip-ups, to mention the obfuscating articles on the book "Communion" by W. Strieber or articles by some Polish pseudo-ufologists, which only ridicule ufology and are probably written under the dictates of the US or NATO special services, which also care a lot about this obfuscation. Already more objective was the material by Anna Węgiełek and Ewa Jabłońska from "Super Express" No. 36/1998 of February 12, 1998, which also did not give the MMSA ruling – which is a pity! It would have done justice to the man whose case effectively silenced the outrage at the cowardice of Chairman Ismay – who not only escaped from the sinking ship – which can still be understood, because everyone wants to live – but it was he who instigated Captain Smith and builder Andrews to speed up the ship by additional knots – because he dreamed of the Blue Riband!

Namely, it turned out that this mysterious ghost ship was the Canadian SS Mount Temple commanded by Captain J.H. Moore, and which failed to help the sinking Titanic.

9.7. Strange aspects of the disaster

Researchers of the incident have always pointed out that ice was sprinkled on the decks of the Titanic after the collision – actually rubbing against the iceberg. Well, the Titanic did not have to collide with the iceberg at all – it could have been hit by the USO, which caused pieces of ice floating around the iceberg to be ejected onto its decks. In this context, it is interesting to note the statement of a Titanic passenger, as shown by Jean Negulesco, who moments after the collision said, "No, it was not that we who hit it, but it hit us..." we'll come back to that response again. In the meantime, recall the description of the collision between the frigate USS Abraham Lincoln and Captain Nemo's Nautilius from Verne's novel – just after the spur hit the side, two whirlwinds rolled onto the deck of the USS Abraham Lincoln, which washed Professor Aronnax, his servant Conseil and Ned Land into the water... Such waterspout could have thrown chunks of orifice on the decks of the Titanic, and could also have been the result of a boiler explosion in boiler room No. 1. The collision of a mass of tens of thousands of tons, accelerated to speeds of almost 40 km/h, would have resulted in powerful acoustic effects, not to mention a strong shock. I remember how, in 1985, our scimitar–rigged MF Pomerania crashed into the pier of the PŻB Sea Ferry Base in Świnoujście, on one foggy day. A downpour of debris poured from the concrete pedestal of the light signal, a sheaf of sparks shot three meters into the air, there was a shriek of plating metal being scraped, and the ferry shook feverishly from the impact and the change in direction of the propellers as the machinery gave "full reverse" and the thrusters tried to push the Pomerania's bow away from the berth... The rumbling was from it like all hell, and yet Pomerania was only 13,000 BRT and moving at 1 – 1.5 kts! The jolt and rumble of the collision was heard by everyone within a radius of many hundreds of meters, and everyone heard the violent spurt of machinery working in reverse. It all ended with the demolition of the red signal light pedestal, the abrasion of the ferry's sheet metal, the fear of the travelers and the curses of the captain... And on the Titanic?

The thing lies in the enormous mass of the ships. The Titanic was moving at 21.5 kts – or 39.82 km/h – and only a few people feel the shock and hear the faint explosion. So the ice edge was so sharp that it cut the side of the ship like a canning knife, NB this is the comparison Józef Konrad-Korzeniowski used – or 1st Officer Murdoch didn't give "all the way back" and "left full rudder"! In those fateful 37 seconds from the moment the obstacle was spotted to the moment the ship hit it, the ship would have had to react to both of these maneuvers, which would have manifested themselves with shocks much stronger than those recorded. These 37 seconds mean that at the moment of spotting the iceberg, Titanic was 407 meters away from it... That's less than half a kilometer. What does this mean? – Namely that there was no time for any maneuvering! A 66,000-ton ship is not a canoe that can be stopped and turned at a distance of two meters – its stopping distance is counted in kilometers. The Titanic could not simply be turned like a canoe. Its titanic inertia turned against it... I suspect that even if the Titanic had thrusters, they would not have been able to steer it sufficiently off course in either direction to avoid scraping against the iceberg and its protruding spurs. Indeed, the best option would have been to give "full reverse" and hit the ice with the bow. At best, it would have flooded the two bow compartments. In the worst case, perhaps it would have been possible to set the Titanic on the ice and thus keep it afloat for enough time to evacuate people from the wreck – that is, for four hours, until Carpathia's arrival. Of course, we can now speculate. Murdoch had to make a split-second decision, and he made it. The other thing is that it was the worst possible one...

Wolf Schneider gives another interesting fact that somehow escaped the attention of researchers of this disaster. Namely, he writes that: "Titanic collided with an iceberg at a speed of 15 m/s," – end of quote. I recalculated and came up with the fact that at the time of the collision Titanic was moving at a speed not of 21.5 kts, as officially reported in all sources, but as high as 29.15 kts – a full 54 km/h!... However, it seems that someone dreamed of the Blue Riband and rushed the ship at the speed of a destroyer of the time going for a torpedo attack. I would very much like to know where Schneider got those 15 m/s from!!!?...

9.8. A course of "ghost ship"

Let's return to the "ghost ship" as seen from the decks of the Titanic and Californian. "Ghost ship" follows a course from NE–E to SW until 11:40 p.m. NDT. Then it stands in a drift and. turns 180°, as if it wants to turn around. Then it starts the machine and at 02:05 a.m. it goes on a course to the SW through a shoal of drifting ice pack and at 02:40 a.m. its lights are out!

The most interesting thing is that it was heading to the wrong position given after the CQD MGY signal. So it would appear that this ship was going to the aid of the sinking Titanic after receiving the first signal, and then turned off the radio station and did not hear the second SOS MGY signal with the correct position. And this turns everything on its head, and Schneider's article does not clarify anything, and confuses this issue even more.

Another question arises here: was the X ship the USO that caused the crash? The ship was facing the Californian with its port side – for its red position light was seen, not its starboard side like the Titanic, otherwise the green light would have been visible. This, in turn, meant that Ship X was facing the bow of the Labrador Current between 11:40 p.m. and 01:10 a.m., which was pushing all ships drifting on the ocean at 2 kts to the south. Such is the abnormal behavior of the "ghost ship" that I don't think it is a ship from this world... – if we reject the the conspiracy theory of (world) history. We now know that it was the SS Mount Temple…

9.9. Even the stars did not favor the Titanic…

Leaving aside all the quibbling about naming this ocean liner defiantly Titanic, which for some was already blasphemy in itself, it should be added that this ship did not even have a sea baptism! This is a rite of ceremonial naming of a vessel involving the uttering of a solemn naming formula and the smashing against the side, or pouring over the side, of a bottle of champagne, wine, grape juice or even seawater. This is precisely what was not done, and thus the ship was already cursed at the very beginning…

Czech writer and astrologer Zoša Klinkorová drew up a horoscope of this ship and the most important moments of its "life." All aspects of this horoscope indicate that the Titanic was an unlucky ship from the very beginning and its voyage was destined to end in tragedy…

Let's start with the horoscope of White Star Lines co-owner and major shareholder John Piermont Morgan, who was a great mystic and would not start anything without a detailed horoscope. As you can see, this time the stars failed him as well… And now I will present his horoscope:

JOHN PIERMONT MORGAN born on April 17, 1837 in Hartford

(CN, USA)

Aspect	Position
Sun	27° Aries
Moon	15° Virgo

Mercury	20° Aries
Venus	19° Aries
Mars	12° Leo
Jupiter	4° Leo
Saturn	15° Scorpio
Uranus	7° Pisces
Neptune	8° Aquarius
Pluto	15° Aries
MC	11° Sagittarius
IC	11° Gemini
Dc	26° Leo
Ac	26° Aquarius
WW	20° Taurus
WZ	20° Scorpio

Such an arrangement of stars, planets and aspects in the houses of the horoscope did not bode well, which also happened. Particularly fatal here is the aspect of Neptune and Pluto, which indicate that a great tragedy will happen (Pluto) having to do with water, sea or ocean (Neptune). Believe it, don't believe it – but after all, the Titanic lay at the bottom of the ocean at a depth of 3810 meters...

And now let's look at the horoscope of the hero of our story himself:

Astrological Horoscope for RMS Titanic

Keel placement on March 31, 1909 at Queens Island Shipyard, Belfast, Ireland	
Sun	10° Aries
Mercury	20° Pisces
Venus	2° Aries
Mars	23° Capricorn

Jupiter	6° Virgo
Saturn	12° Aries
Uranus	21° Capricorn
Neptune	14° Cancer
Pluto	23° Gemini
Moon	7° Leo
WW	20° Gemini
WZ	20° Sagittarius

It shows that already when the keel was placed, a sentence was passed, which was executed three years later... This is a very fateful arrangement of planets and zodiacal constellations.

Is it possible to believe it? Those who want to, believe it, those who don't, don't. One fact remains indisputable – whether there were such or other arrangements of stars, planets and houses of the horoscope – the Titanic now lies at the bottom of the Atlantic and is slowly turning into a mound of rusting iron...

9.10. Water People

I don't believe in such influence of the stars on human life and the existence of the machines produced by it, so let's move on to the subject of Water People. They do indeed exist, as evidenced by the mysterious events that have played out – and continue to play out – on all bodies of water in the world. The Water People were dedicated to their first bestseller titled. "Pacific Vortex!" by the famous American writer of action–seafaring novels Clive Cussler. Polish Television a few years ago transmitted an amazing movie about, among other things, the Water People, and I later wrote an article for „Nieznany Świat" magazine. So it would seem that in the world ocean there is a race of intelligent beings resembling humans and occasionally kidnapping those humans. At least, this is what Robin Cook claims in his book titled. "Abduction," in which he writes that they come from Interterra – the legendary underworld so passionately sought by SS–Reischführer Heinrich Himmler and his expert scientists during World War II, and which can be identified with the mysterious Shamballa or Agharta or Atlantis.

Renowned American ufologist Albert Rosales described over 20 incidents with Water People, and here is one of the fascinating cases of such an Encounter with Mermaids:

9.10.1. CE0/CE-III-E AND B + NL (BOL) IN UKRAINE

Location: Nikopol, Dnipropetrovsk Oblast, Ukraine

Date: August 1995

Time: Day

Incident description:

A few young men went to the local beach on a hot August day, and after swimming for a while, they returned to the shore. There, they were stunned to see four beautiful young naked women emerging from the water. The young men asked them if they were nudists, but the response was silence. They had the impression that the girls did not understand their language at all, but one of the men spoke 3 languages and asked the same question in German, French, and English, but the reaction was the same. The girls returned to the water, and when they started swimming, the young men noticed that the girls' movements were unnatural; they seemed to "glide" in the water. It also appeared that when they dove into the water, they seemed to remain dry. The strange women exchanged strange sounds reminiscent of whistles. (Like dolphins?)

One of the men decided to approach one of the women and touch her, but when he did so, he was struck by something that felt like an electric charge with such force that he was almost thrown back 10 meters from the water.

The strange woman turned around, waved her hand, and effortlessly dove through several large waves; her friends did the same. Soon they reached the center of the Kakhovka reservoir. Soon it started to rain, and the boys returned to the shore when suddenly a huge, luminous sphere of light emerged from the clouds. It descended over the water and began to hover directly over the spot where the strange women floated. Moments later, all four women ascended into the sphere or were absorbed by it. Then the sphere quickly rose and disappeared among the clouds[42].

Unfortunately, as with many cases from the former USSR territories, there is no exact location of the incident, and we are left to speculate. This is due to the inertia of thought among citizens of Ukraine, who still believe that the West desires nothing more than to attack, rob, and kill them, etc. This is a result of communist brainwashing since 1917 and the historical lies of nationalists. It is a shame. Unfortunately, with such attitudes, we will encounter for a long time, especially now that there is a war in Ukraine with Russia. The irony of history is that the threat came not from the West, but from the East.

As for the CE itself, it is interesting that it was indeed women. Although they did not have fins and tails, they could have been Mermaids – beings from the All-Ocean repeatedly observed in all seas and inland waters of the world. After all, why not? Since humans have mastered the lands, why couldn't Water People master the All-Ocean?

---

42. Source: RIA "Novosti" (Russian news agency) and "The Fourth Dimension and UFOs" - newspaper of the Yaroslavl UFO Research Group No. 1995 # 11.

9.10.2. Mysterious Stranger

Location: Rio Tampobata, Chonta region, Peru

Date: 1976

Time: Evening

Event description: The main witness is a woman named Elena, who was paddling her small canoe along the river when a young woman in a small canoe approached her. When the stranger paddled up to the witness, she greeted her and sat next to Elena, chatting with her on several topics, and before leaving, she told Elena that her name was Rogelia and that she would return tomorrow.

According to Elena's statement, this woman was very beautiful, had very fair skin, long blonde hair, and intensely green eyes. She was dressed in a shiny green outfit and fitted, low shoes. Eventually, Elena returned home, and the next day, Rogelia indeed returned, and Elena treated her to breakfast, and after a long conversation, Rogelia left again. From that day on, the visits became very frequent, all in the morning. Elena's husband – Heliodoro went to work in the fields every morning and never saw Rogelia, as she visited their home when he was not there.

One day, Elena told him about Rogelia and her visits, and that she wanted to meet him, but again they could not meet,bo he always left for work early and returned after she had left. Heliodoro did not believe Elena and quickly forgot about it. One day, when Heliodoro came back from work, Elena told him that Rogelia had just left the house, but this only angered Heliodoro, who confronted her.

One day, Elena's little son suffered from a nasty diarrhea, and Rogelia stopped by for a visit. Rogelia then told Elena that her mother was a "doctor" and could take her son to examine him. The two women went to the river, and when Elena got into Rogelia's boat, it started to sink, which frightened Elena, who immediately jumped into her own boat next to Rogelia's canoe. Elena told Rogelia that her boat was too small and it would be best if she came back the next day, and then she scaredly returned home. The next day, Heliodoro came home early from work, around 10 o'clock, and found his wife apparently talking to an invisible person whom he could not see. Seeing this, Heliodoro threw his machete on the ground in front of his house, which apparently startled Elena out of her trance, and she said to him:

"Heliodoro, you must be careful, you almost cut off Rogelia's foot!"

The machete evidently fell next to the foot of the invisible Rogelia. Enraged, Heliodoro returned home, and Rogelia told Elena that she had to go back home. On another occasion, when the waters in the river had risen, Elena could see Rogelia in her small boat floating in the middle of the swift current; she showed her to Heliodoro, but he – of course – could not see her.

One day, when Rogelia was talking to Elena, she mentioned that she had just seen the young son of her neighbor Ernestina and... "liked him so much that she intended to steal him." This caused Elena to quickly visit her neighbor and warn her about the possibility of kidnapping and to keep him safe from strangers. On another occasion, Rogelia approached Elena and angrily told her that she had seen another neighbor who had been sitting in a canoe the night before and was defecating into the river, and evidently, in the same boat, Rogelia inadvertently left a small "beautiful machete." The next day, Elena went to look for that machete, but she only found a small, rusty machete in the boat, so she took it and later returned it to Rogelia.

Once, Rogelia told Elena about the river and mentioned that beneath its waters are "new lands and homes, exactly like those here." But Elena was skeptical and pointed out that she could not live underwater, as she could drown, but Rogelia assured her that this would not happen, as "what is below is the same as what is above."

On another occasion, Rogelia gave Elena a stone as a talisman, but she never said where that stone was from. Elena has this stone to this day. One time, Rogelia said to Elena:

"Elena, let's make a pact between you and me, because I can no longer come here to you".

Astonished, Elena asked her what kind of pact it was supposed to be between them? Rogelia replied that she would return here at midnight and whistle for her, so Elena should step out and confirm this pact. That night, Elena heard a whistle, but she was afraid to leave the hut. Later, in a dream vision, Elena saw Rogelia asking her:

"Elena, why didn't you come out then? I didn't want to hurt you, and I don't want to disturb you, I just wanted to seal a pact with you, so you could live better. But don't worry, I won't haunt you anymore".

After this dream vision, Rogelia kept her word and never visited Elena again. Later, Elena conducted a small investigation in neighboring villages and towns, but no one knew who Rogelia was, and no one had seen her again.

Source: Victor Hugo Velasquez Zea – "Las Sirenas o Yakurunas y la cosmovision Amazonia sobre las Fuentes de agua".

Type: E?

Translation from Spanish: Albert Rosales

Comments:

1. This all sounds very much like "bewitched by a fairy," which was evidently common with events in Europe.In the Middle Ages, and of course it had many variations. According to this source, it is a case of a CE with a type of being that is a river nymph from European myths and legends. (This brings to mind the film "Lady in the Water" directed by M. Night Shyamalan, 2006.)

2. It also evokes all the stories about Icelandic Alfur (Elves) and Huddefolk (Hidden People), who sometimes take care of human children and vice versa. Rogelia was primarily concerned with either Elena or Ernestina's child that she intended to abduct – this was the "pact" she wanted to make with Elena. It resembles all the tales about the abduction of small children or pregnant women that are told across Europe, regardless of nationality or religion, as described by Dr. Miloš Jesenský in his work "Gods of Atomic Wars" - note by R. Leśniakiewicz.

9.10.3. Underwater CE with a Mermaid

Location: several miles off the coast of Florida, FL, USA

Date: 1988

Time: afternoon

Event Description: Professional diver Robert Froster was diving alone in search of mysterious underwater formations when he noticed turbulence in the water. When he looked there, he saw some figure moving toward him. The water around him swirled and surrounded him with a cloud of silt stirred up by it. As this creature moved towards him, it swam in a serpentine motion, rather than gliding through the water. When the strange creature was 20 yards away from him, he saw something odd about its appearance. Appendages resembling arms seemed to reach out toward him, and each of them ended with a hand with claw-like fingers. Then he saw the creature in all its glory. He saw a pair of female breasts, long flowing hair, smooth skin, and a fish tail from the waist down. It looked like a half-woman – half-fish. Froster said:

- I have never seen so much hatred in the eyes of any living being before.

Before the creature could reach him with its claws, Froster shot towards the surface and swam with all his strength towards his boat. After that, he never saw it again.

Source: E. Randal-Floyd – "Great Southern Mysteries"

Type: E

Comment: It appears that the Greys from Orion based here are not the only unfriendly beings on this planet. (Albert Rosales).

9.10.4. My 2 cents

These are just three selected examples from Albert Rosales's dossier on Water People alias Mermaids.

Can these beings be suspected of manipulation as a result of which the Titanic sank on its maiden voyage? Of course! They knew what weaknesses the ship had and what capabilities it had. Such knowledge is half the battle. To achieve the other half, all they had to do was pull the iceberg up to Titanic's course and wait for her to collide with it, which is what happened. Or maybe they even helped it collide with the Titanic – hence the very observation, grotesque but counterintuitively plausible – that the ship was hit by the iceberg, not the other way. This ship X, was precisely the Interterran vessel that followed the events from afar. And its crew could even steer it…

What was the purpose of this operation? To change the existing reality, of course. By the way, the same thing was done in the early 1950s, when another passenger liner SS Andrea Doria was sunk. How was it possible for two modern liners, equipped with radar and other navigational devices, seeing each other! – clashed almost at the entrance to the port of New York!!!????... A question worthy of Hamlet! Of course, it was blamed on radar and a hastily invented phenomenon of radio wave propagation disturbances in this body of water, called radar wave polarization. This explains nothing, least of all why the bow of the MS Stockholm ripped the starboard side of the Andrea Doria and sent it to the bottom… Who knows how the history of the world would have turned out had these two maritime disasters not occurred? And several others, minor but equally mysterious too…

We can only speculate now, because hindsight is 20–20. – that's a good start.

The Titanic's annihilation worked out well for Mankind, becoming a warning against overconfidence in one's own abilities on the one hand, while on the other hand becoming a powerful stimulus for the development of navigation, detection and warning systems, improved day by day, against icebergs, storms or other God's tributes in the waters of the entire world ocean. This has made it possible to avoid many repetitions of the tragedy.

Yet ships are still sinking…

Chapter 10

Tragedy of the DSV "Titan"

Leave the Titanic!
Don't salvage it!
The music is constantly playing there
And they're permanently dancing!
(song by Borysewicz & Ciechowski)

On June 18, 2023 there was a tourist-excursion dive to the wreck of the British steamer – the most famous in its class due to the size of the luxury and number of passengers – RMS Titanic, which sank after a collision with an iceberg on April 14, 1912 in the Atlantic, and its remains are located in the position N 41°43′55″ – W 049°56′45″, about 600 km/334 mn east of Newfoundland.

A submarine, actually a DSV Titan bathyscaph, headed towards the decaying wreck, and with 5 people on board was about to plunge to a depth of more than 4,000 meters in the dark and icy waters of the Atlantic. Headed there and killed in the disaster were OceanGate executive Stockton Rush, one of Pakistan's richest men Shahzada Dawood and his son Suleman, British billionaire and traveler Hamish Harding and French diver Paul-Henry Nargeolet. It is known that the boat imploded near the wreck of the Titanic. An investigation is currently underway to determine when and under what circumstances the disaster occurred. Karl Stanley, who has sailed on the Titan before, said the disaster was foreseeable. In 2019, when he himself was a participant in the OceanGate expedition, he noticed many irregularities. He later shared them all with Stockton Rush, the company's CEO. During an undersea excursion off the Bahamas in April 2019 Stanley sensed that something was wrong. The sounds he heard during the voyage worried him deeply. A day later, he wrote Rush an email sharing his concerns. Well, and he was right – five more victims joined the victims of the RMS Titanic disaster...

The very discovery of the wreck of the transatlantic liner has a taste of sensationalism, because its discoverer captain Prof. Dr. Robert "Bob" Ballard, by the way, performed a top-secret spy mission for the CIA... In addition, Dr. Ballard was known for his search operations for the wrecks of the battleship Bismarck, USS Yorktown, RMS Lusitania and the nuclear submarines USS Thresher and USS Scorpion, so he could undertake it, because he had experience.

There were more than a dozen dives to the wreck of the Titanic using deep-sea submersibles, which James Cameron used in the film "Titanic" and Jerry Jameson in "Rise the Titanic," based on the novel by Clive Cussler. The latter prophetically predicted the disaster of such a deep-sea ship, which was crushed by the powerful pressure – amounting to nearly 440 at there!

And now we have an authentic tragedy – the DSV Titan submersible vehicle, which disappeared that fateful Sunday, June 18. I will not describe it – the media have done it much better than me. I would only like to draw the reader's attention to a certain "unworldly" aspect of this tragedy, namely – it happened in a special place. Well, actually, over the cemetery of 1505 victims of the disaster of this liner!

This area has been declared a marine cemetery and as such is legally protected. Unfortunately – this does not reach some people, and in principle such expeditions should be banned. But the company OceansGate Expeditions, as you can see, had none of this and organized deep-sea excursions for rich tourists. And after all, everyone knows about the fact that the dead should NOT be disturbed! Could this be some kind of revenge for disturbing their eternal peace?

I was immediately reminded of the tragedy of April 10, 2010, which took place in Smolensk in the vicinity of the Severnyy airport. On that day, at 08:41 a.m. CEST, Tu-154M Flight 101 crashed with the Polish delegation to a ceremony at the cemetery of Polish soldiers and intelligentsia in Katyn. In fact, it was supposed to be a pre-election PiS[43] *Parteitag* on consecrated, cemetery land. As you can see, this mindless act on the graves of murdered Poles did not appeal to them and did not happen. Another 96 victims of this catastrophe were added to the Katyn list, although they were not murdered, like the Katyn men...

10.1. The implosion of the Titan occurred differently than expected. New recordings and information

Maciek Kucharczyk writes in GW[44]: Pressure cut off the nose, and the crew compartment was instantly crushed. Previously, people had no inkling, and when the disaster struck, they likely didn't even register it. Such information was revealed during a

43. Polish party "Law and Justice".
44. See: https://wiadomosci.gazeta.pl/wiadomosci/7,114881,31319452,implozja-titana-przebiegla-inaczej-niz-myslano-nowe-nagrania.html.

meeting of the committee investigating the disaster of the DSV Titan submarine diving to the wreck of the Titanic. Recordings of the wreckage lying on the seabed, taken on June 22, 2023, by a search robot looking for the missing unit that disappeared 4 days earlier from OceanGate, were also published. Initially, there was hope of finding it intact along with the five living passengers. The image recorded by the search robot's cameras dashed speculation that the people could have been saved.

10.2. Official investigation and published materials

The recordings were published by the U.S. Coast Guard (USCG), which conducted the search and is now investigating. It was given the highest priority, entrusted to the Marine Board of Investigation, which only deals with the most significant events, an average of one out of a thousand investigated each year by the USCG. The committee began public hearings on September 16. They are expected to last until the end of the month. During them, various experts and individuals associated with OceanGate are appearing before the investigators, who may provide valuable information. The committee itself ordered the publication of recordings of the Titan wreck and an animation depicting its final dive, along with a record of the crew's communication with the mother ship on the surface. From the latter, it follows among other things that the people inside the submarine expressed no concern about its condition and reported no significant problems. Almost exactly 1.5 hours after the dive began, the crew sent a message about releasing two ballast cubes to slow the descent. This was a routine maneuver because the submarine was approaching the seabed. It was at a depth of 3,336 meters, while the Titanic wreck lies at 3,802 meters. Six seconds after the message was sent, the mother ship lost contact with the Titan. The recordings made four days later, now published, show what happened to the vessel. The white element standing vertically on the seabed is the non-pressure aft section, which was freely taking in water. Various auxiliary devices were placed there. It was attached to the rear wall of the pressure hull, where the people were seated. It detached from it when the catastrophic implosion occurred. The remains of the pressure hull itself lay a bit further in two large pieces and many smaller ones. One main piece is the rear hemispherical wall and the crushed remnants of the central cylindrical part made of carbon fibers. This is where the people must have been at the time of the disaster. Not far from the bottom lay the detached front hemispherical wall, devoid of the viewport placed in its center, which could not be found. The remains of the unit were later recovered. The remains of all five crew members were found and identified using DNA. Shahzada Dawood and Suleman Dawood (a businessman from Pakistan and his son), Hamish Harding (a British businessman), Paul-Henri Nargeolet (a French wreck research specialist, Titanic expert), and Stockton Rush (the owner of OceanGate and the main creator of the Titan) died.

10.3. Presented potential cause of the accident

Investigators have not yet presented their version of the events. They will do so only within the next 12 months, issuing a report on the investigation. One of those interviewed was Tym Catterson, a former subcontractor for OceanGate involved in constructing the Titan's hull. He claimed that during the work, he expressed his doubts about the strength of the carbon fiber and titanium structure a dozen times. - I was pessimistic about it, but I only said this much, that I cannot reach in my calculations what his numbers show," he spoke about his conversations with Rush. "I told him that in my opinion, it is poorly constructed and the calculations do not add up," he added. However, the head of the company seemed to dismiss his doubts every time, saying that "a few other engineers working on this think otherwise."

"I concluded that we agreed on the fact that we disagree," said Catterson.

During the hearing, he also presented what he believed to be the most likely disaster scenario. In his opinion and according to his calculations, there was no crushing of the central part of the pressure hull, which was in the form of a carbon fiber tube. So far, this has often been cited as a probable cause of the accident, namely material fatigue after multiple submersions, which finally gave in, accelerated by poor craftsmanship. According to Catterson, however, it was the connection of this central element with the front rim made of titanium, to which the bow's hemispherical wall was attached, that failed. The connection was ensured by special glue and steel fasteners. He argued that the minimal flexing of the fiber hull with each immersion exerted a repeatable pressure on the connection at its ends. Weakening it slightly each time. Eventually, the connection could not withstand it.

Supporting this was, among other things, the condition of the wreckage. The front wall was found detached from the rest of the vehicle without any remnants of the carbon fiber hull attached to it. In his opinion, this proves that the catastrophic failure occurred simultaneously across the entire connection.

"The front was cleanly severed. It must have happened very violently, which means that the people inside had no idea what was happening," said the engineer. The central part, deprived of support, immediately imploded and was partially crushed

10.4. THE DESPOT WHO BROUGHT DEATH UPON HIMSELF

into the rear wall by the force of the water impact. The victim's relatives are demanding a gigantic compensation.

Former employees and associates of OceanGate also testified before the commission. Their statements focused on what has been known since the beginning of the investigation into the disaster. That is, the character of Stockton Rush, who was despotic and disregarded established safety standards as unnecessary restrictions on innovation. According to colleagues' testimonies, he would routinely dismiss and reject any doubts, favoring the opinions of those engineers who agreed with him. He was allowed to do this because he used his vessel in international waters, where he was not bound by the laws of any state or any safety regulations. Outside of common sense.

Tony Nissen, the company's chief engineer, spoke about this, stating that he worked there from 2016 until 2019, when he claims he was fired for refusing to approve Titan's first mission out of safety concerns. He recounted that he repeatedly argued with the boss behind closed doors to avoid showing the rest of the team how different their opinions were regarding the project. - "He fought fiercely for what he wanted and was practically not willing to yield at all. Not by a millimeter," he claimed.

Bonnie Carl, former head of human resources and a potential pilot of Titan, also testified. - "There were young engineers there, and I really mean very young, like those under 20 or just after it, with no experience that I knew of, whom I saw working on the boat with no supervision. That worried me because I knew that I had no idea what I was doing," she described. She left the company shortly after a meeting in 2018, during which

David Lochridge, the head of marine exploration, presented his report containing a series of doubts, remarks, and safety-related recommendations (which was posted on the USCG commission's website). After that, he was fired by Rush. - "It became clear to me then that OceanGate is not a place I want to work," if they have such an approach to safety - said Carl.

So says Maciek Kucharczyk. And we have another piece of evidence that you MUST NOT disturb the dead, because it takes its revenge… They really don't like it!

10.5. And the latest information from February 13, 2025, about the disaster of the submarine DSV Titan diving to the wreck of the RMS Titanic

In the Titan disaster on June 18, 2023, five people died.

During the investigation into the disaster of the submarine Titan, which was diving to the wreck of the famous Titanic, new facts have emerged. The U.S. Coast Guard released a recording that captured a terrifying noise. According to the report, the sound was deemed a "suspicious acoustic clue."

In June 2023, the world was shocked by the news of the tragic disaster of the submarine OceanGate DSV Titan, which claimed the lives of five individuals. Since then, an investigation has been ongoing into the still unexplained explosion. However, a breakthrough occurred on Friday.

The U.S. Coast Guard released a 20-second recording in which a horrifying sound can be heard. The sound was recorded when the submersible disappeared from radar south of Newfoundland. The report stated that this is a "suspicious acoustic clue" in the ongoing investigation.

The recording captures a terrifying noise that suddenly erupted and spread through the water.

The mystery of the cause of the disaster remains the subject of an international inquiry aimed not only at determining the circumstances of the event but also at reviewing safety procedures in the marine exploration industry.

Before the tragedy, the crew of the submarine maintained contact with the support ship Polar Prince, reporting that "everything is fine." However, after one hour and 45 minutes from the start of descent, contact was lost, triggering international searches for the vessel.

David Lochridge, former director of marine operations on the Titan project, demanded rigorous safety testing of the submarine, but his concerns were ignored and he was removed from the company.

The operator of the submarine, OceanGate, reported the deaths of five individuals aboard Titan on June 22, 2023. In the implosion of the submarine, Executive Director Stockton Rush of OceanGate, one of the richest Pakistanis Shahzada Dawood and his son Suleman, British billionaire and adventurer Hamish Harding, and French diver Paul-Henry Nargeolet were killed.

OceanGate has been offering tourists trips to the wreck of the Titanic aboard Titan since 2021. The submersible lost contact with the Canadian ship Polar Prince on June 18, 105 minutes after beginning its descent to a depth of 4 km. The wreckage of Titan was found about 500 m from the Titanic wreck.

The recording captures a terrifying noise that suddenly erupted and spread through the water[45].

45. Źródło - https://www.msn.com/pl-pl/wiadomosci/polska/nowe-fak-ty-o-katastrofie-titana-ujawniono-przera%C5%BCaj%C4%85ce-nagranie/ar-AA1ySdwu?ocid=winp1taskbar&cvid=58b48a48a70e4274ea7d25852d9b5c-

Chapter 11
MS "Jan Heweliusz" – Polish "Titanic"

Poland, too, has its Titanic. It was a spectacular catastrophe that shook the country and which is slowly being forgotten, because the mystery has not been solved to the end. I remind it here by quoting an excerpt from our book entitled "Ghost Trains & Ghosts on Trains" (Jordanów, 2024) – and here it is:

11.1 Unlucky ship

The British have the Titanic, the Italians – the Andrea Doria. Estonians – the Estonia, and we Poles – the Jan Heweliusz. This tragedy affected not only Poles, but also Swedes, Hungarians, Norwegians... Of the 64 people aboard the MF Jan Hewcliusz, only 9 were rescued – the rest drowned or died of hypothermia – exactly like the unfortunates of the RMS Titanic, April 15, 1912... And this in the Baltic Sea – in one of the smallest and seemingly safest bodies of water in the world! This Baltic – which German submariners contemptuously called a shallow plate of noodles – these noodles, are the islands of Hven, Lolland, Falster, Bornholm, Funen, Mön, Usedom, Wolin, Osland,

---

c8&ei=38.

Gotland, Öland, Saaremaa, Hiuma, Zealand and the Åland Islands... In fact – the Baltic is a shelf sea, that is, its depth does not exceed 200 m, while the deepest place – the Landsort Deep off the coast of Sweden – is only 459 m deep.

The Baltic is an extremely busy sea – on its shores there are large and important seaports, between which there is increased ship and ferry traffic – especially on the line from Scandinavia to the rest of the continent and vice-versa, and through the Danish Straits to the North Sea, Norwegian Sea and the Atlantic towards the north and towards the English Channel and further to Africa, the Americas and Australia – towards the south.

And yet, despite this inconspicuousness and density of vessel traffic, the Baltic can show its menacing face. When autumn and winter storms blow the icy Nordwest from the Danish Straits, that's when it's better not to leave port and hole up in a warm house. The winds can rock up to fantastic speeds of 150–160 km/h, and this is already an orcane, lying outside the Beaufort scale... It's about the same in the Howling Fifty or off the coast of East Antarctica. How much is it? The best way is to do the following experiment – speed up the car on the highway to 150–160 km/h and try to stick your head out the window – this will only give the Reader some approximate idea of what the storm wind is from the Danish Straits. And to this you have to add low – mostly negative – air temperature, icy and suffocating water dust carried by the wind and water temperature close to zero Celsius. And then there are the powerful 10-meter short – but all the more dangerous – waves that toss the ship like a cork on the water.

Baltic storms look scariest at night, when shreds of snow-white foam, illuminated only by the ship's lights, dance madly on the black, rolling water, and everything is covered by a dome of black sky... But this is not the scariest thing. The scariest thing is the realization that you are in a small inland sea, within a stone throw from the nearest land, and that in case of an emergency, help will not be able to arrive quickly. Fast enough that you don't get swallowed up by the waves... – is a particularly nasty feeling.

Something like that happened to the passengers and crew of the MF Jan Heweliusz on its last voyage, that fateful night of January 13/14, 1993.

It was not a happy ship. Like its sister ship, also a "railroader," the MF Mikołaj Kopernik, which sailed until recently between Świnoujście and Ystad, carried railroad cars and huge semi trucks. Rarely passengers and passenger cars. It's not that class. Passenger-car ferries, are the aristocracy – while "railroaders" are work oxen. When I was still serving in the WOP Border Control Post Świnoujście – Sea Ferry Depot PŻB, I used to check in with my colleagues for a couple of years, clearing trucks and railroad lorries on these two ferries. And there were some of them, because the fleet of PŻB ferryboats in the 1970s and 1980s consisted of "Dziadek" MF Gryf, "Babcia" MF Skandynawia, the more modern MF Wawel and MF Wilanów, NB, which I first saw in the film "The Olsen Gang on the Track" (directed by Erik Balling, 1975), then the fleet was joined by MF Pomerania (which was then the top of the technical thought of the late Gierek era) MF Silesia (her sister-ship) and MF Rogalin and MF Łańcut. And, of course, both "railroaders" sailing for PLO. The Swedes and Austrians called the Jan Heweliusz – "Havarius" – due to the large number of failures that plagued this ship, NB similarly christened the Mikołaj Kopernik – "Kaputnik" – from the word kaputt... Only that the MF Mikołaj Kopernik sailed until recently, while the MF Jan Heweliusz lies in the 25–meter deep...

The worst adventure the crew of the Jan Heweliusz experienced was in early September 1986, when a dangerous fire broke out on its deck. Three trucks were standing on the car deck, two of which were loaded with polyethylene pellets and chemicals – a real incendiary bomb! – while the third was a refrigerated truck with several tons of hams and bacon. The commission investigating this case concluded that the fire was caused by sparks escaping from the refrigeration unit of this particular refrigerator truck. The very strong wind blowing at the time – also from NW of the Danish Straits – spread them all over the deck and threw them onto the tarpaulins of neighboring trucks. That was enough to cause the tarpaulins to seize up and the cargo of polyethylene and chemicals underneath, too... The flames hit the top and, fueled by strong storm winds, reached temperatures of more than 2000–2500°C! Sensors responded, but the fire destroyed cable connections to the captain's bridge. Before anyone realized the horror of the situation – all three trucks were on fire. Of course, the fire burned through all the cables running above and no rescue and firefighting action could be taken... The fire was extinguished by firefighting, rescue and tugboats arriving from Świnoujście, which brought the ferry to the port.

I was there. It was the most horrible sight I have ever had the opportunity to see. This is what the ships must have looked like after the Battle of Jutland, or the Bismarck or Yamato moments before they went down. It was pitch-black as hell on the Jan Heweliusz. Here and there were crumbling still sizzling chunks of ham, the stench of burnt meat and animal fat mixed with the stench of chemicals, and everything covered with dirty foam from the water cannons and foam generators that extinguished this pandemonium... Most impressive were the several-centimeter-thick sheets of sheet metal, melted and twisted into rolls, as if from a can of sprats in oil. This gave an idea of the power of the raging element!

The next day a rumor went around Świnoujście that this was a revenge of the Gdańsk astronomer for the fact that scientists opened his grave in Gdańsk, which took place on the day of the ferry fire... In fact – both dates matched. Blind chance, or something more???...

And also the testimony of a retired WOP and Border Guard officer from Świnoujście:

I was tasked with commanding the activities involved in picking up a dozen corpses from the Heweliusz which arrived on the ferry Śniadecki. There were corpses of passengers including the corpse of a child, the driver of Yugoslavian origin and then ob. of Austria, he was also there, the Polish wife was not found. It was the first time at that time I saw so many corpses and each one we had to describe, photograph. ...I remember that TVP reported on the news that the corpses were dismembered, deformed, but it was untrue. I gave the truth in the cipher, which irritated Milczanowski and the commission that landed in Goleniów in the evening and were with the Commander of the Branch in Szczecin. Around 3 a.m. the Commander called me and I had to explain everything to Milczanowski. I remember using the words "Mr. Minister since when does TVP tell the truth? They have always lied."

This speaks for itself...

This time, however, nothing foreshadowed the tragic events. Although a few days before the disaster of the MF Jan Heweliusz had a collision with a quay in Ystad and problems with closing the stern gate to the rail deck, but everything ended well and it returned to Świnoujście the next day. Of course – as always in such cases – a team from the Świnoujście Marine Repair Yard was already waiting to repair the damage. How dangerous damage to the wickets to railroad or car decks is shown by the example of another maritime tragedy on the Baltic Sea – this is the sinking of the MF Estonia on September 24, 1994 on a voyage from Tallinn to Stockholm, which was caused precisely by damage to the ferry's bow gate and flooding of the cardeck with water, which led to destabilization of the ship's hull with a known effect – 867 people found their grave in the waters of the Baltic Sea. Collisions with the quay were not rare, but they were not as dangerous as they seemed. I remember how, shortly before martial law was imposed, the MF Wawel slammed the Swede into a quay, smashing the entire bow in the process. It then went with that smashed bow through the entire Baltic Sea spinning those 5 knots, but it got there. The sight was amazing, as the sheets of plating were cut and caved in for a 5–6 meters into the hull, and the front wicket was half-open. If there had been a higher tide, perhaps this voyage would have ended for the Wawel, like the Estonia. At the bottom of the sea... On another occasion, in the summer of 1985, the MF Pomerania tore into the Świnoujście quay, in the process sweeping away with its bow the reinforced concrete signal pedestal at the ferry terminal. Nothing happened to anyone, except the pedestal, which came apart like a house of cards.

11.2 Anatomy of a tragedy

Anyway, this could not have been the cause of the disaster. On its last voyage, the MF Jan Heweliusz took 10 railroad cars, 28 trucks, 35 passengers – including 2 children – and 29 crewmen. They were commanded by the great sailing captain Andrzej Ułasiewicz. The weather was not good: the air temperature was –3°C, the water temperature was only +2°C. The worst weather factor was the wind from the NW – it blew at 110 km/h. After that, the accidents went like this:

January 13, 1993:

- 11:45 p.m. – end of embarkation of passengers and means of transport.
- 12 a.m. – the ferry drops its moorings and leaves the port.

January 14, 1993:

- 03:00 a.m. – first violent heel to starboard, which was compensated by reballasting.
- 04:25 a.m. – a series of tilts to both sides. Wind speed reaches 150–160 km/h, wave height up to 15 m.[46]
- 04:32 a.m. – rapid heeling to starboard.
- 04:36 a.m. – deepening heel to port side, captain sends MAYDAY signal! People are leaving the ferry.
- 04:44 a.m. – signals from the ferry cause alarm at the German MRCC facility on Rügen.
- 05:04 a.m. – MS Arcona rushes to the aid of the Jan Heweliusz.
- 05:12 a.m. – MF Jan Heweliusz turns upside down on its keel. German rescue helicopter from Rügen takes off.
- 05:45 a.m. – a second helicopter from Rügen takes off for help.
- 06:12 a.m. – the Germans are over the crash site and begin to pick up survivors. A third rescue helicopter from Kiel takes off.
- 06:20 a.m. – the Arcona arrives at the crash site.
- 06:35 a.m. – Danish rescue helicopter arrives.

---

46. 12 degrees on the Beaufort scale.

- 09:25 a.m. – German divers search the wreckage of the ferry for living people. They find no one alive...
- 10:45 a.m. – Polish rescue helicopter Mi–14, rescue ship MS Huragan and ORP Heweliusz from Świnoujście arrive at the crash site. They are just picking up the rest of the corpse.

This terrible disaster taught people that only those wearing special rescue suits to protect themselves from contact with icy water can survive in the water. If everyone had them, they would still be alive today. In such conditions, the rule is: as many minutes of life as the number of degrees Celsius on the plus side of the water. And there is no recourse against it...

What actually happened? The investigating commission concluded that the ferry capsized due to a change in the geometry of the cargo and a shift in the center of gravity of the entire ship. Everything was blamed on the monstrous impact of the wind and waves that hit the starboard side after the ship passed through the wind line. When the wind blew into the port side, its pressure was balanced by the water in the tanks that was ballasted to that side. However, all it took was for the ship to get a hit from the wind to starboard and everything changed – the ferry got a heel of more than 30° to starboard, as the force of the wind added to the overballast. The effect could be – and was – only one possible. The ferry lay with its side on the water, and everything that was not fixed flew to the port side worsening an already hopeless situation. Then the ferry turned bottom up. That was the end. Exactly like in the movie "The Poseidon Adventure"...

It is said that the crew is not at fault. Of course, the crew did everything possible to save the people and the ship. The captain is not at fault either, because he could not have foreseen that a strong but steady wind could fluctuate so much. Personally, I am of the opinion that the fault lies with the designers of the "railroaders", who made their hulls completely non-aerodynamic lumps with a huge Cx factor. If the MF Jan Heweliusz had a more streamlined shape, it would be sailing to this day... Of course, someone may object that the MF Mikołaj Kopernik also has an almost identical shape and somehow he did not encounter such an adventure. That's clear, but let's not forget that on the fateful voyage MF Jan Heweliusz went out with some mechanisms out of order, which didn't matter in good weather, but in extreme storm conditions, furious winds of 160 km/h, waves 15 m high, it had to turn into an infernal execution machine – and its trigger became the ferry's huge side surface. The law that proclaims that if something is going to break, it will break for sure, and the usual laws of physics, worked here. There were simply too many negative factors accumulated, which, as in the case of the RMS Titanic disaster, MUST have discharged in a monstrous crash.

And they did unload.

The 16-year-old ferry went down.

As you can see, there is no room for superstition here – after all, the voyage began on the 13th! – or by the curse of an astronomer from Gdańsk and an excellent brewer at the same time – sic! This is a strictly technological catastrophe, and mixing a supernatural factor into it is simply an abuse!... But is it really?

Of course, the boulevard media of the kind of "Fakt" gave mean-spirited, slanderous "explanations" of the kind that illegal immigrants, weapons or something else were smuggled on the ferry, which caused the disaster of the Jan Heweliusz. Reportedly, such data came from Sweden and... the Canadian secret service – the RCMP. Of course, they turned out to be not worth a damn, like most of the sensations let loose by such tabloids, but they did their job and urban legends began to grow around the wreck...

But that's another story.

Chapter 12

MS "Estonia" – The modern "Titanic" of the Baltic Sea

"It's been more than a century since those days," writes Konstantin Isakov in „Archiwy XX wieka" No. 3/2017, pp. 46–47, "when Mankind was shocked by the tragedy of the RMS Titanic, which took more than 1,500 people with it into the four-mile deep of the Atlantic. Much has changed in shipping and the organization of rescues on the water since that event. It would seem that a repeat of such a tragedy in the last decade of the 20th century is impossible. But unfortunately this is not so, over the past few years many ships have become the prey of the world ocean...

12.1. Tallinn's black days

This terrible sea disaster happened on the night of September 27/28, 1994. It became the last tragedy and the last maritime mystery of the last millennium. A mystery unsolved to this day. On September 27, 1994, at 7:15 p.m. EET/ 5:15 p.m. UT, the roll-off ship MF Estonia left the port of Tallinn. On its side were embarked 989 passengers and crew members. The ferry was on a routine cruise between Tallinn and Stockholm. The weather that day was pretty bad – there was a storm at sea, but that didn't cause any concern, either for the ferry's crew or passengers and also for the family members escorting them on such a short voyage. For a ship the size of Estonia, it presented no danger. The ferry was built in Germany, in 1980 for the Viking Line shipping company. It changed hands several times, and in 1993 the ship went into service for the Estonian–Swedish company and was given the name Estonia and served the line between Tallinn and Stockholm. It was a very robust ship, with a displacement of 16,000 tons and was 157 meters long and 24 meters wide, powered by 4 powerful engines that accelerated the ferry to speeds of 21 kts/~40 km/h. During the peak season, it took 1,200 passengers on board. For a year of operation, there were no technical problems with the ferry. And until then, everything was running on a normal track. At 11 p.m. the ship had covered a distance of 200 mn/360 km. The storm intensified, the swaying began, which, however, did not cause some dangerous situations. Passengers calmly went to stand. But already at 01:30 a.m. EET Estonia sent a danger signal, and then disappeared from radar screens. The morning programs of Estonian TV stations brought the country into shock: the Estonia ferry sank and caused many casualties, many family members and residents of the capital shaken by the tragedy came to the harbor from which the Estonia departed on its last voyage. People stood and silently looked at the sea as if hoping that it would return the ship and the people.

12.2. Tragic voyage in investigators' records...

Whenever they saw it sail away from shore, many Estonians remember being overwhelmed by a feeling of pride. A huge white ferry with the name Estonia written on its side, it was the newest and largest ship in the country's fleet. For many, the German–built ship, purchased in early 1993, was a fitting symbol of the country's new self-confidence. It was the ferry that carried many Estonians on their first trip outside the former Soviet empire. Under Communist rule, an anecdote circulated about how one day a white ship would arrive and liberate the nation from tyranny, and many said half-jokingly, half-seriously, that this was the white ship they had been waiting so many years for.

So when the news in the early morning of September 28, 1994 said that the giant, 15,000-ton Estonia had sunk in the Baltic Sea with hundreds of people trapped inside, it seemed like a cruel joke. It simply could not be true!

But it was true – terribly, undeniably true. When details of the accident surfaced, most people in this country of 1.5 million could not avoid being moved by the tragedy. Over the years, almost everyone had taken the Tallinn–Stockholm ferry at least once or twice; and if not, most people knew someone who had. So as Estonians crowded around radios to listen for the names of the people on the list, and it wasn't a question of whether they were dead, or whether they knew anything about it, or the victims – it was a question of how many they knew.

For many Estonians, especially the survivors and relatives of the 852 people who died on the Estonian, the pain and trauma of those days have not been completely alleviated. Evelin Tomson of the victim support group Memento Mare says many relatives, especially those who lost children on the Estonia, are still trying to cope. For many of them," she says, "that night will always be the focal point of their lives."

While investigators have concluded that the poorly designed bow gate was the main cause, the events of that fateful night are still not fully known. They probably never will be. Too many people, including all the officers on the bridge, did not live to tell their version of what happened. In the coming years, Estonia's story is likely to take on a life of its own. Theories explaining why it sank like the one already circulating that the ship hit a Russian submarine will likely become even more varied and stretched. As with the assassination of John F. Kennedy[47] and the sinking of the Titanic, so many aspects of the Estonia tragedy are likely destined to become the stuff of legends and fantasy.

Much of what is known about the accident has been reconstructed based on survivor accounts. The following chronology, compiled by "CITY PAPER – Baltic Countries," is based on sources, including interviews with some survivors. It also includes the findings of the International Investigative Committee, which recently published its final 800–page report on the accident. And the chronology is as follows:

6:30 p.m. EEST, September 27, 1994 – Passengers are beginning to gather at the port of Tallinn, Terminal B. Some are carrying heavy suitcases, while others are carrying bags stuffed with souvenirs. Among those heading to Estonia are: 56 pensioners on a group trip, 21 teenagers from a Bible school and most of the city council from the Estonian city of Võru. Several ticket holders are late and arrive on the ship just as the doors are closing. 989 passengers – mostly Swedes and Estonians, including 189 Estonian crew members.

7:15 p.m. – When Estonia leaves port, the skies are gray and the winds are strong. Still, the weather is no worse than on dozens of other trips. Many passengers put themselves in their cabins or wander around the huge luxury ferry. Some head to duty-free stores to stock up on inexpensive beer, cigarettes and chocolates. Others take motion sickness pills, just in case.

---

47. Currently, President Donald Trump has promised to declassify documents related to the investigations into the Kennedy brothers and Pastor Martin Luther King.

8:00 p.m. – The ship is still close enough to turn back. The sea is choppy, but not enough to spoil the good mood. There is a bar on the ship, alcoholic beverages. There is live music, and some people, undeterred by the rocking of the ship, have taken to the dance floor. Others try the sauna and swimming in the pool below deck.

9:00 p.m. – The ferry sails into stormy weather. High waves agitated in the gray Baltic, six meters high, are large enough to engulf the house. Many passengers, some of them ill, retire to their cabins below the waterline.

11:00 p.m. – The ship is approaching the halfway point of its 350-kilometer voyage. The sea is becoming increasingly rough. Nevertheless, the dance group continues its scheduled performance.

00:30 a.m. EEST, September 28 – The heavy rocking of the ship forces the band to stop playing; the rocking keeps many passengers awake.

Risto Ojassaar said: The dancer, who has just finished performing, heads to the bar on the upper deck to relax. Peeking through the porthole, he sees waves that seem to be reaching deck 8. For now, he is enjoying "*I loved the sea storms,*" he explained later. I thought: "*Oh, Look at that wave! It's magnificent!*"

00:55 a.m. — The first in a series of events that lead to the sinking of the Estonia. Weak, poorly constructed fastenings on the 50-ton bow gate or canopy break under the pressure of unusually strong waves. Many passengers, including one crew member performing a routine inspection on the car deck, hear an approaching metallic bang from the direction of the bow gate, which is supposed to open when the ship is in port, allowing cars to enter and exit the ferry. However, no one suspects that the gate has just broken down. A sailor on the car deck reports the sound to the bridge and examines the inside of the bow. He sees nothing unusual and no longer hears the sound. He therefore assumes that everything is fine.

01:00 a.m. – With the ship moving at normal speed, about 14 knots, the giant bow door is taking the full brunt of the oncoming waves. No one was aware that the already crippled bow door was beginning to break off completely. The watchkeepers on the bridge don't seem concerned about the noise, which was reported only minutes ago.

At the Admiral pub, on deck 5, a staff member is conducting a karaoke contest. This was the concert was supposed to end at 01:00 a.m., but the singing leader says we continue for another 15 minutes because everyone is having such a good time.

01:05 a.m. – The bow continues to be hammered by the relentless waves, and the joints are now completely failing. As the broken loose gate flaps in the raging sea, cutting through the steel plating behind it. They come into contact with the critical inner door, the last barrier between the car deck and the sea. As long as the inner door remains closed, the ship should not sink. But the swinging bow also breaks the locks of the inner doors, which in turn fall slightly forward.

While most passengers have no idea that anything is wrong, some are awakened by noises from the bow. And a few – especially those who have been to Estonia before – are alarmed enough by the sounds to leave their cabins.

On the bridge, another report said there was a creaking near the bow. The crew member who heard the first bang was told to go down and examine the *kardek* again.

About reports of mysterious sounds from the bow, investigators later say the crew should have reduced the shuttle's speed as a precautionary measure – a move that could have prevented the disaster. But officers on the bridge apparently don't do this and yet these are reasons to believe something is seriously wrong. Estonia is not slowing down.

01:10 a.m. – Through the bow gate, which is slightly ajar, water begins to enter the car deck. Via CCTV, a crew member in the engine room sees some water. He believes it is rainwater and calmly turns on the pumps to pump it out. Investigators later note that he did not inform the bridge of what he was seeing.

When the pumps are working the engineer makes his way to the car deck. To his horror, the water reaches his knees.

01:15 a.m. – A catastrophic moment on the ill–fated Estonia: the huge bow door completely ripped out of the ship and crashed into the sea, bouncing off the ship's bulbous bow, which extended from the ship just below the waterline. Many passengers heard a noise that some later described as the sound of a sledgehammer striking and then echoing through the hull. One concerned passenger in the Admiral pub tells his companions: *"We hit an iceberg!"*

As the bow gate opens like a huge whale with its mouth wide open, the Estonia now throws itself straight into the waves, as if trying to swallow the sea in one or two glorious gulps. Almost immediately, with tons of water rushing onto the car deck, the ship tilts dramatically to the right (right again!!!) side by 15 degrees.

Lying on the cabin bed on the middle deck, Risto Ojassaar is knocked onto his back by the tilt. He tries to convince himself that everything is fine: *"I thought: okay, now the ship has tilted and will tilt back."*

On the bridge, the gravity of the situation becomes clear; but the watch officers continue to do nothing without understanding exactly what is happening and why. They continue to operate with insufficient information. They can't see the bow door in their line of sight and apparently don't know that the gate has been ripped open. The panel lights on the bridge glow green, falsely indicating that both: and the bow gate and the inner ramp are locked in place. There is confusion on the bridge. Still no alarm is sounded – an oversight that investigators say later may have prevented many more passengers from being rescued.

A sailor instructed to pinpoint the source of the metallic sounds never reaches the car deck. When he reaches the lower decks, he can't squeeze through because panicked passengers have run up the narrow stairs. Some passengers shout that there is water on deck 1. A crew member falls; stretched out on the floor, he calls out over the radio to the bridge to inform his superiors that passengers are talking about incoming water.

Concerned by reports of outboard water inside the ship, those at the rudder know they need to do something quickly, but are not sure exactly what. They quickly reduce speed and decide to turn to port, positioning the auction side of the ship flush with the wind and waves. They hope this maneuver will counteract the letters that the wind and waves will push the ferry back to an even keel. But, although they probably couldn't have known It's a fatal miscalculation. With the ship tilted toward the angry sea, the waves can now reach the windows and doors of the lower level, blowing them out. Water is now flooding the apartment of the decks, as well as through the bow doors. The sea is pouring into the ship much faster than before, at about 20 tons per second.

The ship tilts further to starboard. It is now clear to everyone that something is seriously wrong; some of the crew realize that the Estonia is going down. There is widespread panic. Many passengers shout to others that they should go to the lifeboats.

Risto Ojassaar has to grab the sides of the cabin door to pull himself up and through the opening. In the corridor, passengers, many dressed only in underwear, head for the main staircase. Ojassaar also heads that way, but the director of his dance group grabs him and shouts: *"No, this way!"* He guesses that only the side staircase can lead them safely outside. Ojassaar said later: *"She saved my life."*

In the casino, gambling cards and chips fly around the room. Slot machines tumble and bounce off the walls. At Cafe Neptunas, on Deck 5, furniture, glassware and china fall from shelves around the bar. The tilt is so severe that some passengers lose their balance and slide into the bulkheads.

01:20 a.m. – The ship's engines have stopped, virtually sealing the fate of Estonia, which is now completely at the mercy of the Baltic Sea. Vehicles on the car deck begin to collide with the bulkheads. The ship is jerking and rocking even further to starboard, and water is pouring over the accommodation decks. Many passengers have already drowned. By now those on the lower decks have virtually no chance of escape; the slanted gangways are virtually impassable. Too many people are crowding the corridors.

At the Admiral pub, the bar moves, sliding across the floor and hitting the opposite wall. People jump behind couches to avoid being crushed. Those in the bar struggle to get out; some of them start running and jump toward the door. Others form a human chain and try to help each other by walking toward the exit.

01:22 a.m. – *Estonia sends its first SOS signal: "Mayday... Estonia"*, says a concerned but calm voice, which is heard by other ships in the area. *"We have a tilt of 20 to 30 degrees and have lost steerage."* Finally, the alarm sounds. A frail female voice is heard over the radio. She speaks only Estonian. "Alarm, alarm," she said. *"There is an alarm on the ship."* By now there is so much noise and shouting, many passengers can't even hear the alarm. A few minutes later, the radio officer transmits his last message to the ships nearby: *"Yes, we have a problem here, strong tilt to starboard... Really bad, looks really bad here now"*. Someone else aboard the ship hears a crew member say: *"We are sinking!"*

The water is already engulfing the entire ship. Risto Ojassaar exerts himself to climb up the side of the gangway. At one point he falls against the glass door. As he looks down, water rushes in from below to above. Exhausted, he finally walks out onto the outside deck. He doesn't see anyone else coming up behind him. Ojassaar later explained: *"One had to be in good shape to climb the stairs. Most of them did not make it."*

Meanwhile, Ojassaar and his dance director are swept off the ship by a wave and are separated. Ojassaar falls into the icy Baltic Sea, plunges so deep into the water that he doesn't think he'll make it back to the surface. *"I thought: I have no air left. I won't make it,"* he recalled. *"Then I caught my second breath."* Jumping to the surface, he sees many life jackets in the water, but no one in them. He climbs onto a nearby raft. The body of his friend is later found in the sea.

The ferry keeps tilting further and further – 60, 70, then 80 degrees. Inside the ship, the floor composed of tiles and carpets gives way, making it even more difficult to make an escape. As the ship tilts, some people lose their grip and perish, falling from one side of the ship to the other. Chairs, tables and shelves fall down the stairs, splashing into the seawater filling the ship. Some passengers sit or stand in stunned silence, frozen with fear.

At Cafe Neptunas, a mother and her adult son climb across the floor in what is now akin to climbing blocks up a vertical building. They pull themselves up by the legs of tables bolted to the floor. When the son reaches the door, his mother, still clinging to the table below, tells him he can't go any further. He begs her to try, but the woman has no energy left. Her son later manages to save himself.

People stop outside the door. Passengers have to wait until they slowly squeeze through by exiting one at a time. One survivor later recalled how he had to shout at people crowding in the doorway, pulling his fingers out of the railing and shouting into their ears to move.

The ship's spacious foyer is particularly treacherous. When the ship tilts, passengers are thrown violently against its walls, injuring and killing some. Walking through the foyer from the stairs to the main exits is like climbing a cliff. One survivor leads his parents and girlfriend through the foyer. Struggling to reach the other side, he looks back: his mother, father and girlfriend are still clinging to the stair railing. Those trapped shout at him to go on, to save themselves.

01:30 a.m. – The ship tilts so far to one side that the bridge – usually the highest point on the ship – almost touches the surface of the sea. At 01:35 a.m., the ship tilts at almost 90 degrees. This is practically on its side. When half of the bridge was submerged, the navigation room clocks out.

Passengers have had about 15 minutes to rescue themselves. Fewer than 300 people have managed to get out. About 750 people are trapped inside, where loud cracking and hissing noises can be heard; some passengers are still inside the ship screaming for life jackets. No one else is getting out of the Estonia alive.

The moon is shining. On the outer deck as passengers and some of the crew scramble for life jackets and rafts. Cutting the lifeboats away from the ship is difficult, and many life jackets are either too big or too small. Inflatable rafts are difficult to open, and desperate passengers try to read the instructions on the raft containers. Some who managed to get out are drunk, while others seem despondent and make no move to put on life jackets. With the ship almost completely tipped over the side, some passengers are panicked others assure that a ship as large as the Estonia should at least stay afloat and not sink.

01:40 a.m. - Many people are stuck in the upside-down hull. […] The ship is sinking fast. There is no time to launch the rafts in any organized way. Many of them were simply thrown into the water by the rocking action of the ship. Those who were lucky enough to get on the rafts and try to pull others aboard, but the sea is rough and continues to throw people overboard. One witness said he had the impression that the waves were deliberately replacing people, throwing some off the raft and sweeping others away. Some people do not have the strength to climb up and simply grasp the ropes around the raft. One man clinging to the raft remembers others in the water desperately tugging at his legs and back with their claws.

01:50 a.m. - Risto Ojassaar looks back from his raft. He can't believe his eyes: a huge white ferry is slipping beneath the waves like a submerging whale. Its bow is pointing upward.

Many of the life raft's passengers and crew notice that the bow is missing a door. They also see people still clinging to the ship's outer railings, not letting go, and then going down with the ship. As it is going down, thousands of bubbles shoot up from below. Estonia eventually settles at a depth of 70 meters at the bottom of the sea.

Hannu Seppanen hugs the raft in the pitch-dark night. Just before Estonia sinks, she hears women screaming. Others recall seeing children crying. As the ship goes underwater, the sound of screams is followed by a sudden, eerie silence.

02:00 a.m. – Over the next few hours, those in the water die of hypothermia, as do some in the wet rafts. Survivors in the rafts struggle against winds of up to 90 km/h. Many are repeatedly blown into the water and have to fight their way back. Others pour icy water from the raft. Some use shoes to scoop up the water.

Ojassaar and two others in his boat are up to their knees in water. If they sit down, they will freeze to death. Ojassaar said: *"Cold water makes you feel so numb and comfortable. This is the feeling when you have death right in front of you."*

The first rescue vessel, the passenger ferry MF Mariella, arrives at the scene of the accident at 02:12 a.m. – about 50 minutes after the first call for help. With great difficulty, Mariella's crew members manage to pull a dozen people out of the water. The rest are still adrift in rough seas, waiting for helicopters to arrive.

03:00 a.m. – Helicopters are arriving. However, many of them are poorly equipped. When rescue teams try to lift the boats out of the water, some break and the rafts plunge back into the sea. Several passengers, assuming they have finally been rescued, die during the helicopters' flight.

News of the tragedy reaches the shore, with people rushing to the ports of Tallinn and Stockholm. An Estonian woman stands near the docks in the Estonian capital, clutching a teddy bear. *"My husband and son were on their way to Sweden,"* she says. *"My son left his teddy bear behind."*

While waiting for rescue, Risto Ojassaar tries not to think about his wife and child. He can't bear it and thinks about their agony while they try to find out if he is alive or dead.

On many rafts, people gather together to warm themselves. One man who escaped from the ship with no clothes on at all stands in the middle of his raft, holding a canopy over his head for four hours. On other rafts, passengers hold the heads of injured companions, protecting them from drowning in the flooded rafts. On another raft, a man shouts for hours, calling on the name of God, while others ask him to be quiet.

09:00 a.m. – The last of the 137 survivors, including Risto Ojassaar, are rescued. The pilots express frustration at finding so few survivors. *"We saw about 40 life rafts,"* said one of them. *"Most of them were empty"*.

In Estonia and Sweden, some relatives receive good news. Ludmila Roden receives a phone call from her husband Ervin, a member of the crew of the. *"I was on the phone all the time. I talk to friends and relatives in the morning,"* he tells reporters. *"I'm happy to tell them I'm alive."* For most, the phone calls only confirm their worst fears.

A total of only 94 bodies have been recovered. Most of the victims are trapped in Estonia and cannot be recovered. Most of the survivors of the accident were young men. Women, children and the elderly had little chance. Except for 11, passengers under the age of 12, none survived.

Final number of deaths: 852.

October 20, 1994. Bodies of Estonians found in the sea are being returned to Tallinn. In a solemn ceremony on the seashore, trucks draped with black ribbons roll off a white ferry carrying 38 coffins. Ships in the area honk their foghorns as a sign of respect. Carrying coffins being taken out of the port on sheets of spruce branches piled on the road. An Estonian official explains: "This is an Estonian tradition. The branches are meant to soften the path of a person's eternal resting place."

December 3, 1997. In their final report, Swedish, Finnish and Estonian investigators point the finger at the German Meyer Werft shipyard, which built the Estonian ferry 20 years ago. The report states: *The Estonian bow gate locking devices caused failure due to wave-induced shock loads, causing opening movements on the hinges. The wicket fixings were not designed according to realistic design assumptions.* Investigators refrain from blaming the crew. However, they suggest that crew members may have been too slow to exchange information while it was still possible to save the ship. (Compiled and written by Eve Tarm and Michael Tarm for the online site "City Paper". This is how it looked on board the Estonia. It looked a little different in light of radio transmissions exchanging correspondence of ships in the vicinity of the Estonian ferry tragedy.

12.3. ...AND IN THE ETHER

And according to Wikipedia, this is what the conversation looked like between Estonia and the ships going to its aid:

- 01:22 a.m. – Engine problems

- 1:21:59 a.m.– MS Estonia: Mayday Mayday, Estonia over.
- 1:22:19 a.m.– MS Mariella: Estonia, Estonia, Mariella reporting.
- 1:23:13 a.m.– MS Estonia: Estonia, Estonia, Silja Europa, Estonia.
- 1:23:22 a.m.– MS Silja Europa: Estonia, Silja Europa here on channel 16.[48]
- 1:23:29 a.m.– MS *Estonia*: Silja Europa.
- 1:23:37 a.m.– MS *Silja Europa*: Estonia, Silja Europa here on channel 16.
- 1:23:57 a.m.– MS *Estonia*: Silja Europa, Viking, Estonia.
- 1:24:00 a.m.– MS *Mariella*: Estonia, Estonia.
- 1:24:01 a.m.– MS *Estonia*: Mayday Mayday.
- 1:24:07 a.m.– MS *Estonia*: Silja Europa, Estonia.
- 1:24:10 a.m.– MS *Silja Europa*: Estonia, Silja Europa, Are you making the Mayday call? Estonia, What's going on? Can you answer?
- 1:24:33 a.m.– MS *Estonia*: Here is Estonia, Who is speaking? Silja Europa, Estonia.
- 1:24:41 a.m.– MS *Silja Europa*: Yes, Estonia, here is Silja Europa.
- 1:24:45 a.m.– MS *Estonia*: Good morning. You speak Finnish?
- 1:24:46 a.m.– MS *Silja Europa*: Yes, I speak Finnish

---

48. This is the so-called UKF rescue channel, which is used to carry out talks on rescue operations at sea.

- 1:24:47 a.m. – MS *Estonia*: Yes, that's the problem we have here, a big tilt to the right side. I think it is twenty, thirty degrees. Could you assist us and also ask Viking Line to assist us?
- 1:25:00 a.m. – MS *Silja Europa*: Yes, Viking Line is right behind us and will get the information. Can you give your position?
- 1:25:06 a.m. – MS *Estonia*: We have a black out [lack of electricity], we can't give it now... I don't know it.
- 1:25:14 a.m.– MS *Silja Europa*: Ok, understood, we will measure up.
- 1:25 a.m.– The power generator went off. The overcast is about 10–15 degrees. The emergency generator has turned on.
- 1:25:26 a.m.– MS *Mariella*: Silja Europa, Mariella.
- 1:25:29 a.m.– MS *Silja Europa*: Yes, Europe here, Mariella... Here is Europe at 16.
- 1:25:36 a.m.– MS *Mariella*: Have you determined their position, or are they on our backtrack?
- 1:25:41 a.m.– MS *Silja Europa*: No, I did not get a position from them, but they must be somewherc ncarby, they have 20–30 tilt and black out.
- 1:25:52 a.m.– MS *Mariella*: It seems to me that they are 45 degrees from our portside.

12.4. Nightmare on the night sea

From the distress signal broadcast by Estonia, it was clear that there was an emergency situation on the ferry, the crew was waking up the passengers with the howling of a siren, and several ferries that were in the area were heading for the crash site. As they approached closer, they saw a terrible picture: on the waves of the rough cold sea, half-naked, frightened and chilled people were struggling to hold onto a raft. Only a dozen managed to rise from the water.

At around 03:00 a.m., rescue helicopters from Finland and Sweden arrived and began lifting from the water those who could not be helped by the ferry crews. For many of them, help came too late – even being lifted out of the water did not help – people died of hypothermia aboard the ships and helicopters that picked them up from the water. On September 28, at 9 a.m., the last rescued people were pulled from the water. All 137 people were rescued, 95 people were officially declared dead, while 757 people were declared missing without a trace. The Estonia disaster turned out to be the largest maritime disaster in Europe after World War II.

12.5. Explicit and implicit reasons

An official commission of inquiry composed of representatives from Finland, Sweden and Estonia concluded that the immediate cause of the disaster was the bow gate – the above-water part of the ferry used to board cars.

In heavy storm conditions and at high speed of the ship, the gate could not withstand the impact of the waves encountered, which simply ripped it out flooding the ferry's cardeck. Then the water flooded the cargo hold, which immediately caused a large tilt to the starboard side. By the time the crew realized what was happening it was too late – the ship lay on its side and went down within minutes. The MF Estonia sank in just half an hour. When the commission's conclusions were learned on all ferries of similar design, they began to make examinations of the bow doors. The German shipbuilders who built the ship disagreed with the conclusions. They presented documents showing that the Estonia's bow gate was calculated to withstand much greater forces, and that its damage could have been caused by an explosion. However, there was no evidence of an explosion aboard the Estonia. And then people began to talk about the secret causes of the disaster.

They were all related to some mysterious cargo that the Estonia was carrying.

It is said that just before the ferry bounced, two vans came on board without customs inspection. What they were loaded with is unknown. According to one of them, the Estonia was used for drug smuggling. The ferry may have carried another batch on its last voyage, but the smugglers learned that police were waiting for them in Stockholm. And that's when the members of the smuggling team decided to open the bow gate and throw the contraband out to sea. Having done so, they were unable to close the bow gate, as a result of which the ferry began to take on water. However, naval experts did not believe too much in the veracity of this hypothesis, believing that a similar step in storm conditions would be tantamount to suicide, and the Swedish prison was certainly better than the bottom of the Baltic Sea.[49]

---

49. The mere opening of the bow gate was not enough to push cars off the deck. The **Estonia** type roll-off ships still have a bow car gangway to lower, along which vehicles enter and exit the ferry deck. Leaving the gangway on the high seas in stormy conditions would be tantamount to disaster. NB, the MF **Wawel** had a similar adventure in December 1981, hitting the Ystad harbor berth with its bow. Thanks to the fact that the sea was very calm, **Wawel** was able to return to Świnoujście. The ferry had a damaged bow gate and, with a higher wave, the car deck could have been flooded, but even in that case, all entrances to the decks were tightly sealed and outboard water would not have been able to penetrate the ferry's engine room.

Another hypothesis is that MF Estonia was transporting weapons that formerly belonged to the Soviet Union. Such a possibility was solemnly confirmed by the head of the Swedish customs authorities admitting that in 1994, the UC there had an agreement with the Swedish Army according to which cars loaded with electronics purchased from the Russian Army and delivered from Tallinn aboard the Estonia were not inspected at the Stockholm port. But in 2005, the Swedish government, when asked by the commission, proved outright that there was no military cargo on board the Estonia on the day of the crash.

Supporters of the "military" theory consider two versions of it, namely: some claim that some extra-secret Soviet weapons were exported on the Estonia, which the Russian special services could not allow to be taken to the West. It was they who organized the diversion. The others claim that the diversion was the work of the secret services of the West threatened by the disclosure of their secret operations with the export of secret weapons from the territory of the former USSR and who decided, literally and figuratively, to drown the whole affair in the waters of the Baltic Sea.

In addition, there is also a hypothesis in circulation that the ferry was carrying radioactive materials, possibly including nuclear weapons components.[50]

But this hypothesis – however fantastic it may be – has its confirmation, namely, the sunken ship was covered with a concrete sarcophagus similar to the one at the Chernobyl NPP, and the waters around it were declared an exclusion zone.

---

50. This hypothesis is justified insofar as during the USSR era, ferries on the Mukran (Sassnitz) – Klaipėda line carried nuclear fuel for the East Germany nuclear power plants and radioactive "ashes" after their use. After the Americans revealed this practice, these cargoes were carried by special trains through Polish territory.

Also noteworthy is the fact that the authorities of the three Baltic countries categorically refrained from raising the wreck of the ferry, although it lies at a depth of only 83 m, while, for example, the Russian SSGN K–141 Kursk was raised from a depth of 150 m!

In 1995, a treaty was concluded by the countries concerned – including Russia – prohibiting any work on the wreck of the Estonia. This treaty also includes the United Kingdom. This is explained by the creation of an underwater cemetery for the victims of the disaster and not to disturb them, but many believe that there is an international conspiracy of silence around the Estonia in order to keep the true causes of the disaster secret. It is also interesting to note that several crewmen, including the captain's helper, pictured in the lists of those rescued later mysteriously disappeared from both the lists and the country.

In early 2009, the Estonian government disbanded the investigative commission after it had already published its fourth statement, whose deductions were that the most plausible cause of the ferry's sinking was its design flaws and harsh weather conditions. At this, the official investigation into the causes of the disaster closed definitively, and opponents will not receive answers to the questions that plague them. At least not in the official way…

12.6. Opinions from the KKK

From the weather map for the day, it seems that it was not fun there… A powerful storm, wind and wave. Many such ships could go down in such conditions. (Hades)

Note how much the fate of the "Estonia" resembles that of the "Jan Heweliusz". In both cases, a storm raged in the Baltic, in both cases many people died unprepared to abandon ship, and in both cases conspiracy theories arose about the cargoes they carried, obviously linked to the spec-services of Russia and other countries. I'm afraid they are worth as much as the paper on which these rantings were written, but the public wants to believe the gibberish. If there really was a trefid cargo there, it would have been quickly extracted, already for safety reasons (radioactive contamination of the Baltic waters off the coast of Finland) already for politics – the West would give a lot for such a treat to denigrate the Russians in the eyes of the world. This is obvious, and therefore the reason is different, and only the question remains: what is it? (Arystokles)

Look at the fact that, like the RMS Titanic, RMS Empress of Ireland, HMHS Britannic, RMS Lusitania, SS Andrea Doria or MF Jan Heweliusz, the ill-fated Estonia also sank by plunging to starboard! Is this li just a coincidence? It already looks like some kind of curse to me...! (Daniel Laskowski).

12.7. But that's not the end of the case

These events shocked the whole world. On the night of September 27/28, 1994, in the Baltic Sea there was the sinking of the roro ship MF Estonia with almost 1000 people on board. For the umpteenth time the forces of Nature showed their might. The ship went down. But was the cause of this tragedy only the storm. And yet it turns out that new facts have come to light...

Not long ago on TV appeared a Norwegian series titled "Estonia – disaster at sea" (2020) in which this disaster was shown from a completely different side – from the side of witnesses, families of the victims and investigative journalists not entangled in political games.

Particularly interesting is episode 5 entitled. "Going Underwater," which shows the expedition of the German ship MV

Fritz Reuter, led by investigative journalist and director in one person Henrik Evertsson, who examined the wreck using a DSV robot. Incidentally, the expedition's advisor and consultant was Jakub Olszewski, who has already scored two expeditions to the wreck. It should be clarified that the Germans are not signatories to the treaty on the burial site of the victims of the Estonia ferry disaster, nor are the Norwegians, which allows them to freely investigate the tragedy. And the results of the investigation are shocking…

12.8. Who clashed with Estonia?

That was all until the dive to the wreck of the ferry on September 21–22, 2019, under the watchful eye of Finnish border guards on the ship FSG Turva, who allowed the inspection of the wreck. Due to the depth and cold water, a DSV robot was used there, which circumnavigated the wreck of the Estonian and took photographic documentation.

The DSV filmed two holes cut in the wake in 1996 by Rockwater divers. Turning the wreck 10° to starboard allowed visual inspection of the starboard side partially buried in soft Baltic clay. This inspection yielded the sensational discovery of a large hole measuring 1.2 x 4 meters 1/3 of the ship's length from the ferry's bow at the height of the fender at the pool and sauna. It now becomes understandable why the Estonia went down so quickly, as stated by Eng. Linus Andersson.

The video also cites the opinions of two maritime disaster specialists – Lieutenant Commander Frank Børresen of the Norwegian Navy and Prof. Jørgen Amdahl, who unanimously ruled that the hole was caused by a collision between the ferry and an unidentified floating object – with Prof. Amdahl stating. Amdahl said that his calculations show that Estonia was hit with a force of 500–600 tons, so it could have been a 1,000-ton ship moving at 4 kts or a 5,000-ton ship moving at 1.2 kts. So it could not have been a detached bow gate weighing only 55 tons, which bore no signs of collision with the side of the ferry, other than traces of collision with its bow pear. The hole could not have been punched in the side of the ferry by some floating trunk or something like that, it's impossible!

Therefore, what kind of reef? The answer is – no! There are no underwater rocks in this body of water. The bottom is made of glacial till and is covered by soft Baltic clays. The rocks are not there. This hypothesis has been definitively rejected. So...?

12.9. Testimony of witnesses...

... Estonian survivors say that the ferry's tilt was preceded by two strange sounds resembling the rumble of an explosive going off or hitting the side of the ferry. This is repeated in all the testimonies – Nota bene, which no one took seriously and no one took into account in the investigation!

Particularly interesting is the testimony of Karl Eric Reintamm, who was one of the first to get out on the deck of the ferry, looked at the water on the right side, and... in the water he noticed a large, long and wide floating object that was moving. Was it a submarine? This he does not know. He didn't serve in the military, so he has no idea, but he's absolutely sure that something was there, and it was brighter than the dark water... Prof. Amdahl even concluded that it could have been a small Kobben-class submarine, whose parameters match his calculations of the size and mass of the object that collided with the MF Estonia.

What were the two booms? Personally, I believe that the first was the result of the collision of the Estonia with this mysterious object, while the second was accompanied by the detachment of the bow gate on the kardek. Initially, the ferry began to take on water with its starboard side, and then water from the kardek began to pour into it in addition. As it flooded most of the starboard compartments, the ferry tilted to starboard and turned 120° to the right, as a result of which it settled on a clay slope and, under the influence of its weight and an additional 10,000 tons of stones and sand, turned another 10 degrees to the right, so that the starboard gate and its damage were exposed.

The detached gate alone could not have sunk such a large ROPAX[51] ferry like Estonia. I remember in December 1981, a few days before martial law, the Polish ferry MF Wawel returned to the port of Świnoujście with a hole in the bow tilt gate for a car deck.[52] Fortunately, the sea was calm and the ferry was able to travel at 5 kts. Wawel's captain said that even in the event of a high wave, nothing would have happened, because it was enough to close and seal all the hatches so that a few tons of water would only be on the car deck, which did not threaten the stability of the vessel. But for safety reasons, the ferry returned to the country with no passengers and only a skeleton crew. I suspect that the same would have to be done on the Estonia to

---

51. ROPAX – basically a variation of the passenger–car ferry, with increased cargo space and reduced public rooms and passenger cabins; ROPAX's are sometimes erroneously referred to as "typical" passenger–car ferries; ROPAX's evolved from "normal" passenger–car ferries when, after the abolition in shipping between the countries of the European Union, passenger transport began to lose importance on many lines, and at the same time cargo transport increased – on some lines were introduced (as additional or only, in place of the existing passenger–car ones) pure cargo vessels were introduced, on other lines "classic" passenger–car ferries were and still are (the middle of the first decade of the 21st century) replaced by ROPAX–type ships. (Wikipedia).
52. The RORO ferries of the time had two doors: bow and stern, which allowed for quick loading and unloading of the vessel.

prevent her from sinking if the bow gate was torn out. Finding a hole in the side of the latter dramatically changed the situation and tragedy was inevitable.

12.10. Submarine?

Karl Eric Reintamm's testimony seems to indicate this unequivocally. The point seems clear – the ferry was rammed by a submarine, so was the MF Estonia deliberately rammed by an unknown submarine, with the intention of sinking it? Was it a criminal sinking? But by whom and for what purpose? To answer these questions, one must go back in time to the early 1980s – the very apogee of the Cold War.

In those years, mysterious submarines – such normal and miniature ones – appeared in the Scandinavian waters of the Baltic Sea. They were observed in all territorial areas of Denmark, Norway, Finland and peculiarly most in Sweden. There they were seen even in internal waters. Of course, the media fueled the atmosphere of uncertainty and danger, all services were on stand-by, while ZOP ships combed the coastal waters covering every suspicious target with missiles and torpedoes. I have written about this more than once and will not repeat myself. Out of all this, one Soviet submarine was captured, which entered the Swedish navy's base in Karlskrona and settled on the reefs there. And that was its only "success." I wrote the word in quotation marks, because if the submarine had not entered the rocks, they would have had a button...

But the psychosis of fear by the Russians remained, although it is not at all said that only Russian submarines were there. NATO submarines were also hanging around and one of them caused a collision with a fishing boat.

It is also puzzling that the deal on the wreck of the Estonia was joined by Britain. One gets the impression that the English are also keen that the truth about the tragedy should not come out. I wonder why? I have an ugly suspicion that the English know exactly what happened there, and who knows if the Estonia didn't collide with a British submarine that was patrolling a sector off the coast of Finland at the time...

NB, the Finns also reported sightings of mysterious vessels in their territorial waters and may have asked for help from the British or another NATO country to combat the scourge. It could have been the Norwegians, it could have been the Germans. Poland and the Baltic states have only been members of NATO since 1999, so they cannot be considered. Besides, what could the Poles support the Finns with? We have one old Kilo class ship and, since 2002, three equally old Norwegian Kobbens, which were rather unfit for the job already, and which are now going for scrap[53]...

What can I say? Was it a criminal sinking? Yes, it may have been a criminal sinking. The idea was to hide something from the world and to prevent that something from getting to the West. I don't know what it could have been – the authors of the film claim that it was some electronic components of Russia's new weapon of mass destruction – WMD, or outright some copy that NATO intelligence swung at Russia. That it was a criminal sinking is also proven by the fact that the ferry was rammed, not treated with a mine or torpedo.

The thing is that mines and torpedoes leave traces: smudges, shrapnel, casing debris, by which the manufacturer, and therefore the user, can be traced. If the Estonia had been torpedoed by a Russian Federation submarine, there would have been no

---

53. Satus in 2024.

signing of the agreement, but the Scandinavians would have raised an uproar about Russian piracy, etc. If it had been fired by the British, it would have been exactly the same from the Russian side. This is obvious – just remember the events of October 20, 1981. Meanwhile, hush, hush! – And as Polish say like in a Czech movie – nobody knows anything…

Time. The catastrophe occurred at night, between 01:20 a.m. – 01:30 a.m. EEST, which is when most of the passengers went to bed. Only the crewmen on duty remained on watch. The perfect time to commit mass murder on unsuspecting victims… And that's why the target of these murderers would have to be defined. Was it the shuttle's cargo, the people traveling on it or perhaps the crewmen? This is what one would have to look for answers to.

12.11. Unknown wreck?

There is a possibility that the Estonia impaled itself on some drifting wreckage that went to the bottom after the collision. It sounds possible, but in that case this mysterious wreck would have to be found – if not on the surface, then on the bottom, but always. But was it moving at its own speed within 4 kts?

So far, this mysterious wreck has not been found, so this hypothesis has little grounding in reality…

12.12. USO vel UAO?

There is another possibility – an Unknown Submarine Object that collided with Estonia and sank it. This is reminiscent of some of the events in the waters of the Bermuda Triangle and the Devil's Sea. And above all, the fictional events described by Jules Verne in his novel "Twenty Thousand Leagues Under the Seas" (1869–1870), the starting point of which was the authentic events that took place up to and in 1866 – it is about the observations of the "runaway rock" or the case of damage to the ship SS Scotia and several others – I refer those interested to this novel, which, despite all these years, is still relevant and works on the imagination!

Well, it can be hypothesized that the Estonia was rammed by just such an object. According to the stories of witnesses who saw it – it did not resemble a submarine and, interestingly, it was visible on the waves despite the prevailing darkness. Rather, modern submarines do everything in their power (and their designers above all) to be invisible in the sea depths as well as on the surface. They are painted gray or black with special anti-radar paints. The hulls are covered with anti-sonar rubber. Civilian vessels are painted white or orange-yellow and with reflective paints. So whose ship was it? Aliens from outer space? The Water People – inhabitants of the world ocean? Someone we don't know yet...? This may explain the tight veil of secrecy and the Baltic governments' desire to hide the truth. Well, because I don't know if the inhabitants of these countries, including Poland, would be happy knowing that in their territorial waters are loitering units of Aliens or Water People, whose intentions are unclear to say the least – given the fact of the massacre committed off Finnish shores.

On the other hand, They can always reproach us for what we have done to the Baltic Sea in our stupidity, and words like "cloaca" or "sewage" are very, very mild and inadequate. Not to mention that more people have died in the Baltic Sea than anywhere else, to mention the wartime shipwrecks of Operation Hannibal. The torpedoing of the Wilhelm Gustloff alone claimed more lives than the Titanic disaster! – about which later. So according to the dyke.

By the way, this "Baltic solidarity" is becoming understandable. Governments want to hide the fact of foreign penetration of the Baltic, hence all this agreement on where to bury the victims of the disaster.

I would still like to remind you that not so far away again from the site of the disaster there is something called the Baltic Anomaly – BSA[54] Some say it is some kind of alien structure hidden in the depths of the Gulf of Bothnia. So far it is not known exactly what it is. Worst of all is the considerable depth at which the BSA is located. Diving to it is very difficult, and we won't soon find out what it is…

So what to do? First of all, implement a reinvestigation of the case and with all the chicanery. Examine the wreck of the Estonia thoroughly and find all the trefty goods that were carried on that fateful voyage. This is exactly what can – for now – be done. Well, and finally speak the truth.

12.13. And one more from the last-minute:

The Swedish government has said it will allow the wreck of the ferry Estonia to be re-examined. The ship sank in the Baltic Sea in September 1994, and 852 people died at the time.

The Swedish State Accident Investigation Commission has requested a new examination of the vessel. Interior Minister Mikael Damberg said yesterday that the government will consider the option of adjusting the law to allow the wreck to be

---

54. Described in the blog Wszechocean: see. *http://wszechocean.blogspot.com/2011/08/czy-na-dnie-batyku-znajduje-sie-ufo.html* (1-7) and *http://wszechocean.blogspot.com/2012/02/ufo-na-dnie-batyku-afery-ciag-dalszy.html* and *https://wszechocean.blogspot.com/2013/12/batycki-falcon-millenium-czy-batycka.html* i *https://wszechocean.blogspot.com/2018/10/nowa-hipoteza-o-bsa-i-innych.html*.

examined. The wreck site is protected from penetration by laws adopted by Sweden, Estonia and Finland that prohibit diving.

"A lot of new information has emerged about what the shuttle wreck looks like now. Therefore, I believe that the need to finally clarify the causes of the disaster" – said Bengt Runestedt to Swedish radio, the son of one of the victims.

In September 2023, a documentary was aired on a commercial television station, showing a hole in the ship's hull, which had not been documented anywhere before. The film's authors suggest that the Estonia ferry may have sunk as a result of being hit by a submarine.

According to an official report adopted in 1997 by the governments of Sweden, Estonia and Finland, the cause of the vessel's sinking was the detachment of the bow door, which caused water to enter the car deck.[55]

And one more thing, namely - recently, several intentional damages to undersea fiber-optic cables have been found in the Baltic Sea, causing disruptions in the worldwide exchange of stock exchange information, trade, etc. etc.

As ex-Major of the GRU Viktor Suvorov a.k.a. Vladimir Bogdanovich Riezun (Rezun) states in his works - one of the tasks of the GRU's Marine Spetsnaz Brigades is to attack undersea cables carried out with the help of surface vessels and/or submarines - DSVs. This is what we have been seeing since the war in Ukraine began, where the Russians have been trying to bring haos to NATO countries with the help of Chinese ships from their "shadow fleet" - illegal transporters of oil and other goods to and from Russia. Recently, the Chinese ship MS Eagle S was captured, which was loaded with electronic reconnaissance equipment. That ship broke another cable from Estonia

55. Source – Radio Szczecin, dated December 19, 2020

to Finland. And this would indicate a target for Russia's next aggression against NATO countries.

12.14. Opinion of a ufologist

Back in October 2021, I asked Swedish ufologist Clas Svahn for his opinion on the subject, and he answered me as follows:

"There are so many opinions and so few facts about Estonia. I will wait for the analysis that is being done at the moment. But so far there is no indication that the ship collided with anything else. I was working that night (I wrote one of the first articles about the disaster in the world) and the weather was terrible. People I've talked to say that water was often seen on the car deck, and the ferry was poorly maintained. We'll see what the ongoing investigation says."

Well – I take your word for it. So far, this investigation is stalled and we will have to wait a long time for its results…

12.15. Letter from a Reader

Hello, I am an unconstant reader, a fan of conspiracy theories and a lover of "moon cave" type stories.

I once wrote to Editor Witkowski and was pleasantly surprised by the factual response to, altogether insignificant, suggestion about the "Great" pyramid.

Why am I writing?

The topic of "ferry", I deliberately do not use proper names, you know hahaha systems…, rarely appears in publications "from the frontiers of science".

Just a misfortune. Disaster.

I have an acquaintance, like you associated in the past with the "uniform", I never, but it so happened that living "here" we use in conversation our broken language of our eastern "neighbors" – From his point of view, both eastern and southern. In various stories from the end of the last century (sorry for the generalities but it's easy to identify the guy if I give details), so in various stories from the "eastern Baltic region" of the 1990s, "Big Brother" appears, and sometimes it is understood only by people coming from countries east of the Oder.

To the point. On the occasion of various incidents at the "exit of brothers" from our countries, it turned out that some devices remained in place, and even there were times when an attempt to cross the border (towards "to the owner") ended in a blockade from the simple fact of refusal to provide information "what is the cargo" – border and other services were no longer friendly as before. Well, with such a "story" a friend ended it more or less like this.

"To this day, no one knows where these three *** are, and they did not leave the country... you know, and then the ferry sank".

I was slightly shocked, despite various other stories, mostly of a smaller scale. Which is understandable.

And now I read your article/post... well, it seems that it had no right to reach Sweden (I don't even know where the ferry went, to Sweden?).

I can of course add vaguely (because what do I know?) some detail but I neither know the type nor the markings or model. Just a convergence of stories from absolutely different sources that I can hint at. So aliens are rather ruled out... (A.P.).

And my answer:

Dear Sir,

Thank you very much for your voice on this issue and your interest in this topic. It is rather obvious that the "Estonia" was deliberately sunk. By the Russians? – perhaps. There is a small but nasty "but" in all this, namely – I do not think that the Russians managed to bribe or otherwise force the governments of the Baltic countries – except Germany and Norway – to collude in silence over the wreck of the "Estonia". In that case, the Swedes would be the first to raise an uproar that the Russians are bribing them, and there would be a stink all over the world. The Danes, too, by the way. Well, and Poland with its sick Russophobia too. Maciarewicz et consortes would immediately exploit this for propaganda. But Maciarewicz sits quietly on this issue…There must have been something else here though – what? We can guess at it. In this case hypotheses non fingo, because we have too little background data, and the boundary data are not certain either. What is certain is that the MF "Estonia" lies at the bottom of the Baltic Sea.

Sincerely –
Robert Leśniakiewicz

૱

Chapter 13
Slovaks and Czechs on the "Titanic"

And here is the material sent by Dr. Miloš Jesenský on the issue of the Slovak and Czech victims of the disaster, which is little known in our country. He writes as follows:

13.1. Did the Slovak become, along with the ship, a victim of an ancient curse?

It has been 112 years since the fateful night on April 14, 1912, when the Titanic's imposing hull disappeared beneath the surface of the North Atlantic while an orchestra was playing. About one thousand five hundred passengers and crew members perished in the wreck of the ship considered unsinkable by its creators, making the event one of the worst maritime disasters of peacetime. The wreck of the legendary ship, which sailed from Southampton in the United Kingdom to New York in the United States on April 10, 1912 under the command of veteran Captain Edward J. Smith (1850–1912) and eventually became the site of a major tragedy, is associated with a number of disturbing mysteries and enigmas. These include the question of the presence of Slovaks or Czechs on board, as well as bizarre reflections on the curse of a mysterious ancient Egyptian mummy that was allegedly secretly transported below deck. So where does reality end and fantasy begin?

13.2. The revenge of an ancient priestess?

Speculation about an ancient Egyptian curse is truly rampant in this case. *Stories are circulating that the mummy of a priestess of the god Amun Ra is responsible for the sinking of this ship, we read at least on the "Záhadného sveta", which summarizes the most widespread version of the event. Its owner got into financial trouble and therefore sold it. However, every other owner had the same experience and buying the mummy always brought only bad luck. And so it ended up in the museum. It was to be bought back from the museum by William Thomas Stead, who was aboard the Titanic at the time. He wanted to secretly transport the mummy to the U.S., as he feared that due to its reputation the transport would be banned. And the mummy attacked! The ship hit an iceberg that shouldn't have been there at all, and sank to the bottom. So could an ancient curse have caused the sinking of the "unsinkable" Titanic?*

This disturbing question has inspired several artists, among them in 1999 German director Rasmus Hirthe (*1971), creator of the short film "Titanic. The Only True Story" ("Titanic. Die Einzig wahre Geschichte"), an homage to the silent, black-and-white horror films of the 1920s, quietly whispering disturbing messages. The masterfully built tension, unsettling atmosphere and expressionistic poetics, despite the deliberate stylization of the old film's dark magic, depict the storage of a mysterious sarcophagus in the hold of a luxury ship, in which a demonic mummy later comes to life, accompanied by his grave followers, to take possession of the victims among the passengers and eventually them with the ship sent to a sea grave.

But could this be the case in reality?

When I was still a boy, I came across the article "Revenge of the mummy" in my grandfather's library, flipping through old volumes of the interwar travel magazine "Dookoła Świata," recalls writer and researcher Robert Leśniakiewicz. – I don't remember the number and author after half a century, but it was written about an archaeologist who found the mummy of a priestess of Amun Ra. According to the author of the article, she looked quite ordinary, but on her face there was a "strange, sinister smile, full of falsehood and contempt." But when I looked at her, I saw no hatred in her, rather bitterness, doubt and skepticism, indicated by her tightened lips and large, dark eyes. It was as if she wanted to confirm to us, after millennia had passed since her death, that everything in life is just futility.

The popular Polish author does not believe in the ancient Egyptian curse, and his American colleague Stefan Andrews remains similarly skeptical: *Of course, the mummy itself did not sink the Titanic. The records, waybills and customs declarations make no mention of any mummy on board, nor did any of the rescued sit with the mummy in the lifeboat. What's more, the ill-fated mummy is well known, is in the British Museum's collection, and was undoubtedly kept safely in museum deposits during Titanic's first and final voyage.*

But how did it appear in the terrible history of the sunken ship?

13.3. In a museum, not on a steamship

The artifact known as the Unlucky Mummy arrived in England in the last decade of the 19th century. Basically, it is a sarcophagus lid, made of wood and plaster, covered with hieroglyphics that reveal the owner's affiliation with the priestesses of the supreme god Amun Ra. It was brought here by the amateur archaeologist Thomas Douglas Murray, about whom the well-known English investigator of paranormal phenomena, Reverend Augustus Montague Summers (1880–1948) noted that it was because of her that he lost his hand and his two servants lost their lives in a strange combination of unfortunate accidents in Egypt. From then on, the mummy was destined to bring misfortune to all in whose hands it fell, until, thanks to Lady Warwick Hunt, it ended up in the British Museum. At the time, its sinister effects were also of interest to London reporter Bertram Fletcher Robinson (1870–1907), who was also warned about the "elements guarding the mummy" by the world-famous author of the Sherlock Holmes stories and enthusiastic connoisseur of all things mysterious, Sir Arthur Conan Doyle (1859–1930). The warnings of a friend did not help, Robinson died suddenly at the age of thirty-six, and speculation about the curse became widespread in connection with journalist William Stead (1849–1912), who was one of the victims of the Titanic. But what connected the mysterious ancient Egyptian artifact to the ship, whose construction began on the docks just two years after Robinson's death? A bit of detective work will reveal what role the original owner of Murray's mummy played in this, when he invited his friend Stead to the British Museum on the basis of disturbing rumors. Here, while viewing the mummy, they allegedly felt that the facial expression on the lid was the manifestation of an anguished living soul. The pair of gentlemen even planned to hold a sort of spiritualistic séance, during which the "anguish and distress from the eyes of the coffin figure" was to be removed, but the museum management did not agree to this strange ritual.

In 1912, Stead became a prominent passenger aboard the ill-fated ship. The hopeful Nobel Peace Prize winner set out on the trip at the personal invitation of then American president and also staunch pacifist William Howard Taft (1857–1930) to attend a convention at Carnegie Hall. However, he never made it there. He was last seen reading a book in the Titanic's first-class smoking room shortly before the unfortunate collision with the iceberg. However, soon after his death, testimony emerged from one of the survivors, who recalled how Stead had debated the mummy curse several times in the social hall. It was no different even on the memorable eve of the disaster.

13.4. Czechs were not on board

It seems that the only surviving passenger aboard the Titanic of Egyptian origin was not the resurrected ancient priestess, but Hammad Hassab (1885–1965) from Cairo with a ticket for ship No. PC 17572. He was rescued from the waves by the crew of the ship Carpathia, on which Dezider Engel, who lived in Lower Otrokovce near Hlohovec, was also serving at the time.

In 2012, publicist Tomáš Vasiľko spoke with his descendants living in Trnava, and Engel's great-grandson revealed to him: Dezider Engel was born in Budapest in 1855. He was a waiter by training, and at the age of twenty-two he left to serve on a ship. From 1903 he served on the ship Carpathia. Here he made it until 1912, up to the manager of the ship's restaurant on the Carpathia, where he also worked at night when half-drowned and chilled survivors from the Titanic were rescued. "Since it was very cold, they gave them dry blankets and tea. They deployed them wherever possible. The crew also provided them with cabins," Milan Pavlík recalls, recounting his great-grandfather's story, which also includes touching and tragic scenes. "Many women kept their children warm under their shirts. The survivors also told them that there was a shootout on the Titanic when some men tried to get into the lifeboats."

Dezider Engel sailed on the Carpathia until the outbreak of World War I, after which he retired from naval service. "He was worried that the ship would fall into one of the sea mines," explains M. Pavlík, and recall that his ancestor guessed the ship's fate quite accurately, as it was sent to the bottom of the Celtic Sea on July 17, 1918, as a result of a torpedo attack by the German submarine U-55. After twenty years in America, Engel moved to Lower Otrokovice in 1936, where he died and was buried in the local cemetery.

But let's go back from the lifeboat crews to the Titanic before the fateful night of April 14–15, 1912, and look at the passenger lists. Since neither Slovakia nor the Czech Republic existed at the time, we need to take a closer look at the list of Austro-Hungarian sailors. There were a total of 49 on board: forty-four in third class, four in second class and one even in first class. Of these, only seven in third class and one in second class survived. In August 2018, the Czech editors of National Geographic magazine meticulously checked other names: *"Although Mr. Emil Taussig had indeed traveled on the Titanic, he was not of Czech descent, the popular daily Národná politika claimed on Wednesday, April 17, 1912. Journalists at the time also claimed that Taussig, from Prague, had survived the voyage, so they congratulated him and his family. Unfortunately, Taussig's first-class passenger was an American and did not survive the tragedy – but his wife and daughter were rescued on boat No. 8. Perhaps most famously, Josef Kielbasa claimed to have survived the disaster and even deprived Captain Smith himself of a seat on the boat. Except that Kielbasa was an obvious liar – in addition to omitting many details from his story, he isn't even on the crew list. In many places, Kielbasa was wrong: he claimed that the cups began to fall after impact (no one but him noticed this), misstated the names of known crew members (such as radio operator Philips), and completely mischaracterized the chronology of the accident – including when the panic broke out and who was where. Kielbasa's recollections of the SOS signal that was transmitted are also false – the Titanic transmitted a different, more common CQD signal. Also to be reduced to fairy tales is the talk that the band that played to the sad end were also Czechs. Also highly improbable is the story of Viktor Halva, who claimed that he fell off the deck and made it to the lifeboat on his own strength."*

13.5. In search of Mary from the Titanic

Shortly after the disaster, Czech newspapers wrote about a certain Maria Lovásikova, who had traveled to Philadelphia to visit her brother as a galley helper. However, her name is not on the list of personnel or passengers, as Tomáš Vasilko confirms, but at the same time reminds her of her possible Slovak origin: *"It is said that a certain Mária Lovásikova from Žilina , but her name is not on the passenger list, should have died on the ship. Publicist Patrik Martinik, in his post for the "Titanic World" website, states: Mária Lovásíková was born in 1870 in Hričovské Podhradí. She was in the third grade and was one of the first victims below deck. She wanted to go to America, it was her dream. Due to the lateness of her szyfkarta, she was not declared dead until October 31, 1961, almost fifty years after the accident."*

In 2009, just weeks after news broke in the media that the last Titanic passenger, Englishwoman Millvina Dean, had died at the age of 97, investigative journalist Peter Getting began his search for Slovakian Mária Lovásikova. And he began with a statement from the then People's Court in Žilina, preserved in the archives: *Mária Lovásikova, born in 1870 in Hričovské Podhradí in the district of Žilina, had been missing since 1913. In 1913, she traveled to America on the Titanic. That ship sank and there has been no news of her since.* From this information, he then deduced that Mária was unmarried, and that the report of her death was made by Juraj Lovásik, the son of her brother Ján Lovásik, to whom she was to go to America in connection with: *Ján was working in America and later died there, and son Juraj had his son declared dead along with Mária. The announcement was made in December 1960, and it took a year to submit any reports on both cases. Since no one responded, in 1962 both siblings, Ján and Mária, officially "died".*

In Hričovské Podhradí, the reporter also tracked down Maria's last direct relative, Emilia Cupánová, who told him: „ "A long, long time ago, some people were interested in this, but today it's hard to find anything. There were rumors that she worked on the Titanic in the galley as an auxiliary force, allegedly to save money on tickets." At the same time, however, Peter Getting reminds us that a minimum of verifiable data is all that is needed to solve this mystery: hile there are many documents, materials and facts about the Titanic itself, this differs from those about Maria. Personal items or photographs from this period are missing, people in our area in the early 20th century were probably busy with other things than taking care of their home archives. Thus, we do not know Maria's face. They don't even have a photo of her brother Ján in the family, and the news of his death in America in the 1930s was brought only by visitors who went abroad to work.

Some documents have survived, however. Card files kept by immigration authorities at Ellis Island show that several Lovásiks from Hričovské Podhradie – spelled as Hricov, Rics or Alsokricso – came to the United States at the time, and the bearers of this surname are also frequently mentioned in the town chronicle of the said village in Upper Považie. According to Peter Getting, the director of the Žilina State Archives, Dr. Jana Kurucárová, while reading the records in the church metrics, even made an interesting discovery, correcting existing data: *Mária Lovásiková was not born in Hričovské Podhradí in 1870, but married couple Štefan Lovásik and Maria Pekariková stayed there during the period they lived there and had seven children. Mária Lovásiková was born three years earlier than stated in the 1960 public notice, on January 21, 1867.*

It is not unusual that the entries in the books of that time did not have a uniform diction, the priests often recorded them phonetically, simply from hearsay, so deviations in names and surnames were quite common. It is therefore quite possible that Mária Lovásiková's mother, who remarried as a widow, may have been registered once under her family name and another time under a changed name. "*In addition to Maria, the church book also lists her brother Ján and information that the entire family lived in house No. 24,*" Dr. Kurucárová adds.

The author of the report "Maria from the Titanic," which appeared in a July 2009 issue of the "Plus 7 dní" magazine, carefully considered the possibility of mystification: *At the time of the disaster, cases of alleged witnesses to the disaster. All over the world there were witnesses to the crash who had never been on the Titanic. Several imposters were also in the former Austro–Hungary. Interestingly, the list of ships communicating with the sinking Titanic included the SS Frankfurt – the same ship on which Maria's brother Ján sailed to America a year later, and could not fail to hear the story...*

However, it is questionable for what reason Juraj Lovásik would mention the Titanic to his relative Maria, when during the proceedings establishing his death it was enough to say that no one had heard of it for half a century? And why would the tradition about Maria be so strong in the family if it was just distorted facts or fiction? We probably won't know the exact answers after such a long time and because of the lack of documents – Juraj Lovásik took the secret to the grave, having died only a year after Maria was declared dead.

So our search must continue.

13.6. THE REMARKABLE STORY OF MICHAL NAVRÁTIL

The search for the Slovakian victims of the Titanic is a real challenge that, according to today's press, is almost impossible to meet. For example, on April 18, 1912. "Slovak National Newspaper" wrote: *The names of those who died in the disaster are not yet known. What is known is that the ship's captain Smith, officers and sailors were mostly killed. According to one Parisian report, between the 1st and 2nd class travelers of the sunken steamer there were no travelers from our homeland, but it is possible that among the travelers in the 3rd class were also our compatriots.*

Compared to the venerable editors of the even more venerable patriotic magazine, we have a great advantage today in that we can confirm the existence of a Slovak in the second class cabin, who was Michal Navrátil (1880–1912) from Serede. In 1902 he emigrated to Nice in the south of France, where he opened a thriving tailor's shop. He soon married Marcella Caretta from Genoa, with whom he had two sons – Michel Marcel (1908–2001) and Edmond (1910–1953), known by the affectionate nicknames Lolo and Momo. For this reason, however, the marriage did not last long and after the divorce the children remained in the care of their mother. So he returned and decided to take the children and secretly go with them to Chicago. In Monte Carlo, he bought three second-class tickets on the Titanic for £26 and boarded in Southampton under the false identity of his friend Louis Hoffman. Michal's granddaughter, Élisabeth Navrátilová, told their touching story in her 2002 book "Children of the Titanic." Even years later, the elder Lolo remembered how the huge steamer touched their childhood imagination: *It was a fascinating ship. My brother and I played on the front deck and were amazed.* Even the older, then four-year-old Lolo remembered little of the night of the disaster at sea, except how he and his brother were woken up by their father along with an unknown man: "*They hurriedly dressed me and picked me up. When I think about it now, I am very emotional. They knew they were going to die,*" he confessed to his daughter many years later. The Navrátilovs reached the lifeboat at the last minute. According to Élisabeth Navrátilova *Michal handed the children over to the people in the boat, he did not push himself into it* – according to another testimony, the second officer Charles Lightoller prevented him from entering the boat, who, with a revolver in his hand of the party, strictly adhered to the "Women and children first" rule. However, despite the noise and chaos, Lolo remembered his father's words: "*When your mother comes, and she certainly will, tell her that I loved her and still do. Tell her that I expected her to come to us and that we will be happy together in the New World.*"

Marcelle Carett lived in Nice for more than two weeks being in despair, until on April 21, 1912, she saw an article in the newspaper "Le Figaro" about "ocean orphans" looking for a family, accompanied by a large photograph of her own children. Her next meeting with them in New York was a big event, with only a few journalists absent. Meanwhile, the body of Slovak Michal Navrátil was retrieved from the cold waves of the Atlantic as the fifteenth in a row. In his coat pocket he had a pistol, a gold watch and a pipe. And because he was traveling with the papers of his Jewish friend Hoffman, he was buried in Canada in a Jewish cemetery.

13.7. Dead passengers return...

At the end, there remains the strange story of Józef Hancko (1874–1962), a native of Tekow, who bought a ticket on the Titanic, although, like the other passengers, he had no idea that it was his first and last voyage beyond the horizon of death. His fate was later described by Józef's grandson Cyril Hancko, who came from the United States years later to visit his relatives in Tekow. In this way, the mosaic of his grandfather's life began to form an interesting, if unexpected, picture.

When Józef Hancko traveled to the US in 1912 to visit his brother-in-law and work, he missed his third-class ticket on the Titanic. He was supposed to board at Cherbourg, where he arrived, but due to lack of time to pass the mandatory medical examination, he was not allowed on board and had to travel on another ship. Later, the residents of Tekow learned from the newspaper that the Titanic had sunk and rightly believed that their compatriot had died. But Jozef Hancko was not lost overseas after all: *"After a long time he found a job, but his first paycheck was stolen,"* his grandson explains. *"But he was very industrious, saved something and sent dollars to his wife. In Tekow they thought he was dead, so when the letter came, his wife fainted. He returned home as an American in 1915, when the war was already underway and he had to enlist. Józef didn't want to go to war, so at first they locked him up because they thought he had come from America as a spy. Later he served as an interpreter for the commander of the Austro-Hungarian soldiers, as he knew German, Hungarian, English, Serbian and Croatian."*

Thanks to this, he also managed to survive the war years, as they say – the one who avoids the gravedigger's shovel will not die soon, as Cyril Hancko reminds us with a smile: *" Józef was born for the second time, and it was said that now he would live a long time. And Józef Hancko only died at the age of eighty-eight due to the flu."*

Thus ended his life's journey. He passed away peacefully in bed, among loved ones, not abandoned and drowning in the cold and dark depths of the Atlantic.

13.8. Passengers from apartment B-51/53/55

One of the stronger moments in the second part of the film "Ghostbusters," which has not lost its impressive scale even after almost forty years, is the nighttime arrival of the ghostly, spirit-filled Titanic in New York Harbor in 1989. Similar feelings arise when we look at the empty trunks of a wealthy couple, now belonging only to the elusive spirits of the past. But the suitcases are here, heavy and so massive that strong hands of a living person must grasp their handles. Why are they empty! They were only recently discovered in the attics of nearby houses and in the attic of the mansion in Kovarcach, to which our traces are currently leading. On a drizzling autumn day, as the blowing wind strips the yellowing leaves from the trees of the surrounding park and tosses them into the air, we gaze at the rain-soaked façade of the restored baroque residence, which now serves as a social gathering place for society. It is from here, from the luxurious residence on the edge of the village in the Topoľčany district, that American billionaire Thomas Cardeza (1875 – 1952) set out on his journey with his mother Charlotte (1854 – 1939). His wife Mary (1880 – 1943) stayed at their Slovak residence, while Thomas and Charlotte boarded the ill-fated Titanic in Cherbourg, France on April 12, 1912.

13.9. Prominent passengers from Kovarica

But who were the other participants in the drama who later fought for their lives in the darkness and icy cold of the North Atlantic? The man's full name was Thomas Drake Martinez Cardeza. His mother Charlotte came from the family of English textile magnate Thomas Drake. Her marriage to James Cardez, a wealthy lawyer from Philadelphia, in 1874, added an earldom title to their family, as her husband's relatives descended from an ancient Spanish family from the province of La Coruña. Their only son Thomas grew up in luxury and studied at prestigious American schools. He later became an influential financier, but in body and soul, he was a traveler, not counting his love for hunting and the company of women. Paradoxically, he inherited his adventurous nature from a horse, and when the head of the family died prematurely, he accompanied his mother on trips during which she circumnavigated the globe twice on her own yacht. During one of the African expeditions, Thomas Cardeza met the Hungarian nobleman Henrich Aponi (1885-1935), the last owner of the estate in Oponice, known for its historical library and valuable collections. The men, who knew how to fully enjoy life, quickly found common ground. And this was not only on safaris through African savannas and forests, gambling in Monte Carlo, or at the Moulin Rouge cabaret in Paris. Soon they formed such a close-knit pair of bon vivants that Baron Aponi offered the world traveler Cardeza the rental of his residence in Kovarť. Thirty-one-year-old Thomas agreed, and in 1906, he moved with his wife Maria, who had interrupted her promising career as a theater actress in New York, to the new residence in Slovakia. Additionally, there were claims that the Cardez family was indeed involved in economic espionage within the then Austro-Hungarian monarchy, which is possible but remains unconfirmed.

In any case, the Americans astonished the locals with their eccentric lifestyle - not only did they possess the only car in the world, play tennis, roller skate, and walk hand in hand with a chimpanzee, but they also established a beautiful park near their residence, which, among other botanical gems, attracted visitors with a globe made of living plants depicting the continents. A small zoo also appeared, featuring little bears that entertained local children. However, the housewife Mary Cardezová did not indulge in self-service luxury in Kovarť - she helped local residents wherever there was a need and generously donated to charitable causes.

After returning from one of the African trips,In early April 1912, the Cardez family decided to have a short stay in America. While Mary stayed at home to manage the estate, Thomas and his mother began packing their suitcases – exactly those that were found a hundred years later in attics. There was even a record of the luggage count – one of those details that history sometimes preserves in contrast to significant things: fourteen trunks, four sailor bags, and three baskets. In addition to a luxurious dress, Charlotte Cardezová took jewelry valued at four million dollars from the vault of their residence in Kovarce, including a heart-shaped diamond. If we remember the gem known from the Oscar-winning film featuring Cate Winslet and Leonardo DiCaprio, then we are on the right track: this is the real Heart of the Ocean (!!!).

13.10. Luxury sank in a maritime grave

As previously mentioned, the Cardez family boarded the Titanic on April 12, 1912, during a stopover in Cherbourg. They were headed to another family residence in Germantown, Pennsylvania, USA. On the ship, they rented the most luxurious first-class suite No. B-51/53/55 right next to the shipbuilder's cabin, which had a lounge, two bedrooms, and its own outdoor terrace. In today's currency, their ticket number 17755 cost over one hundred thousand dollars (originally £512 and 6 shillings). Furthermore, the comfort of the prominent couple was ensured by maid Annie Moore Ward (1874–1955) and butler Louis Gustave Joseph Lesueur (1876–1939). Upon boarding, they fully participated in the whirlwind of social life aboard the ship's traveling elite. However, like other wealthy individuals, they enjoyed a comfortable, pleasure-filled voyage for only two days, until the surface of the North Atlantic closed forever over the Titanic during the memorable night of April 14 to 15, 1912.

The Cardez family boarded lifeboat No. 3 around one o'clock in the morning. It was filled with distinguished passengers and was launched under the command of First Class seaman George Alfred Moore (1880-1943) with only forty people aboard, even though it could have accommodated twenty-five more. Thus, four dozen wealthy men sailed away from the sinking ship. While several dozen children traveling in second and third class perished in the sea water, Charlotte Cardezová also saved her dog, a Pekingese named Su-Yat-Sen, who accompanied them from Slovakia. Five hours later, they found themselves among the rescued aboard the Carpathia, and Thomas Cardeza, when asked how he was one of the first to get on a lifeboat so quickly, replied to reporters: I helped my mother onto the boat and waited for the other women and children from that part of the ship. When there was no one left, after summoning men to fill the remaining vacancies, I did it.

Another version states that the billionaire refused to leave the deck without her son and said in an interview with the Washington Post:

Panic erupted on the steamer due to the lack of lifeboats. It was dreadful. But getting into the boat did not mean survival. Four of us perished before the Carpathia rescued us. They were killed by the terrible cold of the icy waters of the Atlantic Ocean.

Since then, the Cardez family has not publicly commented on the maritime disaster or the events of that memorable night. Certainly, the hostile social climate contributed to this after it was revealed that the insurer paid them around £37,000 for the sunken jewels, which is about seventeen million current dollars. There was a general sentiment that the billionaire family profited from an accident in which over 1500 people did not even save their lives.

However, Thomas Cardez was undoubtedly moved by this tragedy. Soon after, he converted to Catholicism and was baptized. In 1913, he returned with his mother to Kovarce, where they stayed intermittently until the end of World War I. In memory of the dramatic events, Thomas ordered one of the rooms in the residence to be decorated like the cabin of the Titanic. After 1918, the Cardez family mainly resided overseas, in the United States. After his mother passed away in 1939, Thomas became the sole heir to the vast financial empire. His wife Maria worked for the Red Cross until 1943, when she died of leukemia. Thomas Cardeza outlived her by nine years, after which he donated his entire fortune to Thomas Jefferson University in Philadelphia for blood disease research.

13.11. Polish Passengers on the "Titanic"

When it comes to Poles traveling on the Titanic, the "Encyclopedia Titanica" lists the following names:

- Mrs. Leach Aks or Leach Rosen + son Frank (/) third-class passenger, born March 20, 1891 in Warsaw, rescued;

- Mr. Jacob Birnbaum (/) first-class passenger born August 24, 1884 in Krakow, died;

- Mr. Harris Cornblatt (/), third-class passenger, born in 1882 in Warsaw, died, body unidentified;

- Mr. Benoit Picard or Berk Trembiski (/), third-class passenger, born November 27, 1878 in Warsaw, rescued;

- Mrs. Rosa Pinski or Róża Pińska or Pinskaja (/), second-class passenger, born in Warsaw (32 years old), rescued;

- Miss Sarah Roth (/), third-class passenger, born October 10, 1880 in Tarnow, rescued;

- Mr. Woolf Spector or Spektorowski (/), third-class passenger, born in 1889 in Zambrow, died, body not found...

As can be seen from the above, all these Polish citizens were of the Mosaic faith. There were no native Poles on the Titanic.

Bożena Aksamit has a slightly different opinion: there were few Poles on this ship, probably a dozen, the shipowner did not record nationalities on the passenger lists. Hundreds of our fellow countrymen emigrated overseas, but traveling on the Titanic was too expensive for them: the cheapest ticket cost 8 pounds, while the most expensive first-class ticket cost 250 pounds, which was a huge amount of money at that time. Very poor people could not afford a ticket to America.

Poles emigrated primarily on German transatlantic ships, mainly from Hamburg, where it was much easier to get. Some did indeed sail from England, but there they opted for cheaper vessels. The ports from which Poles departed largely depended on which shipping line intermediary they encountered. Their representatives traveled to villages, presented the advantages of emigration, and encouraged people to leave. They handled all the formalities afterward, because in addition to the ticket, one had to buy a visa, pay taxes, and obtain a passport. The intermediaries profited from this, but a person who wanted to leave for overseas and had never left their village before would not manage without their assistance.

As for the Titanic, Polish-sounding names - Ostrowska, Kozłowski, Pawłowicz - are mainly found on the list of passengers in the cheapest, third class. There are several dozen such names. They were often Poles who had already been emigrating for some time - in the United Kingdom or France.

It is known that among the passengers was, among others, Berek Trembecki, a Pole of Jewish descent, who worked in London. He became fascinated with the Titanic and decided he would sail on it. He managed to survive. Father Józef Montwiłł from Suwalki, who was sailing across the ocean to take on a parish in Worcester, Massachusetts, drowned after refusing a place in a lifeboat. He stayed and, together with Anglican priest Thomas Byles and German Benedictine Joseph Peruschitz[56], administered the last rites until the end. His body was never found.

While reviewing the passenger list, I found other Polish-sounding names, namely:

- Mr. Eliezer Giliński (/)?, age 22, third-class passenger;

- Mr. Ernest Morawek, age 54, second-class passenger;

- Mr. Stefo (Stefan) Pavlovic (Pawłowicz), age 32, third-class passenger;

---

56. Source: https://www.gospodarkamorska.pl/edukacja-praca-na-titanicu-by-lo-kilkunastu-pasazerow-pochodzacych-z-polski-14196.

- Mr. Vasil (Wasyli) Plotcharsky (Plotczarski), age 27, third-class passenger;

- Mr. Selman Slocovsky (Słokowski) (/)?, age 20, third-class passenger;

There may have been other Poles or people of Polish descent there, but I did not find them due to the English-language spelling of names and (in the case of Jews) foreign-sounding names – e.g., Goldberg.Ruby, etc.

ଓ

Chapter 14
The criminal Operation Hannibal

14.1. The biggest evacuation operation

It is widely believed that the Titanic tragedy was the greatest and most depressing of all maritime tragedies. This was de facto the case until the spring of 1945. The war was still raging in Europe and the Pacific, thousands of lives were lost daily and material goods going into billions of dollars, pounds, marks, rubles were wasted... I would now like to tell the Reader about the tragedies, next to which the Titanic disaster is porridge with milk. I am referring here to the criminal action of the German administration and the Kriegsmarine known by the code name Operation Hannibal. It's like the Titanic tragedy times ten. Or twenty. Polish Wikipedia puts it this way:

Operation Hannibal (German *Unternehmen Hannibal*) – German military operation to evacuate by sea soldiers and civilians from Courland, East Prussia and the so-called Polish Corridor in occupied Poland between mid-January and May 1945. The operation was carried out due to the progress of the

Soviet offensive in the East Prussian and Pomeranian operations, as well as auxiliary operations.

The Soviet East Prussian operation by the 3rd Belorussian Front commanded by General Ivan Chernyakhovsky launched on January 13, 1945, together with the 2nd Belorussian Front commanded by Marshal Rokossovsky, later cut off East Prussia between January 23 and February 10, 1945. German Grossadmiral Karl Dönitz ordered Admiral Oskar Kummetz and Rear Admiral Konrad Engelhardt to plan and carry out the Rettungsaktion (evacuation operation). Dönitz sent a message to Gdynia in occupied Poland ordering evacuation to ports outside the zone of Soviet operations. The operation was given the code name "Hannibal." In his postwar memoirs, Dönitz stated that his goal was to evacuate as many people as possible ahead of the Soviets.

The gigantic number of military personnel and refugees turned this operation into the largest evacuation in naval history (in 15 weeks, between 494 and 1,080 ships and transport vessels of all types, including fishing boats and other vessels, also using Germany's largest naval vessels, transported between 800,000 and 900,000 refugees and 350,000 soldiers across the Baltic Sea to the Third Reich and German–occupied Denmark). The number of evacuees in this operation was three times the number evacuated at Dunkirk.

1. Baltic Front, 2.Baltic Front and 3. Baltic Front on October 9, 1944 cut off 32 German divisions in the territory of Latvian Courland with a total of about 200,000 men and 20,000 soldiers of the SS Latvian Legion. In January 1945, the GA "Courland" was created from the units cut off there by the Red Army belonging to the GA "Courland".

The evacuation plan for the Gdańsk–West Prussia District, developed on Albert Forster's staff, was given the codename "Eva–Fall" and was approved as early as September 4, 1944. Forster, reckoning that the evacuation routes of the population from East Prussia would pass through Gdańsk Pomerania, and that the region taking over the evacuation of the population from both areas would be West Pomerania, invited both Gauleiters to a conference to coordinate the evacuation. Forster's proposal was completely disregarded by the Gauleiter of East Prussia, Erich Koch, who claimed that his area did not need to be included in the evacuation because it would not be captured by the Red Army. This apparent ignorance on the part of Koch caused the evacuation of Prussia to be carried out in haste and in complete disarray, and the groups of refugees and evacuees arriving in Gdańsk Pomerania from the fall of 1944 caused more and more disruption, worsening the already difficult situation of the population of Pomerania. The evacuation of the population from the area also soon turned into a disorderly flight.

From the south rushed:

Operation Vistula–Oder (January 12–March, 1945)

Warsaw– Poznań Operation (January 24–February 23, 1945)

East Prussian Operation (January 13–May 9, 1945)

Kriegsmarine commander Karl Dönitz on January 21, 1945 gave the order to begin Operation "Hannibal," that is, to evacuate the personnel of the submarine training flotillas from Gdynia and Piława. This task was to be carried out with the flotilla's own ships:

School ships – U–14, U–17, U–56, U–57, U–58, U–59, U–152, U–721, U–746, U–1197, U–2502, UD–4

Training ships – U–721, U–747, U–778, U–822, U–828, U–903, U–924, U–999, U–1007, U–1065, U–1205, U–1306, U–2521, U–2524, U–2533, U–3010, U–3012, U–3020, U–3023, U–3025, U–3501, U–3507, U–3511, U–3513, U–3514, U–3517, U–3522, U–3524, U–3529

Battleships – U–1110, U–2503, U–2518

Supply ship – *Memel*

As well as several ships and vessels, the largest of which were: MS *Wilhelm Gustloff* (25 484 BRT), *Hansa* (23 130 BRT), *Hamburg* (22 117 BRT) and *Deutschland* (21 046 BRT) and transport ships: SS *Cap Arcona*, MS *Goya*, MS *(General von) Steuben*, *Thielbek* and *Athen*.

These ships were to evacuate all personnel of the 2nd Submarine Training Squadron (2. Unterseeboots–Lehr–Division) and its equipment by early February.

Civilians were to be taken as space was available, if there was any left on the transport ships. The Party never approved of civilians leaving their homes, houses or fleeing their homes, as this would have been seen as defeatism and severely punished, although a plan to rescue German civilians and German troops remaining outside their country had already been drawn up in January 1945, when the German government obtained the secret English operational order "Eclipse."

According to documents of the MOK Ost (Marineoberkommando Ost in Kiel), the Red Cross (German – DRK) and the logbooks of various vessels, it appears that by the end of March

1945 some 1.23 million Germans had been evacuated to ports in the West (among them were also Allied prisoners of war, French forced laborers and Polish citizens).

During a meeting at Headquarters, Adm. Dönitz disagreed with the generals of the land forces, who began to pile up problems related to evacuation by sea, as the transports were being carried out despite enemy counteractions. The only thing that could stop the entire operation was the dangerously depleting supplies of coal (the Ruhr and Upper Silesia were already occupied at the time) and propellants, which would have prevented units from going to sea. Losses during this operation had to be reckoned with, as they were inevitable, and this was mainly due to the insufficient number of escort units.

The evacuation continued until the end of the war. A large convoy gathered in the area of the island of Bornholm, where the convoy commanders tried to negotiate a surrender with the Western Allies. It ended with the landing on Borholm. GA "Kurland" fought in Courland until May 1945. Part of the army left the Courland Peninsula and was evacuated to Western Pomerania and the Hel Peninsula. At the time of the surrender, this army group numbered about 180,000 soldiers. (Wikipedia).

14.2. Secrets of German training grounds

But that's not all, because most likely (actually, certainly) the local Torpedo und U–bootswaffe Versuchenanstallt working on new types of submarine weapons was evacuated from Gdynia (then Gotenhafen). Its remnants can be seen today in the waters of the Gulf of Gdańsk and the Hel Peninsula. It was the artifacts and documentation of this institution that the Russians were looking for right after the war. Unfortunately, we do not know whether they found anything or not…

Personally, I am of the opinion that this was not only about the secrets of the T u.UVA but also about other German retaliatory weapons training grounds deployed along the Polish Coast: the V-weapons training ground in Łeba – Rąbka, the SS airborne training ground in Władysławowo, the V-weapons training grounds in Ustka, Kołobrzeg and Międzyzdroje and, of course, the rocket weapons training grounds near Peenemünde, which, admittedly, was ruined by a British air raid in August 1943. Of particular interest was the SS aerial weapons training ground in Władysławowo (d. Grossendorf), for it was there – according to urban legends – that the trials of Hitler's UFO, the V-7 Hauneb, took place, and under the supervision of the Waffen-SS General himself u. SS-Obergruppenführer Hans Karl Friedrich Franz Kammler, who was a confidant of Hitler himself and head of his secret projects. This promotion placed him above Albert Speer, who was minister at the time, and Reichsmarschall Air Chief Hermann Göring, making him the de facto second in command. His end is also mysterious, and he most likely managed to escape to South America and on to the US, where he most likely worked in the rocket program there.

Echoes of these events were included by Janusz Meissner in his novel "Wraki" – "Wrecks" (WL, 1950) later filmed by Ewa and Czeslaw Petelski in 1956.

Not surprisingly, it was furiously sought out by the Russians, who seized all the training grounds and missile bases in Poland, East Germany and Czechoslovakia. That's a subject for passionate stories and historical studies, but we'll deal with the Baltic Titanics of that time period. The first of these, the most famous, is…

14.3. ... MS Wilhelm Gustloff

This beautiful cruise ship was launched in Hamburg in 1937. It was named after an assassinated NSDAP member, and Adolf Hitler himself was at the ship's launch. It became the flagship of the Kraft durch Freude (KdF) organization. During the war it was renamed a hospital ship. Until 1945, it was moored in Gdynia. As a result of the Soviet offensive and during the German withdrawal from Poland, the ship, as a transport ship, was used to evacuate the German population and healthy and wounded soldiers (including personnel of the 2nd Submarine Training Flotilla) from Gdynia before the advancing Soviet troops during Operation Hannibal. Re-launching the ship and adapting it to the role of an evacuation unit required a lot of work.

This staff of the 2nd OP Training Flotilla also included personnel and documentation from T u. UVA and other institutes working on retaliatory weapons, which was hunted by Soviet intelligence. This alone can explain the activity of Soviet divers on the wreck of the Wilheln Gustloff. Other hypotheses speak of the search for the famous Amber Chamber, which the Germans looted in Tsarskoye Selo.

Incidentally, I recommend to the Reader an excellent sensational novel by Christopher Piers entitled "Gustloff - the mystery of the Amber Chamber". "Gustloff - the mystery of the Amber Chamber", Publishers Initium, Krakow 2024, in which the author sheds interesting light on the events of January 1945.

The vessel set out on its last voyage on January 30, 1945, escorted by the torpedo boat Löwe. On board the Gustloff were 173 crew members, 918 officers and sailors from the Second Submarine Training Division (2. U–Boot Lehr Division), who were to man or supplement the U-boat crews, 373 women from the Kriegsmarine Auxiliary Corps who were military telephone operators, telegraphists, typists, draftsmen or nurses, 162 wounded Wehrmacht soldiers, and 4,424 refugees, including officers of the Todt organization, Junkers, policemen, Gestapo men, NSDAP activists and families of Nazi officials fleeing the areas occupied by Soviet troops. A total of at least 10,000 people were on the ship, according to the latest estimates, as confirmed by a dispatch sent from the vessel. The ship was hit with three torpedoes by the Soviet submarine S–13 commanded by captain–second lieutenant Alexander Marinesko. A total of 6600 people died in this hecatomb.

It was the greatest maritime tragedy in the recorded history of mankind (the largest known number of victims of the sinking of a single ship). However, the torpedoing of an auxiliary vessel, going in a convoy of warships, was completely in accordance with the laws of war, specifically the London Agreement of 1936, regulating the rules of submarine warfare. During the preparation of the ship's last voyage, a number of cardinal errors were made, the most important of which were – using an armed Kriegsmarine auxiliary to evacuate civilians, allowing it to be heavily overloaded, and sending it on a voyage with an escort.

Currently, the wreck is located at the position N 55°07′27.7″ – E 017°42′14.6″. It is considered a marine graveyard and diving to the wreck and its vicinity within 500 meters is prohibited.[57]

Edmund Kosiarz in his booklet "Treasures of Wilhelm Gustloff" (Yellow Tiger Series, MON, Warsaw 1977) writes:

Among the numerous personnel of the submarine fleet, it was decided to evacuate sailors from the 2nd School Division of

---

57. Source: *https://pl.wikipedia.org/wiki/MS_Wilhelm_Gustloff*

Submarines[58] [...] and several auxiliary and logistical units. The most important among them was the communication service staff, largely composed of women, without whom the U-boats could not operate at sea. In addition to them, the evacuation also included training subunits, which comprised not only people but also heavy training torpedo devices weighing up to several tons, depth charge launchers, and other equipment (what kind???).

By the way, Wilhelm Gustloff was referred to as Beischiff II ULD, meaning accompanying ship of the 2nd School Division of U-boats, and served as its command point, thus becoming a warship. After the war, until the late 1960s, the wreck was designated only as UNDERWATER OBSTACLE NO. 73.

In addition to equipment and documentation, treasures were loaded onto Wilhelm Gustloff, namely:

Treasures were loaded onto Wilhelm Gustloff and Hansa. But it is doubtful that priceless works from the Amber Room were in the heavy crates. Rather, they were the treasures of Kriegsmarine: the submarine fleet personnel with all their equipment.

Another Polish author, this time a writer of thrillers, sees this issue somewhat differently. Finally, novels have appeared in Poland that connect past events with the present and are exceedingly sensational. One such novel I recommend to the Reader is Krzysztof Piersa's "Gustloff: The Mystery of the Amber Room," which meets all these requirements, and thus we have a series of mysterious crimes – sophisticated murders of old combatants, a complicated investigation by the Gdańsk police, the mystery of the wreck of the German liner MS Wilhelm Gustloff, and the

---

58. Original: II U-Bootlehrdivision.

case of the titular Amber Room and other treasures of the Nazis plundered in Poland and the USSR.

The action takes place in the present day on the Coast – in the Tricity and in Königsberg. The characters act somewhat in the style of Indiana Jones and Dirty Harry Callahan. We deal with mysterious documents containing encrypted messages from wartime history. Along the way, the secrets of the Gdańsk Judenrat (Jewish collaboration council) are revealed, along with a clever revenge on the Nazis which was planned and executed with truly hellish ingenuity. It was they who, through their intrigues, exposed the German freighter to fire. This was their revenge for the sending of several thousand Jews to death camps.

To all of this, we also have a brief course on using the Enigma and breaking codes, along with dizzying plot twists. In a word, there is something enjoyable for everyone: both for conspiracy theorists and for historians of World War II. A true delicacy, as Vincent V. Severski described it – and he was right. It is read easily, lightly, and pleasantly; the crazy adventures of our heroes, love, deadly threats, and fast-paced action are undoubtedly the qualities of this holiday novel. And most importantly – it contains another hypothesis regarding the resting place of the Amber Room – the most valuable artifact plundered by the Germans from Peterhof[59].

According to other authors and researchers, the Amber Room was transported in the hold of a small vessel, the SS Karlsruhe, which was sunk in January 1945. Searches conducted by an international team of divers did not result in finding this work of art. One crate was recovered, in which parts of some machines were found. Like Gustloff and other wrecks from Op-

---

59. The Amber Room was located in Tsarskoye Selo.

eration Hannibal, the wreck of the SS Karlsruhe is a war cemetery, and diving there is prohibited.

According to another version, the Amber Room was destroyed by Soviet soldiers, who demolished the castle in Königsberg as a "seat of fascism"[60]…

I am afraid that the ex-major of the GRU Viktor Suvorov alias Vladimir Bogdanovich Rezun is correct, who bluntly claims that the Germans burned the Amber Room during their retreat from Leningrad.If it somehow survived and was transported to the West, sooner or later its artifacts would be revealed, and so far there have been none and there are none. Unless it rests in one of the spectral "golden trains," which is, however, another matter…

14.4. MS "Goya"

Less well known is the tragedy of another German transport ship MS Goya. This ship was also used by the Nazis in Operation Hannibal. It was built in 1940 at the Akers Mekaniske Verksted shipyard in Oslo. Already that year, she sailed as a support ship (transport ship) for German submarines. From 1943 she belonged as a base ship for Kriegsmarine submarines. Later it served as a target ship in the port of Memel (Klaipeda). In 1945 she was reclassified as a transport ship for the army and, as part of Operation Hannibal, intended to carry German refugees from Pomerania, among other places. Contrary to oft-repeated opinions, it did not have the status of a hospital ship, but a military transport ship. At the time of its sinking, it carried not only civilians and wounded, but also military personnel, including 200 soldiers of the 35th Armored Regiment.

---

60. "Expedition to the Bottom - Amber Chamber" episode 3, (USA 2022).

On its last voyage, Goya sailed in a convoy of ships carrying German refugees from East Prussia and Gdańsk. On April 16, 1945, off the coast of the southern tip of the Hel Spit – four hours after leaving port – she was attacked and damaged by Soviet bombers. Goya sailed in a convoy with smaller transport ships – Kronenfels and Aegir. The speed of the convoy was limited by engine trouble on Kronenfels, which was even forced to stop the machine for 20 minutes for repairs. On the evening of April 16, Goya was detected by the torpedo-armed Soviet submarine mine-layer L-3. Despite a relatively strong escort – the convoy's cover was provided by two mine-layers, M-256 and M-328 – at 11:52 p.m., within a dozen miles of Rozewie, L-3 fired four torpedoes, two of which hit the ship. The first hit the bow, while the second hit the midship, destroying the engine room and causing an explosion that broke the Goya in half. The ship sank shortly after midnight in four minutes. Such a rapid sinking made any planned rescue operation aboard the Goya impossible. At least 6,000 people died in the icy water; a higher death toll (around 7,000) is possible, as there were likely people on board who were not included on the passenger list. The escort ships managed to pick up only 182 people, 9 of whom soon died. Some sources say that 98, 165 or 334 people were rescued.

The commander of the submarine, Captain Vladimir K. Konovalov, was honored for this action with the highest Soviet war award – the title of Hero of the Soviet Union. Incidentally, the modern nuclear submarine SSN V.K. Konovalov appears in the novel "The Hunt for Red October" by Tom Clancy.

The wreck of the Goya rests at the position N 55°12′ – E 018°18′ and has been declared a war grave, where diving to the wreck and its vicinity within 500 meters is prohibited.[61]

---

61. Source: *https://pl.wikipedia.org/wiki/MS_Goya*

14.5. SS General von Steuben

The third large ship that was sunk during Operation Hannibal was the SS General von Steuben. It was a German passenger ship that had been converted into a troop transport ship during the war. It shared the nasty fate of the two previously mentioned. It was sunk by the Soviet submarine S–13 under the command of Capt. Marinesko. Rumor has it that Marinesko could not bear the consciousness of murdering so many people – he broke down and committed suicide.

On its last voyage it set off from Piława (today Baltiysk in East Prussia) to Swinemünde (currently: Świnoujście) on February 9, 1945. On board were, among others, active SS officers with their families and naval cadets. The ship, sailing without shadowing, was escorted by the torpedo boat T 196, a TF–10 (torpedo catcher) auxiliary ship. Detected by the Soviet submarine S–13 commanded by Capt. 3rd rank Alexander Marineska. On February 10, 1945 at 0:50 a.m., north of Słupsk Shoal, it was hit by two torpedoes. The first hit below the pier, while the second hit the boiler room. A huge panic ensued. There was no way to organize evacuation and rescue. After 3 minutes, the boilers began to explode, and the ship burst into flames. After 5 minutes, the ship was lying on its starboard side. Under these conditions, the crew was unable to lower the lifeboats due to lack of time, and also because the davits were covered with ice. After seven minutes, the Steuben went down. The torpedo boat T 196 rescued a total of about 300 people, more than half of whom were soldiers. About 4,500 people died.

The wreck is currently located at position: N 55°13'26" – E 016°40'48". It was only discovered by ORP Arctowski in May 2004. The wreck is a war grave, and for this reason diving is forbidden within 500 meters of it, however, these prohibitions are broken and elements of the wreck are stolen (a rudder wheel and a machine telegraph, for example, have been lost in this way). Legally only research diving expeditions to the wreck take place.[62]

14.6. SS "Cap Arcona" and other victims

Another victim of Operation Hannibal is the German passenger liner SS Cap Arcona, named after the only German cape – Arkona on Rügen. It usually sailed on the Hamburg–South America route. This turbine ship was one of the many passenger ships that received one more funnel than needed – for aesthetic reasons. It usually carried the wealthiest passengers, but also emigrants to South America. One of the flagship figures associated with the ship at the time was its first captain, Commodore (the most senior captain) of the HSDG[63] fleet Ernst Rolin. The ship's peaceful service lasted almost twelve years, during which the turbine ship, commanded by two captains – the aforementioned Ernst Rolin and Richard Niejahr (the second Commodore of the HSDG fleet) – made 91 voyages, carrying more than 200,000 people.

From 1940 it was taken over by the Kriegsmarine and was used in the Baltic Sea. In 1942, with the participation of Cap Arcona in Gdynia, Herbert Selpin's film "Titanic" was made (mainly interiors). "Titanic." Devoted to the disaster of this ship, but with a strong propaganda, anti–English idea. Beginning in 1944, it began transporting refugees from East Prussia to the west as part of Operation Hannibal. On April 26, 1945, 6,500 prisoners from Neuengamme concentration camp and about 400 survivors of the death march from Wesoła camp (German:

---

62. Source: *https://pl.wikipedia.org/wiki/SS_General_von_Steuben*
63. Hamburg–Südamerikanische Dampfschifffahrts-Gesellschaft – Hamburg Shipping Society – South America.

Fürstengrube, a sub-camp of KL Auschwitz) were transferred to the ship. The prisoners were also placed on other, smaller vessels Thielbeck and Athen. All ships were moored in the Bay of Lübeck with the presumed intention of sinking them with the prisoners to hide evidence of war crimes. Its commander, Captain Heinrich Bertram, protested against taking so many people at once aboard a logistically unprepared ship, but relented in the face of violence.

On May 2, 1945, after the cessation of hostilities on land, the Allied command gave the following ultimatum in open text:

We call on all naval vessels sailing under the flag of the Third Reich to make an immediate port arrival. All German ships encountered at sea after 2 p.m. on May 3 will be bombed. I repeat. We call on all...

Captain Nibmann, commanding the ship Athen, knowing the contents of the British warning, raised the white flag (despite the stationing of an armed SS detachment and armed Kriegsmarine sailors on board), communicated with the Neustadt harbor commander and arrived in port at 1:45 p.m. Captain Nibmann knew that the ships in the harbor roadstead did not comply with the radio warning. On the flagstaff and masts of the prison ships fluttered the flags of the Third Reich and none of them bore the markings of the Red Cross. Captain Nibmann, making a port call before the British ultimatum expired, saved the lives of 1998 prisoners of the Athen ship (which after the war, as part of war reparations, sailed under the Polish flag as the Waryński).

The other three ships, despite all awareness of the Allied warning, remained in the roadstead with their flags raised up to and including the moment of the air attack. Cap Arcona's captain intended to light the ship at night after the British warning (he had previously been captain of the official registered hospital ship Monte Rosa), but this was categorically forbidden. On the ship's deck, there were numerous arguments between SS sentries and Cap Arcony's civilian crew, who were not prepared, on the eve of the war's end, to share responsibility for the premeditated crime that had been planned. The Thielbeck ship also failed to raise the white flag.

On May 3, shortly after 2 p.m., the ships, standing on the roadstead, were attacked by Hawker Typhoon aircraft of three RAF squadrons (197th, 198th and 263rd). The aircraft of the 198th Squadron fired 62 missiles at Cap Arcona and Thielbeck (40 of which were accurate). The 197th and 263rd squadrons attacked the ship Deutschland IV with bombs and rockets.

A thousand survivors of the attack swam to shore, but there, according to witnesses, the SS, Kriegsmarine sailors and armed civilians shot at survivors in the sea and killed those who made it to shore. Nonetheless, about 350 people managed to survive as British soldiers arrived on the spot.

Of the Germans who killed the prisoners, those who did not escape before the arrival of the British were either slaughtered by the British soldiers, who, seeing what was happening, hardly took any prisoners, or by the prisoners (the British did not resist when the prisoners attacked the fleeing Germans). In the case of the remaining Germans (those who escaped earlier), the investigation to find them was unsuccessful.

On May 3, the command of the 2nd Tactical Air Army issues "order No. 71":

Hospital ships and Red Cross evacuation ships will be in the basin. These ships will be illuminated and are not to be, I repeat: not to be attacked.

The suspension of hostilities applied to the Hamburg region. Denmark and Norway were further under German Nazi control, there was a practical danger of German criminals and dignitaries fleeing to these still-occupied countries, and due to the mined nature of the basin, Allied naval interception operations were out of the question. The Germans repeatedly failed to comply with the Allied warning of May 2 in those days – up to and including May 4, the British sank 21 transports and ships in the body of water covered by the May 2 warning, as well as 7 smaller vessels.

The moral responsibility for the criminal hecatomb of prisoners lies with SS-Reichsführer Heinrich Himmler and Hitler's successor, Grossadmiral Karl Dönitz.

Some SS men serving on the sunken ships went on trial in Hamburg (at the Curio-Haus) from March 18 to May 3, 1946.[64]

In general, the entire Operation Hannibal was one great war crime, which caused many times more casualties than the RMS Titanic disaster, and it should be mentioned, because recently voices have been raised in Poland that German refugees are innocent victims of "communist crimes" against defenseless civilians and demand its condemnation. Well, no. A distinction must be made between Nazi Germany's crimes in Poland and Europe and the deliberate sinking of these ships. Civilians fled in fear of the Russians and Poles coming from the east – because they feared retaliation for the crimes committed by the Wehrmacht and SS formations in Poland, Lithuania, Latvia, Estonia, Belarus, Ukraine and Russia. It finally reached them that they were to blame for causing and waging war in Europe, the establishment of concentration camps, the extermination of entire nations, the murder and persecution of political opposition,

---

64. Source: *https://pl.wikipedia.org/wiki/SS_Cap_Arcona*

etc. and that the nations of Europe could take fierce revenge on them – and rightly so. This is, after all, how the propaganda of Dr. Josef Goebbels presented this thing. The result was only one – genocide, which has not been accounted for to this day…

In addition to the German units mentioned here, during Operation Hannibal the following were also sunk:

MS *Stuttgart* bombed in Gdynia, 1000 casualties – wounded German soldiers;

SS *Thielbek* – 2800 victims, mostly prisoners of Stutthof and Neuengamme Concentration Camps…

…and several smaller units.

Needless to say, these wrecks are particularly dangerous for the environment due to the cargoes they carry and the fuel that can escape from the unsealed tanks at any time and contaminate huge areas of the sea and adjacent beaches. As far as the Baltic is concerned, the thing is not new – these phenomena have been observed before, and environmentalists have signaled the dangers associated with it. The result was as usual – that is, none. Except for a handful of scientists, no one cared. The established dogma was that artificial fertilizers, especially those containing NPK, must be used to increase crop yields, and this was to be the remedy for all the ills of agriculture. And this is true both in Poland and the rest of the Baltic Sea countries.

This green in the sea is not the color of life at all, but on the contrary – it is the color of death, because this mass of algae will fall to the bottom of the sea and there decompose anaerobically into hydrogen sulfide – H_2S and methane – CH_4. Dead fish and other marine organisms will enrich the Baltic waters with organophosphorus compounds – such as phosphine (phosphoric) – PH_3, which is a toxic and flammable gas at the same time.

And on top of all this, add the C-weapons dumps lying on the seabed since the 1940s, and containing, among other things Sarin – $C_4H_{10}FO_2P$, Soman – $C_7H_{16}FO_2P$, Tabun – $C_5H_{11}N_2O_2P$, Luizite A – $C_2H_2AsCl_3$, Iperite – $C_2H_8Cl_2S$, Clark I – $C_{12}H_{10}AsCl$, Clark II – $C_{12}H_{10}AsCN$ and others – a total of 50,000 tons of CWAs – chemical warfare agents. As you can see, most of them are infernally toxic phosphorus and arsenic-organic compounds. Of course, on top of that, there are also incendiary bombs with white phosphorus and ordinary bombs with crushing explosives – these are even more, as much as 500,000 tons! Andrzej Sikorski in "Przeglad" No. 27/2024 gives an interesting statistic of accidents with CWA's on the Polish coast:

In 1955, 120 children from Żywiec who were staying at a colony in Darłówek were injured on the beach. In 1966 four fishermen from Darłowo were burned (with iperite), in 1977 12 fishermen also from Darłowo, Kołobrzeg and Ustka, in 1979 four fishermen from Darłowo and Ustka, and in 1997 eight fishermen from Władysławowo. In the latter case, a soldier burying this 6-kilogram block of iperite in the ground half a year later was diagnosed with pulmonary sarcoidosis.

And then there are the 6,000 tons of oil found in the tanks of shipwrecks from both World Wars and post-war disasters: MS Wilhelm Gustloff, SS General von Steuben, SS Stuttgart, MS Goya, TS Franken and many others. Well, and to top it all off, municipal wastewater poured into rivers flowing into the Baltic – to mention the last two inflows of Warsaw sewage into the Vistula, and biologically and chemically contaminated flood waters flowing down the Vistula and Oder... In a word, there is everything in our sea, except perhaps radioactive poison, although we can't be sure of that either, as several nuclear power plants have been erected over this unfortunate sea, which may have dropped some radioactive nastiness into its waters unnoticed. It's also the strange affair of the sinking of the MF Jan Heweliusz in 1993 and the MF Estonia in 1994. There may also be ships supplying the Nazi atomic research centers at Mosty (Luftmuna 4) and Arkona.

In breaking news:

They are warning about dangerous chemicals in the Baltic Sea. Appeals have been made

On the German coast of the Baltic Sea and the North Sea, seawater foam is heavily contaminated with PFAS chemicals - warns Greenpeace.

Seawater foam on the beaches of the German Baltic and North Sea coasts is heavily contaminated with PFAS chemicals - reported the environmental organization Greenpeace on Monday in Hamburg.

PFAS are perfluoroalkyl and polyfluoroalkyl substances resistant to water and grease, which are used in the production of outdoor and sports clothing, carpets, and food packaging, such as pizza boxes or baking paper. Due to their resistance to degradation in the environment, PFAS chemicals are referred to as "forever chemicals."

Greenpeace ecotoxicologist Julios Kontchou has called for a ban on the use of PFAS in everyday items.

As reported by Greenpeace, nine samples were taken in November and January on the German islands of Norderney and Sylt, in Sankt Peter-Ording, and along the Baltic Sea - in Boltenhagen and Kühlungsborn.

All samples indicated exceedances from 290 to 3777 times the Danish limit for water in bathing areas, which is 40 ng (nanograms) per liter. The German limit, which will only come into effect next year - 100 ng/l - for the 20 most common PFAS has also been clearly exceeded. To date, there are no limit values in German bathing areas.

According to Greenpeace, nearly all applications have PFAS-free alternatives available. Nevertheless, the chemical industry wants to cling to PFAS and so far rejects all proposals for regulation at the European level.

- We appeal to the German government to protect people and the environment from the unjustified interests of the chemical industry. The use of PFAS in everyday items must be banned immediately - called ecotoxicologist Julios Kontchou.

The PFAS group includes over 10,000 chemicals - points out Greenpeace. Many of them are harmful to health and the environment. Some are carcinogenic, affect the hormonal system and reproduction. Many of these substances remain in the human body for a long time. PFAS do not degrade and accumulate in the food chain[65].

The future of the Baltic looks no longer green but black. But fools and greedy stoners are not frightened by this, because they have profit – and profit counts more than anything. Only that they will have no one to leave this profit to, nor take it with them to the grave... Working as a volunteer at the Hel Marine Station of the University of Gdańsk, I had the opportunity to see seals and other marine animals infested with toxins leaking from unsealed containers and bomb bodies. Similar observations have been made by the staff of the Marine Institute in Gdańsk. And this also applies to wrecks from the Vistula La-

---

65. Katarzyna Domagała-Pereira - https://www.msn.com/pl-pl/wiadomosci/other/alarmuj%C4%85-o-gro%C5%BAnych-chemikaliach-nad-ba%C5%82tykiem-wystosowano-apele/ar-AA1ylNFc?ocid=winp1taskbar&cvid=ce5e7dab4fd44fc88aa57631f6ec7f27&ei=7.

goon, which, as a closed body of water, is even more threatened by contamination. The threat continues to grow, and so far there is no smart one to deal with it.

And now about another aspect of the war in the Baltic that projects further into the history of the Cold War – it is this...

14.7. FZT Graf Zeppelin mystery

And another subsection on the mysteries of the Baltic. This time it won't be about disaster victims, but about what happened in such a small body of water as the Baltic Sea in the last months of World War II and immediately after. Despite the fact that the cannons fell silent, the battle for the Third Reich's secrets continued in all countries, and one of them was the German aircraft carrier FZT[66] *Graf Zeppelin*, which fortunately did not get beyond the trial phase.

The Kriegsmarine saw no special reason why they should have aircraft carriers in their ranks. Yes – super battleships like Bismarck or Tirpitz, pocket battleships like Admiral Graf von Spee, Lützow, Gneisenau or Scharnhorst and other heavy ships – yes, submarines especially Type XXI – by all means, but aircraft carriers? Somehow not so much. German military personnel saw no use for them. Big and expensive to build and operate... One of the four aircraft carriers that were to be built as part of the surface fleet expansion program, better known as "Plan Z," and of the four, the Graf Zeppelin was the only one that was close to being completed and put into service. And the "Baltic Wrecks" website goes on to state that:

The order for the aircraft carrier "A," the future Graf Zeppelin, was placed in November 1935 at the Deutsche Werke shipyard in Kiel, as the second of a planned series, but the only one

---

66. From Flugzeugträger = aircraft carrier.

almost completed. The Graf Zeppelin vessel was designed with a flight deck extending the entire length of the hull and an island superstructure on the starboard side on which a funnel was also placed. The fuselage itself was divided into 21 watertight compartments housed inside two hangars placed one above the other, each 16 meters wide. Communication between them and the takeoff deck was provided by three aerial elevators. Aircraft launches were to be carried out via catapults, space for two was provided in the forward part of the flight deck. The ship was to be powered by 16 high–pressure boilers grouped four at a time in four boiler rooms. Each boiler room transmitted steam to one of four turbine units, which in turn powered the ship through four propellers. The overall power output of the machines, 200,000 hp, was to allow the aircraft carrier to accelerate to a speed of 35 knots. Aircraft carriers of this type were also to be partially armored. The sides were to be protected by 100mm thick armor, covering the engine rooms and ammunition magazines. The hull under the hangars was protected by 50 mm of steel, in addition, the flight deck was clad with 30 mm of armor. The entire structure provided cover against shrapnel and aerial bombs. The Graf Zeppelin aircraft carrier, which was more than 90% completed, was assigned to the construction of a harbor barrage and towed to Stettin. There it was stripped of most of its machinery and armaments. („Baltic Wrecks").

On April 24, 1945, slightly damaged by field artillery, the ship was captured in by Soviet troops, who then towed it to Świnoujście. In 1947 it was decided to send it back to Leningrad (now St. Petersburg) with the intention of using it for research purposes. FZT A Graf Zeppelin sank on August 17, 1947 while being towed in the Baltic Sea. Its wreck lies at the location specified by the coordinates: N 55°31'03" – E 018°17'09", at a depth of 87 m [67].

Wikipedia gives the following information:

Design work on German aircraft carriers began in the spring of 1934. The decision was made to build two vessels Flugzeugträger A (Graf Zeppelin) and Flugzeugträger B (Peter Strasser – in honor of the creator of German naval aviation) with a displacement of 23,430 tons. Work on the ship had been underway since December 28, 1936. On December 8, 1938, the first aircraft carrier was launched in Kiel in the presence of Adolf Hitler and Hermann Göring and named in honor of aviation designer Ferdinand von Zeppelin. Work on both vessels continued until the spring of 1940. However, despite considerable progress in construction, they were abruptly interrupted by order of Adolf Hitler. Work was not allowed to resume until 1941, but only on the Graf Zeppelin, which had been launched three years earlier. During this time, the ship's hull was towed first to Gdynia and then back to Kiel. In 1943, due to the deteriorating situation on the Eastern Front and shortages in the supply of materials, construction was once again halted. The aircraft carrier Graf Zeppelin, which was more than 90% completed, was earmarked for the construction of a harbor barrage and towed to Szczecin. There, most of the machinery and armaments were dismantled from it.

On April 24, 1945, the ship, slightly damaged by field artillery, was taken in by Soviet troops, who then towed her to Świnoujście. In 1947 it was decided to send it back to Leningrad with the intention of using it for research purposes. The Graf Zeppelin sank on August 17, 1947 while being towed in the Baltic Sea, probably as a target ship as a result of hit tests conduct-

---

67. See Baltic Wrecks – *http://www.balticwrecks.com/pl/wraki/graf-zeppelin/*

ed on it. It is possible, however, that it was sunk by the Soviet Navy under pressure from allied armies, which did not want to allow the USSR to have an aircraft carrier in its possession.

On July 12, 2006, the aircraft carrier's hull was found by the oil exploration and production company Petrobaltic in Baltic waters 55 km north of Władysławowo at a depth of 87 meters. The RV St. Barbara research vessel used by the company, equipped with specialized underwater sounding equipment, tracked and recorded the wreck, the first to do so. On July 26, 2006, the hydrographic ship ORP Arctowski conducted an underwater survey of the sunken vessel. On July 27, 2006, the Polish Navy officially confirmed that the sunken wreck was the Graf Zeppelin. (Wikipedia)

On the subject of its sinking, Mieczyslaw Fedorowicz writes:

The captured German fleet was divided among the world powers by a tripartite Anglo–American–Soviet naval commission. The Graf Zeppelin was classified in category "C" and awarded to the Soviet Union. Units under this category had to be sunk or scrapped sooner or later.

The ship was originally planned to be used as a testing station. However, this proposal put forward by Admiral Kuznetsov, was rejected. The government decided, in accordance with the recommendations of the tripartite commission, to sink the ship. By Decision No. 601–209ss of March 19, 1947, it was decided to destroy all captured vessels belonging to the "C" category. This fact the command of the SWF[68] has decided to use to conduct tests on the viability of ships.

Preparation for the decommissioning of category "C" ships was handled by a special commission under the command of Vice Admiral J.F. Rall, established on May 17, 1947. It was

---
68. Soviet War Fleet.

planned to conduct experiments on the effects of explosions of air bombs, artillery shells, mines and torpedoes in two layouts.

The first layout envisioned the explosion of charges placed on board, while the second assumed simulated attacks from water and air. The lifting of the ship was handled by the 77th Division of the ASS KBF.[69]

Already on August 17, 1945, an inspection of the wreckage was carried out.

36 punctures in the sides from shells and shrapnel measuring 1.5 x 1 meter were signaled. Propulsion machinery, boilers, generators were blown up. Explosion-damaged watertight bulkheads were found in the engine room area. A 0.8 x 0.3 meter hole and a 0.3 meter gap were detected in the underwater part of the fuselage. The flight elevators blew up and the flight deck was perforated from bullets or shrapnel.(…)[70]

So it is correct – the ship was deliberately sunk by the Russians, who made it a target ship. The purpose of the exercise was obvious – to develop a method of fighting the Americans and British aircraft carriers as effectively as possible for future warfare... As can be seen from its wreckage, experts say – the Graf Zeppelin sank after detonating several 2000-kilograms[71] aerial bombs on its deck and additional bombing by horizontal and dive bombers. The Nazi aircraft carrier went down after detonating a ton of explosives on the launch deck and 5-6 bomb hits out of 90 dropped.[72]

---

69. Awaryjno-Spasatielnaja Służba Krasnoznamiennogo Baltijskogo Flota – Emergency and Rescue Service of the Baltic Red Banner Fleet.
70. „Graf Zeppelin" – history of the german aircraft carrier – *https://tu.swinoujscie.pl/2017/12/graf-zepplin-historia-lotniskowca/*
71. Most likely, these are standard 200-225 kg bombs.
72. Documentary "Drain the Oceans – World War II," National Geographic Channel.

I think we should not give credence to the stories about American and British pressure, because Stalin would have simply ignored them. With 11 million troops in Europe, he could afford to do so, and besides, he knew that Truman no longer had any atomic bomb at his disposal to put any pressure on him... Besides, he needed knowledge of German technology and how to fight aircraft carriers, which the Red Fleet did not have, because it did not fight them in naval warfare.

And everything would have been fine, had it not been for a certain letter from a witness of a sighting and CE3 with a UFO, which took place in 1947 in Świnoujście, and which the authors of the book "NLO prosit posadki"(Profizdat, Moscow 1991) A.S. Kuzowkin and N.N. Niezapomniaszczyj received, and which went like this:

Greetings to you Fyodor Fyodorovich!

You asked me 11 questions, which I answer as best I can and one at a time. These flying discs were seen by many people. It was in the spring, in 1947 – when exactly, I can't remember. It was in Germany – in Swinemünde (today Świnoujście) on the shore of the Baltic Sea – 400–500 meters away. Around 10 or 11 o'clock in the morning, it was nice and warm weather then, even the grass was not swaying – there was an absolute calm.

There were many discs flying there, and in the middle of the formation there was a larger object – it resembled a tire from a GAZ 51. The objects would rise vertically, then lay flight to horizontal and slowly fly away. They were as bright as duralumin. There was a rainbow glow on the larger ones. The larger ones held at an altitude of 150–200 meters, while the smaller ones lowered toward the ground. Some of them were within two meters of me! I wanted to catch one of them, but I didn't catch up. Two plates flew around the artillery positions, while the larger ones hung motion-

less in the air and swayed from side to side. Then the small discs flew up to the larger ones and all together slowly moved away. I tried to reach them with my bayonet, but I was unsuccessful...

I think it will be better for you to contact the then commander of the 612th daplot – Major Belyaev. He said at the time that it was the Americans who photographed our cannons and ships in the northern zone of the OWR[73]. Others said that there had been an explosion of some device on the aircraft carrier Graf Zeppelin – classified, of course – although, as everyone knew, it had been sunk in the sea. The color of the object was similar to the dial of the "Meridian" radio receiver, with dots around the perimeter of the disc. These discs flew from the sea to the south. At that time, something happened to our SON.[74]

When it was all over, they began to collect statements from us and had us sign an undertaking to keep everything absolutely secret. Then I was transferred to Pilau and told no one about anything.

Unfortunately, the authors did not give the name or address of the sender, and the name and patronymic Fyodor Fyodorovich does not say anything...

So the question is: was the Graf Zeppelin while in Soviet hands from April 24, 1945 to August 17, 1947 examined by their scientists and designers? This is obvious. For over two years, it could have been looked at thoroughly and all the research done, and then going by the pressure of the Western Allies simply sunk while being towed to Leningrad as a target ship for bombers and/or anti-ship missiles being an improved version of the V-1 flying bombs and V-2 ballistic missiles. Blowing a thirty-

---

73. Garrison. The entire event took place on the grounds of Fort West, where the plot artillery positions were located.
74. Artillery tracking station.

foot hole in the deck could have been done by exploding a ton of TNT in the warhead of such a missile. So was the aircraft carrier the first victim of a new generation of weapons – rocket weapons? This is precisely one of the mysteries of the Graf Zeppelin, but not the last.

The UFO sighting over Świnoujście must have already taken place after the sinking of the Graf Zeppelin, that is, after August 17, 1947. What the observed flying saucers were we can only guess. Of course, they could have been Vril or Haunebu vehicles from the research centers in Peenemünde and/or placed aboard the would-be aircraft carrier. Either way, this letter and the information it contains is a mystery that remains unsolved to this day.

The third mystery is related not so much to the Graf Zeppelin as to a ground facility. It is specifically about the warehouses of Luftmuna 4 in Mosty, West Pomerania. Luftmuna is the term for ammunition depots for the Luftwaffe. To date, historians have failed to explain this World War II mystery. In the Szczecin Lagoon, Allied planes sank the ship MS Artushof, whose cargo arouses surprise: in the holds were, among other things, 38 graphite-carbon poles and half a ton of graphite pressed in rolls. Could this have been material for a nuclear reactor? Was the ship to unload them at a small harbor near the secret Luftmun 4 facility in Speck (today Mosty)? On its grounds is a circular pool 7 meters deep, confusingly similar to the pool at Haigerloch, where US troops discovered a German nuclear reactor.[75]

This reactor was very primitive, but it worked, and that was the most important thing. The Germans were able to obtain uranium-235 in it for atomic bombs, which were detonated in

---

75. Bogusław Wołoszański – „Zagadka Luftmuny", in „Sensacje XX wieku".

several places in the Reich: at Jonastal, at Ohrdruf, at Rügen, and near Gomel, in the USSR.[76] They were no marvels – their power was less than 10 kt TNT.

According to Bogusław Wołoszański, the Germans read, with the help of a primitive Schwetfisch tube computer, the encrypted dispatches of the Soviet agents lodged in the American Project Manhattan. These dispatches contained specific data enabling the construction of a nuclear reactor and an A-bomb... And of course they succeeded – the first A-bomb was detonated at Rügen.[77]

Ivan Barykin wrote on this subject in his series of interviews with SS–Obersturmbannführer Walter Schulke in the pages of "Tajny XX wiekka" magazine, and I have posted translations of these materials on the Internet[78].

In his accounts, Schulke recounts an experiment with a bomb of monstrous force that was conducted near Peenemünde. So this address would have been a match. Admittedly, Schulke was talking about Rügen there, but whether this was definitely the case, I can't guarantee. Perhaps there was a misunderstanding, because the names Rügen – in German and Rudden – are phonetically similar to each other...

And again: do all these events have any connection with each other?

---

76. R. Leśniakiewicz – *https://wszechocean.blogspot.com/2017/08/hitlerowskie-poligony-broni-a.html*. As for Gomel, there was an explosion there involving an explosives magazine or a thermobaric bomb.
77. Ibidem.
78. http://wszechocean.blogspot.com/2014/03/hiperboloida-ss-gruppenfuhrera-kammlera.html; http://wszechocean.blogspot.com/2013/03/kod-antarktydy.html; http://wszechocean.blogspot.com/2013/03/kod-antarktydy.html; https://wszechocean.blogspot.com/2014/02/bronie-odwetowe-v-w-rosji.html; http://wszechocean.blogspot.com/2015/02/superbomba-dla-fuhrera.html.

First of all, Bogusław Wołoszański may be wrong – the MS Artushof carried a cargo of graphite not to, but from Luftmun 4. The Germans were not building a nuclear reactor, they were rolling up the business – they did not want the reactor to fall into the hands of the Russians pushing from the east and south. Most likely, they wanted to move it somewhere safer. Western Pomerania was liberated by the 3rd Strike Army, operating in the direction of Goleniów, Wolin, Kołobrzeg and Białogard, and the 6th, 61st and 47th Armies going to Szczecin. Opposing them were the troops of Army Group "Vistula." In February and March 1945, the 1st Belorussian Front developed its success in the northwestern part of Pomerania, reaching Kamień Pomorski on March 6, 1945, and the next day the Baltic coast in the area of Dziwnówek and Pobierowo and the Szczecin Lagoon in the area of Stępnica. Goleniów was also captured on the same day. The other armies of the front, i.e. the 47th A and 61st A, slowly pushed back the German troops in the direction of Dąbie and Gryfino, encountering strong resistance and numerous counterattacks. The 1st AWP (Polish Army), after liquidating the Świdwin grouping, approached Kołobrzeg with its main forces, and separated part of its forces to liquidate the German grouping near Trzebiatów. In the west of Pomerania, a strong German bridgehead was maintained in the area of Dąbie and the northern part of Gryfino. On March 14, troops of the 1st FB launched an attack aimed at eliminating this bridgehead. On March 19, they succeeded in tearing the bridgehead into two parts (Dąbie and Gryfino). After an unsuccessful German counterattack, the retreat from the bridgehead began and by March 20 it was liquidated. Remaining on the left bank of the Oder River, on the island of Wolin and the island of Uznam, the German troops were not pressed by the Red Army until the start of the Berlin Operation on April 20.[79]

79. Wikipedia.

Well, and it was through the islands – taking advantage of Soviet military involvement in other directions – that the German nuclear pile and most likely the personnel operating it were evacuated. That's why Soviet submarines fiercely tracked and drowned ships with fleeing Germans, the victims of which included MS Wilhelm Gustloff, SS Goya and SS General von Steuben... The idea was to prevent the Germans from using state-of-the-art technology against the incoming Soviet and Polish troops. That's why these wrecks were intensively penetrated by Soviet divers – they were looking for artifacts and technical documentation carried by these ships.

It was a bit different with the aircraft carrier. It was sunk deliberately after dismantling everything that was possible and novel from it – and could be useful in the course of World War III operations. It was an empty shell, which was finally sent to the bottom of the Baltic Sea, having been trained on it by aerial bombardment and perhaps shelling with V-1 type missiles. The Russians captured a total of 22,000 units of these weapons, so they had skolko ugodno material for research.

What was mentioned above is just my hypothesis, which came to me after Bogusław Wołoszański's program on Luftmuna 4 and the possible production of uranium or plutonium charges for Nazi A-bombs, one of which was detonated quite nearby – on the island of Rügen or Rudden...

And this is what was at stake in the final weeks of the war.

14.8. The Mysterious Fate of the USS Independence

And yet another aircraft carrier – this time American – whose fate is just as mysterious as that of the Graf Zeppelin. This ship was the American aircraft carrier USS Independence (CVL-22).

14.8.1. Operation Crossroads

USS Independence joined the Operation Magic Carpet fleet starting on November 15, 1945, transporting veterans back to the United States until its return to San Francisco on January 28, 1946. Assigned as a target ship for the atomic bomb tests of Operation Crossroads, it was positioned half a mile from the detonation site on July 1. The veteran ship did not sink (although its smokestacks and island were crushed by the blast), and after participating in another explosion on July 25, it was transported to Kwajalein and decommissioned on August 28, 1946.

14.8.2. Sinking and Disaster

The highly radioactive hull was later moved to Pearl Harbor, and then to San Francisco for further testing. Ultimately, the ship was sunk near the Farallon Islands off the coast of California on January 29, 1951, by placing two torpedoes inside the hull. Controversy later arose concerning the sinking of the Independence, as it was claimed that at the time of sinking the ship was loaded with barrels of radioactive waste, which subsequently contaminated the nature reserve and commercial fishing associated with the Farallon Islands. However, in 2015 it was determined that "any risk to public health was minimal," which could be expected after such a period of time. In 2009, the wreck of the Independence was confirmed to be located at a depth of 2600 feet (790 m) in Monterey Bay National Marine Sanctuary off the Farallon Islands at approximately N 37°30'00" - W 123°05'00" through a deep-water multibeam sonar survey conducted from the RV NOAAS Okeanos Explorer. In March 2015, scientists and technicians from the American National Oceanic and Atmospheric Administration (NOAA) aboard the research vessel RV Fulmar used an autonomous underwater vehicle DSV Echo Ranger to investigate the wreck, utilizing

Echoscope 3D imaging sonar to produce a series of images. The vessel rests upright with a slight tilt to starboard, and most of the flight deck remains intact, although there are gaping holes in the flight deck leading to the hangar below. No signs of radioactive contamination were detected, although barrels of waste are still visible on the hangar deck, some of which are rusted and open. A NOAA spokesperson described the wreck as "surprisingly intact." In 2016, a mission led by Dr. James P. Delgado, a deep-sea archaeologist, in collaboration with Ocean Exploration Trust and the National Oceanic and Atmospheric Administration, brought researchers closer to the wreck than ever before. Using robotic exploration vehicles, the team examined the USS Independence for the first time since its sinking 65 years earlier, streaming footage online. During the investigation of the wreck, researchers found evidence of at least one Grumman Hellcat aircraft, as well as partial remains of an SB2C-4 Helldiver and 40 millimeter and 20 millimeter anti-aircraft guns. (Wikipedia) Footage and images were shown on TV in the 6th episode of the series "Expedition Down" titled "Atomic Secrets of the Cold War" (season 2, episode 6)

14.9. The End of the Japanese Giants

This chapter would be incomplete if we did not mention three Japanese naval giants – the two super battleships IJN Yamato and IJN Musashi and the super aircraft carrier IJN Shinano. These were vessels with a displacement of over 72,000 tons and super-powerful armament with guns of an unprecedented caliber of 460 mm. They overshadowed the German giants of Plan Z, such as Bismarck and Tirpitz, which had a displacement of 50,300 tons and a main artillery caliber of 381 mm, as well as the Japanese Nagato-class battleships with 410 mm guns and the American Iowa-class battleships with 406 mm guns. By far the largest warships of our time, without a doubt. Of course, apart from aircraft carriers[80].

The battleships Yamato and Musashi did not utilize all their combat capabilities. And despite being conserved, they fell prey to bombers and torpedo planes. These giants went to the bottom after taking several bombs and torpedoes.

The situation was different for IJN Shinano. It was initially intended to be the third hyper-battleship of the Yamato class. However, exhausted by armaments, Japan in 1940 was unable to supply the materials for its construction, and Shinano was reclassified as an aircraft carrier.

Wikipedia states:

In 1942, a decision was made to continue the construction of this ship, but as an aircraft carrier. Its basic parameters—the displacement and dimensions—were retained, as the hull was almost complete. The powerful main artillery and part of the armor were replaced by large fuel tanks and storage for spare parts, as the ship was designated as a supply center for smaller aircraft carriers. A large, single-deck hangar measuring 168 m could accommodate up to 120 aircraft, but it was assumed that only 40 to 50 would carry out combat operations from the ship; the rest were to be used to replenish combat losses of the accompanying carriers. The combat unit was located in the bow of the ship, while the aircraft during transport had their place at the stern.

Shinano became the largest aircraft carrier and, together with Yamato and Musashi, the largest ship of World War II. It was only 11 years later that the American aircraft carrier USS Forrestal achieved a similar displacement. Shinano was launched on October 8, 1944.

---

80. See: Witold Supinski, "One hundred years of warships", Warsaw 1965.

On November 19, 1944, the ship was commissioned into the Japanese fleet. It set out on its maiden voyage from Yokosuka to the Kure shipyard, where its final outfitting (including the installation of watertight bulkhead doors) and crew training were to take place. Many dockworkers were still on board. On November 29, 1944, south of Honshu Island, the aircraft carrier Shinano, sailing under the protection of destroyers, was spotted by the American submarine USS Archerfish (SS-311). It fired 6 torpedoes at the aircraft carrier, four of which hit the starboard side: three amidships, and the fourth struck the stern. This caused increasing list on the ship, which could no longer be controlled. Despite attempts to tow by the escorting destroyers, Shinano capsized and sank. Although the aircraft carrier remained afloat for several hours after being hit, due to panic among the inexperienced sailors and dockworkers, as well as the malfunctioning of the ship's rescue systems, most of the crew perished.

The dark legend states that the aircraft carrier was hit by only one torpedo and sank due to the lack of watertight compartments. In any case, this giant also rested on the seabed as a result of technical shortcomings and the incompetence of the crew and dockworkers, who paid for it with their lives. Do the fates of this ship not resemble those of the German FZT Graf Zeppelin?

All these wartime tragedies claimed many more victims than the RMS Titanic…

ೞ

Chapter 15
The disaster of the "Titanic" of the heavens

Our book would be incomplete if we didn't mention in it the disaster of the Titanic of the heavens – the great airship. Of course, we are talking about the great German passenger airship LZ–129 Hindenburg. This is how Dr. Miloš Jesenský writes about it:

15.1. Pride of the Third Reich

It was early afternoon on May 6, 1937 at the air base in Lakehurst, NJ, hundreds of people gazed impatiently at the sky. At any moment, the German airship LZ–129 Hindenburg – the largest flying machine in the history of the world – could land there. Around 7 p.m. the silvery aircraft finally appeared. The spectators' excitement very quickly turned into horror. During the maneuver of mooring the airship to the mooring mast, a spectacular fire broke out:

"I kept running away, because flames were raging near my head," recalled Robert Buchanan, who was a member of the ground crew at the time. *"It looked as if someone had eject the gas,"* he recounted. The rainy weather that day saved his life. *"I*

was wearing a pullover that was quite soaked. I think that's what saved me."

Werner Doehner was aboard the airship that day. At the time of the crash, his father was in the dining room, and then he didn't see him again. *"Everything started to burn in the blink of an eye,"* recalls Doehner, who was 8 years old at the time of the crash and is the last surviving passenger of the Hindenburg. *"My mother climbed out of the window, throwing my younger brother out as well. Mom jumped out and broke her pelvis."* Doehner saved himself, but he later lay in the hospital for months with second-degree burns.

The Hindenburg was the most luxurious aircraft of all time, wrote British publicist Nigel Blundell. "It was a flying palace in the sense of the comfort it offered rich clientele flying across the Atlantic. The airship was so huge and lofty that it became for aviation what the Titanic was for shipping. And the irony remains that, like that great steamer that plunged into the depths of the Atlantic, the Hindenburg also crashed twenty-five years later."

Thirty-six people found death in the burning wreckage of the airship – and in addition to one member of the ground staff, there were 22 crew members and 13 travelers, including war hero Ernst Lehmann, who died in the hospital as a result of severe burns. The commander of the airship, who was not shot down even once during the Great War, and whose airship LZ-26 was dismantled under the Treaty of Versailles, continually said as if in delirium: *"I can't understand it, I can't understand it..."* The cause of the tragedy, which was the next tragedy of the largest means of transport after a quarter of a century, remains a mystery to this day.

15.2. WHAT WAS THE CAUSE OF THE DESTRUCTION OF THIS TITANIC OF THE HEAVENS?

The first steerable balloons appeared in the second half of the 19th century, but the first truly functional airship, the LZ–1, was built in 1900 by Ferdinand Count von Zeppelin (1838–1917), and later, thanks to powerful financial support from the German government, more and more perfect flying machines came out of the production halls of his factory. As early as 1909, von Zeppelin had accumulated enough money to establish the air cargo company DELAG Gmbh. which branded its aircraft with the prefix LZ. The old nobleman's initials became synonymous with all German airships.

The DELAG company prospered and by 1914 had transported 33,722 people. After the outbreak of World War I, all airships were adapted to the needs of the army, which used them for reconnaissance and bombing. Night raids by Zeppelins quickly became the terror of French and British cities.[81] Therefore, it is no wonder that after the war Germany was banned from building these aircraft. This restriction lasted until 1925, when post-war agreements and treaties were revised. The former chief designer of the DELAG Gmbh. company, Dr. Hugo Eckner, founded the Zeppelin Luftschiffbau company and announced a nationwide fundraiser for the development of German air navigation.

His initiative was met with widespread response. Dr. Eckner soon raised capital of 4 million marks, which he used to build an actual super airship. The flying giant LZ–127 Graf Zeppelin was completed in September 1928, which made its first transatlantic flight to the US the very next month, and made an around–the–world circumnavigation from August 8 – 29, 1929.

81. Airships were used primarily for rallies to London and Bucharest – translator's note.

The success of the LZ-127 inspired Dr. Eckner to build even more perfect airships that would be able to secure air transportation around the world. The first of the new-generation zeppelins, the LZ-128, was never completed. After the crash of the British R-101 airship in the fall of 1930, Dr. Eckner concluded that his flying craft should be filled with non-flammable helium instead of the dangerous and explosive hydrogen. However, a serious problem arose, for the natural sources of this gas were located only on U.S. territory, and its export to Germany was embargoed. The Americans needed helium for their own flotilla of airships, and besides, they feared – and rightly so – that German zeppelins would bomb American cities on the US East Coast.

After waiting fruitlessly for several years for the helium embargo to be ended, Dr. Eckner's construction team began working on plans for two huge hydrogen airships. And first to be completed in March 1936 was the LZ-129, which was without a doubt the greatest flying machine of all time. People of the interwar period were fascinated by everything that was the largest, and even today it is considered a phenomenon in the field of aviation – even the world's largest modern aircraft, the Airbus A380, is 3.5 times smaller in comparison… The shadow of this project was that it was financed in the lion's share by Hitler's NSDAP and was presented as a symbol of the Nazi regime. So the builder, willingly or unwillingly, had to accept that his design decorated with hakenkreuzes would become part of Goebbels' propaganda. From its gondola an orchestra played military marches, leaflets poured out urging people to support the policies of the NSDAP, and also in 1936 its flight graced the opening of the 11th Summer Olympics in Berlin.

"It was the Concorde of its day," Carl Jablonsky of the Navy Lakehurst Historical Society said of the 245-meter Hindenburg, and compared it to an aerial giant that cut the trip over the Atlantic from 4–5 days in half. It was named after German Reich President Paul Ludwig Hans Anton von Beneckendorff und von Hindenburg (1847–1934) and was built by Luftschiffbau Zeppelin in 1935. It cost about GB£500,000 at the time. It had a brand new duralumin skeletal structure, its length was 245 meters – it was only 25 meters shorter than the Titanic! – width was 41 meters, the total volume of this giant was 200,000 m^3 of gas distributed to 16 chambers, its total weight was 240 tons, of which payload was 112 tons, it was powered by four Mercedes Benz diesel engines of 890 kW each, which allowed it to develop a cruising speed of 135 km/h. Its shell was made of cotton fabric impregnated with a mixture of iron oxide and cellulose acetal and drawn with aluminum powder, which gave it a beautiful silver color.

The initial plan to fill the airship's balloons with helium was prevented by the embargo, so the designers used flammable hydrogen. And since hydrogen has a 10% higher payload, this allowed the airship's payload to be increased and additional passenger cabins to be added. Extreme precautions were taken and fire regulations were made stricter.

The Hindenburg could take on board 72 passengers (50 on transatlantic flights) and 61 crew members at a time. [...] The Hindenburg made its first flight in March 1936, and by the end of that year it had made 54 flights, including 36 flights to the United States and Brazil. In June 1936, it made a record-breaking double flight over the Atlantic in 5 days, 19 hours and 51 minutes. During the airline's nine-year history from Friedrichshafen to Pernambuco, Graf Zeppelin made 144 flights and carried more than 10,000 passengers!

For the first of 18 scheduled flights to America in the 1936/37 season, LZ-129 took off from Frankfurt Airport on May 3, under the command of Captain Max Pruss, and Zeppelin flight manager Ernest Lehmann. He flew with him to the US with 60 crew members and 35 passengers. The flight proceeded without complications until the North American coast, where on May 6 the airship entered a zone of strong contrary winds. Due to the bad weather in New Jersey, Lehmann decided to postpone landing for a few hours. By that time, more than 1,000 journalists and reporters had gathered at the base in Lakehurst. Some had cameras with them, and one had a movie camera. There was also a radio reporter to provide live commentary on the arrival of the aircraft. And it is thanks to Herbert Morrison's radio microphone that we have an authentic statement that went on the air about the tragedy that occurred seconds after the mooring ropes with which the airship was to be attached to the ground were lowered.

Morrison began his report with the words: "The ropes had just been lowered. A number of people grabbed them at the airport. The rear engines are braking the airship just so that they can be held... It is starting to burn!... It is terrible!... Flames shoot five hundred feet up..."

Then suppressing tears he shouted: "This is the most terrible event I have witnessed. One of the biggest disasters in the world. Dear God! All the travelers! This is unbelievable! He finished his comment with the words, This is a terrible disaster. Lying here on the ground is a huge smoking wreck."

15.3. Hindenburg annihilation

And now, with the airship's fuselage devouring a flaming inferno before the eyes of Morrison and hundreds of other witnesses to the crash, let's pose the question of what actually happened?

By the time the giant aircraft sailed past Manhattan skyscrapers on the afternoon of May 6 at such a height that travelers waving their hands from the airship's portholes could look into the face of a photographer atop the Empire State Building, the flight seemed to be going smoothly. At 7 p.m. EDT, the touchdown operation began. At 7:21 p.m., the first mooring rope was thrown and ground personnel began the procedure for mooring the airship. The force of inertia moved the airship forward and the altitude rudders were in dangerous proximity to the mast. Captain Pruss wanted to repeat the approach maneuver, but at exactly 7:25 p.m. spectators noticed a flash in the rear of the aircraft, followed by an explosion that was seen from 15 miles away! The Zeppelin began to plummet downward and people began to jump out of the windows. Most of them killed themselves as a result of the fall from the high altitude, or suffered serious injuries – mainly broken limbs. Those who were more conscious climbed down the mooring ropes, but the most fortunate were those who managed to escape from the airship's gondola already on the ground – these did not suffer even a scratch.

Sailors from the base ran to the burning wreckage and tried to pull out as many people as possible, however, against their efforts, 13 passengers and 22 crew members, including the commander, did not survive the disaster. One member of the ground crew was also killed, having been brought down by the burning wreckage.

The crash became famous primarily due to media coverage. There were many reporters waiting at the airport, in addition to which there is also a transcript of Morrison's statements, a videotape record and a whole host of photographs. Later, Morrison's account was accompanied by film footage, which is among the biggest radio events in the history of the medium.

The US government set up a special commission to investigate the causes of the crash. After thorough questioning of witnesses, analysis of photo and film footage, and specialized expert opinions, it concluded that the explosion of the hydrogen balloon and subsequent fire of the entire airship was caused by a spark of static electricity that jumped from a soaked rope, or from the mooring mast.

Although this has not been proven – today, the version that is considered the most likely is that the fire was caused by an electric spark that resulted from the accumulation of static electricity. This theory is supported by the fact that the airship was constructed in such a way that electrical charges could not spread through it, and the plating was separated from the aluminum skeleton by non–conductive cables. During the flight, the airship passed through an atmospheric front, during which the mooring ropes moistened and became conductive. The friction of the airship's surface against the air created a charge of static electricity, and the moment the ropes touched the ground the entire airship's skeleton was grounded. And this also meant that an electrical discharge jumped between the plating and the skeleton. According to witnesses, St. Elmo's fires could be seen around the airship before it landed.

The puzzling tragedy of LZ–129 was thus explained anew by former NASA employee Prof. William van Horst. He pointed out that the airship's covering was saturated with a mixture of iron oxide, cellulose acetal and aluminum powder, which gave such a shiny silver glow to the entire airship's covering, but above all it was a highly dangerous explosive. Thus, all it took was one electric spark from a mooring pole...[82]

The next popular theory relates to a video recording of the crash, in which the airship can be seen making a relatively fast rotation even before it caught fire. Some experts suggest that there was a rupture there in one of the bonds or frames of the skeleton, which then perforated the balloon and caused a hydrogen escape, which in turn ignited from an electric spark. However, this is probably only theoretically possible, as no evidence indicates that the zeppelin's plating was perforated.

A further contentious area surrounding this disaster is which chemical compound did this hypothetical spark ignite? In addition to the possibility that only hydrogen burned, there is the certainty that the plating, which contained thermite[83], burned in the first place.

The German side firmly rejected this hypothesis, for it stated that all airships were protected against the possibility of fire. It was inconceivable to the fanatical Nazis that such a perfect product of German technology could have been destroyed by the forces of Nature. So they assumed that the fire could only have been caused by the explosion of a bomb planted aboard the Hindenburg.

---

82. The mixture mentioned by the author is not so much an explosive mixture, but an incendiary mixture called thermite. Thermite burns by emitting huge amounts of heat and the temperature of its flames reaches 3500°C – translator's note.

83. The latter possibility is indicated primarily by the orange–yellow color of the flames. Hydrogen burns with a bluish, almost invisible and smokeless flame, while the airship burned with a bright, mossy flame of burning plating and thermite saturating it, if hydrogen burned – the flame would be of a completely different color and would not produce any smoke, but at most a column of white vapor, because the result of the oxidation of hydrogen is water vapor – translator's note.

FORTUNES OF THE FIRST AIRSHIPS

– FROM THE GREAT WAR

Causes of airship destruction	Quantity	Comments
Destroyed in battle	46	
Engine or fuel explosion	6	
Impact of atmospheric factors	10	Including SLX.
Ground accidents	25	
Fires in the air	5	3 confirmed accidents, 1 Dixmunde – undoubted, 1 – LZ–59 – insufficiently documented.
Dismantled for spare parts	42	

According to the anthology "Ludzie przestworzy", Warsaw – Poznań, 1930.

15.4. A MURDEROUS ASSASSINATION ATTEMPT?

Immediately after the crash, a sabotage hypothesis emerged, which was mainly promoted by representatives of the Zeppelin company and, above all, Dr. Hugo Eckner. Zeppelin's airships were considered a symbol of the power of Nazi Germany, so they could have been a greedy target for opponents of Hitler's regime. This hypothesis was supported by the fact that the fire broke out in the aft part of the airship, far from the ropes anchoring it to the mast.

In 1975, the hypothesis became the material for a script for an American techno-thriller titled. "Hindenburg," directed by Robert Wise and starring George A. Scott, Anne Bancroft and William Atherton, which begins with what happened shortly before the Hindenburg took off on its 37th trip across the Atlantic from Friedrichshafen, Germany, to Lakehurst, USA. What no one expects is that mechanic Boerth (William Atherton) has placed a bomb on its deck to destroy the air giant after it lands in America. The flight goes smoothly, but Gestapo Lt.[84] Ritter (George Scott) suspects something. The drama begins when, as a result of the delayed landing, the time until the bomb detonates is dangerously shortened. The Hindenburg disaster, which remains unexplained to this day and whose investigation was abandoned by Hermann Goering himself for fear of losing prestige, enabled screenwriters Nils Gridding and Richard Levinson to write a script based on the sabotage hypothesis. The story received unexpected support 35 years after the event. Michael MacDonald-Mooney, in his book also claims that the disaster occurred not as a result of an unfortunate accident but sabotage, the perpetrator of which was a young, 25-year-old anti-fascist Erich Spehl from the Black Forest , who died in the flames. He further claims that the American and Nazi au-

---
84. In fact, the colonel – translator's note.

thorities got along because they did not want an "international scandal."

Another movie with the same title is the techno-thriller "Hindenburg – The Last Flight" (2011), directed by Philipp Kadelbach. The plot in a nutshell is as follows: The world's largest passenger airship, the 245-meter Hindenburg, takes off on a flight from Frankfurt to New Jersey. On board is a set of passengers, including Helen (Greta Scacchi) and Jennifer van Zandt (Lauren Lee Smith). When designer and aviation enthusiast Merten Kröger (Maximilian Simonischek), who is just at the airport in dramatic circumstances, learns of a bomb planted aboard the airship, he decides to prevent a disaster and save Jennifer. At the last minute, the man jumps aboard the Hindenburg.[85] What it ended with – we all know.

Incidentally, there had already been a whole series of airship accidents and crashes before the Hindenburg disaster – the vast majority caused by bad weather. None of these, however, involved zeppelins, which held the unbroken safety record for this type of transportation – the Graf Zeppelin flew 1,600,000 kilometers without an accident and carried 12,000 passengers. The Zeppelin company hardy declared that not a single traveler was injured in its airships.

All of the airship fires, it was widely believed, were caused primarily by the use of explosive and flammable hydrogen to fill their balloons. This seemed obvious and resulted in the filling of the balloons with non-flammable helium, but a careful analysis of the Hindenburg accident showed that this was not at all as obvious as people thought. As I wrote earlier, the cause of LZ-129's annihilation was the ignition of its shell, which was coated with a varnish containing dusty aluminum and Fe^{+III}

---

85. Source: https://www.filmweb.pl/film/Hindenburg-2011-595563/descs

iron oxide. This is none other than thermite – a mixture used in incendiary bombs, which burns according to the following reaction:

$$Fe_2O_3 + 2Al \rightarrow Al_2O_3 + 2Fe + Q \text{ (heat)}$$

which produces temperatures of more than 3,000 degrees C! Thermite is used, among other things, as fuel in the space shuttle's auxiliary rockets, so it's not surprising that LZ–129 literally flamed out in a matter of minutes![86]

15.5. Consequences of the disaster

The Hindenburg disaster changed all that. Impressive video footage and an evocative radio report from the landing site completely changed the public's faith in the safety of this means of transportation. Thanks to this event, the embargo on helium to Germany was ended, but it was soon reinstated due to the deterioration of the international situation. Nevertheless, Hitler ordered the completion of the sister unit of the ill-fated LZ–129, which was to be filled with non-flammable gas and new plans for even larger aerial giants. German chemists, however, failed to fulfill the Führer's whim and the airship LZ–130 Graf Zeppelin II had to be filled with hydrogen.

"The Hindenburg airship disaster did not have the same repercussions as the Titanic disaster, and after a while it was almost forgotten," according to Slovak historian Tomáš Klubert, who specializes in the history of aviation.. "Both disasters, however, continue to fascinate specialists and laymen to this day, not least because they were the result of disregarding the power of the forces of Nature. The Titanic and Hindenburg were the clearest technical symbols of their era, and their disasters preceded the appearance of even worse cataclysms. The

---

86. "What Happened to The Hindenburg?" – TV BBC 2002.

monstrous steamer was meant to show the power of the British Empire (and Europe as a whole) over the rest of the world, a power that was to last for centuries, but shortly after its sinking it irrevocably disappeared in the flames of the Great War."

The flying giant, on the other hand, was a symbol of the Third Reich, which its leaders claimed would exist for 1,000 years, but which soon ended in flames and debris, like the ill-fated airship. In both of these catastrophes another fact is puzzling and astonishing – from the Titanic disaster to the outbreak of World War I elapsed exactly the same time as between the Hindenburg disaster and Hitler's attack on Poland!

After the start of World War II, the commercial use of German airships ended, and their combat use did not interest anyone. The German aerospace industry needed huge amounts of aluminum, so the metal-intensive, non-functional zeppelins were dismantled. On May 6, 1940 – exactly three years after the Hindenburg crash at Lakenhurst – the LZ-130 was destroyed by the Wehrmacht. The same fate befell the old LZ-127 and the unfinished LZ-131. However, some accounts from the Czech Republic indicate that at least one airship remained and may have served Hitler's scientists as an experimental launch platform for V-rocket missiles – as we wrote about in the book "WUNDERLAND: Pozaziemskie technologie Trzeciej Rzeszy" (WUNDERLAND: Extraterrestrial Technologies of the Third Reich) (Ústi nad Labem 1998 and 2007, Warsaw 2001 and 2006). After the end of World War II, no one had any intention of building such huge airships. This was due to the turbulent development of airplanes, but also the still vivid memory of the Hindenburg tragedy, which marked the beginning of the end of an era in which luxury was valued as much or more than speed...

15.6. Flight QF-32

Our book would be incomplete if we did not mention one of the most dangerous episodes in the history of civil aviation. It is the contemporary history of the flight of the Airbus A380-842 of the Australian airline QANTAS with the registration VH-OQA on flight QF-42 from Singapore to Sydney, which took place on November 4, 2010, at 10:05 SGT[87].

Wikipedia states the following about it: On November 4, 2010, during the Qantas Flight 32 flying from Singapore Changi Airport to Sydney, there was a failure (explosion) of engine number 2. The aircraft had to make an emergency landing in Singapore for technical reasons. Neither passengers, crew, nor people on the ground were injured, despite engine components damaging the wing and falling onto the Indonesian island of Batam. Qantas grounded all A380 flights. Investigators determined that the cause of the explosion was an oil leak in the Rolls-Royce Trent 972 engine. In 2010, two types of micro-cracks were detected in the wings of the aircraft: in the ribs and in the supports securing the wing covering. The cracks were caused by design errors. In 2013, Airbus redesigned the A380 wings. The introduction of changes in production delayed the delivery of 25 aircraft in 2013. The first aircraft after the modifications were delivered in 2014, and repairs also included all produced units (during scheduled inspections). In 2012, the costs incurred by the manufacturer to repair the wing ribs in most delivered units amounted to €251 million, and in 2013, an additional €85 million.

Damage and problems that occurred after the engine explosion in the A380:

---

[87]. According to the film "Titanic in the Sky" from the series "Catastrophe in the Sky" episode 13/99, Canada 2024.

- Significant fuel leak from the left center fuel tank (there are a total of 11 tanks in the A380, including one in the horizontal stabilizer);
- Significant fuel leak from the internal tank on the left side of the fuselage;
- A huge hole in the fairing of the flap actuator mechanism;
- Failure of the rear fuel pump, which resulted in the inability to transfer fuel;
- Occurrence of a fuel dumping problem;
- The explosion of the engine created a huge hole in the upper part of the wing;
- Partial dysfunction of the slots on the leading edge of the wing;
- Partial failure of the brakes and aerodynamic spoilers;
- Destruction of flaps by engine fragments;
- Total loss of hydraulic fluid in one of the two systems of the jet;
- Failure of the landing gear deployment mechanism;
- Loss of one generator and associated onboard systems;
- ECAM warnings (Electronic Centralized Aircraft Monitoring) of a huge imbalance in fuel distribution (due to leaks from the left-side tanks);
- Problem with balancing the aircraft for landing due to remaining fuel in the trim tank at the tail;
- Damage to the front spar of the left wing by engine fragments;
- Loss of the anti-skid system;

• Inability to standardly shut down engine number 1 due to severe damage to onboard systems;

• Inability to shut down engine number 1 using the fire switch, meaning the engine's fire suppression system was not operational[88];

Onboard this colossus were 440 passengers and 26 crew members. Everyone survived the landing, but afterwards, a few individuals were poisoned by smoke from the burning engine before it was extinguished...

But that's not all, as problems also occurred with other Airbus aircraft:

• On April 14, 2011, another incident occurred. At J.F. Kennedy Airport in New York, an Airbus A380 belonging to Air France brushed its left wing against the tail of a Delta Air Lines Bombardier CRJ-700 while taxiing. No one aboard either aircraft sustained injuries.

• On June 19, 2011, an Airbus A380 (prototype MSN004) registered F-WWDD, while taxiing at the Le Bourget airport near Paris, collided its wing with a building.

• On July 21, 2011, an Airbus A380 of Korean Air, while landing at Tokyo-Narita Airport on runway 34L, scraped its engine on the runway surface. There were 168 passengers onboard. No one was hurt. The plane was towed to the parking area. After an inspection lasting about an hour, the plane flew to Seoul.

• On November 4, 2011, an A380 of Qantas flying from Singapore to London made an emergency landing at Dubai Air-

---

88. Source: https://dlapilota.pl/wiadomosci/airbus/co-sie-stalo-podczas-feralnego-lotu-a380-linii-qantas.

port. The reason was a failure of one of the engines (an oil level problem). There were 283 people on board. No one was injured.

• On October 1, 2017, the Airbus A380-861 with registration F-HPJE, on Air France flight 66, made an emergency landing at Goose Bay base in Canada due to what was reported as severe damage to one of its four GP7000 engines. The aircraft was flying from Paris to Los Angeles, with 496 passengers and 24 crew members on board.

As can be seen, each of the incidents mentioned above could have ended fatally and the "Titanic syndrome" is still in effect. Despite the fact that these machines are packed with sensors (about 25,000!) and computers, accidents still occur, and fortunately, it is people who make decisions and not some AI, a point that Stanisław Lem highlighted in his stories...

15.7. The Mystery of Flight MH 370

When writing about the air disasters of giants, one cannot overlook the most mysterious event that took place on March 8, 2014, when a huge Boeing 767 of Malaysian Airlines disappeared without a trace somewhere over the Indian Ocean on flight MH370 from Kuala Lumpur to Beijing. This case has been described in our book "The Mystery of the Seventh Arc" (Jordanów 2020), in which we presented some of the more interesting theories and hypotheses regarding this tragedy.

To this day, it is unknown what happened to this plane and nearly 300 people on board. Essentially, one thing is almost certain – this plane fell into the waters of the Indian Ocean, somewhere west of the southwestern coast of Australia – about 2-3 thousand km from Perth. The problem is that there is an underwater plateau at a depth of 4000 m and more. So far, reconnaissance using side-scan sonars has yielded no results, while the analysis of currents and winds occurring in the Indian Ocean seems to indicate this particular area. Evidence of this may include debris attributed to this aircraft washed up on the shores of eastern African countries and archipelagos in the central and western parts of the ocean, including Mauritius, the Maldives, Madagascar, and the Mascarene Islands. But despite this, the fate of flight MH370 remains an unsolved mystery.

Chapter 16

Titanic – Assassination or conspiracy?

Once again, we return to the Titanic tragedy. And finally the word falls – ASSASSINATION. In the first chapters we wrote about the possibility of assassination of the travelers sailing on the Titanic – a dozen millionaires who had a weighty influence on the fate of this world. This is the opinion of Wiktoria Leśniakiewicz – our historical consultant. According to her, the disaster generally fits into the background of an era that was coming to an end. Which had only two years of existence left. In the world, the colonial division continued all the time. Let's not forget that a nationalist boil was just rising in Europe, which had to burst. And it burst two years later in Sarajevo. And then the Great War – also known as World War I – broke out in Europe.

This time we are concerned with the ship itself. Well, because not only big, but also luxurious. Expensive tickets, that's a fact, but the very crème-de-la-crème of the world at the time traveled on it. In addition, also the middle class – that middle class and migrants to a better world, who were fed up with the misery of Europe and the despicable conditions in it. All this buoyed White Star Line's coffers and posed a competitive threat. The loss of such a luxury colossus would have been – and de facto was – a huge blow to the company.

In 2024, a startling report appeared on the Internet that this was a meticulously prepared, devilishly precise thought-out, planned and executed assassination attempt. The target was both the ship and its passengers, especially the richest ones. And here is what the author of this material says:

… it is the Jesuits who are responsible for the Titanic tragedy. To allow the creation of the US Central Bank, they built the world's largest passenger ship and named it Titanic. The sinking of the Titanic was a plan by the Jesuit order to get rid of opposition to the creation of the US Central Bank. The people on the Titanic were against the Central Bank – they had to die. Among them were J.J. Astor, I. Strauss, B. Guggenheim, and many other millionaires who opposed the Central Bank in America. Therefore, they had to be taken out of the way and found themselves on the Titanic. The owner of the company owning the ship was J.P. Morgan, who himself was an agent of the Rothschild family who were bankers for the Pope and the Vatican. Major Jesuit targets were brought on board, and the captain was E.J. Smith. His resume shows that he was a Jesuit coadjutor, that is, a Jesuit who took the oath but did not wear the vestments.[89] The coadjutor blends in with the scenery and never looks like a Jesuit priest. This experienced Captain Edward Smith orders the ship to sail at full speed through an 80 square mile ice field, and on a moonless night. As many as 8 telegrams were sent warning the captain of the danger, he was warned 8 times to slow the ship down. "Slow down Titanic," "You're sailing too fast!" – not once did he listen. He knew there was ice, he knew he had a field of icebergs ahead. He knew he should slow down but didn't – and so you look and ask how it happened that this man sailed

---

89. He's kind of an agent of influence – to use modern secret service terminology.

blindly into the field of icebergs and didn't slow the ship down without being more careful. The only conclusion you can draw is that he is a coadjutor of the Jesuit order.

The entire leadership chain of the Jesuit order told him "sink the ship" and he did so aboard the Titanic. This was documented in a National Geographic video published in 1986. [...] This videotape shows that as the Titanic sailed along the coast of England – it had various stops. At one stop, a Jesuit man boarded it. His name was Francis Brown. When Brown boarded the Titanic, he took pictures of all the wealthy people. He took pictures of Captain Smith, and then before the Titanic sailed into the Atlantic, Francis Brown got off. And then, of course, the Titanic sank. Well, Francis Brown receives a camera from his uncle Bishop. He's told to take pictures of all those First Class passengers who are going to be killed. And that's exactly what he does. He takes pictures of everyone and anyone who is there and who will die. And one of the rich passengers offers him a ticket. Well he knows that the ship is going to sink, but he timidly made contact with his provincial superior. In turn, the latter replied: "abandon this ship." Like Brown, another Jesuit agent J.P. Morgan did not make that sea voyage despite the fact that he had a trip to America booked, Morgan also "accidentally" canceled the trip at the last minute, of course Morgan had his own suite booked and some 55 people cancelled their reservations on the Titanic at the last minute. J.P. Morgan was one of them. He said he was sick. And by the way he said "don't load my valuable paintings on the Titanic", so his valuable artwork wasn't there and he didn't lose anything.

How do we know that a crime was committed on the Titanic? The moment the iceberg was spotted, 1st Officer Murdoch tried to avoid the deadly object. This was quite reasonable, but

Murdoch also ordered the ship to put it in reverse gear.[90] Author Will Wade asks the obvious question: why did Murdoch, wanting to get out of the way of the iceberg, throw full braking by shifting the full power of the engines into reverse? In fact, in the instructions from Knight's Modern Seamanship of 1910, it clearly contradicted Murdoch's decision. The instructions are clear: "avoid reversing engines," indicating that Murdoch performed the maneuver to cause a collision. Author Will Wade was unable to explain Murdoch's conduct against the ship's driving instructions.

But the actions of the captain and Murdoch were not the only signs of treachery on the night the Titanic sank. We saw all kinds of anomalies on the Titanic, for example, when it was sinking red emergency flares should have been used so that other ships alongside could see that the Titanic was in trouble. Well, some people removed the red flares and replaced them with white flares, which made it look like they were shooting white flares and having a party. And then the loading of the lifeboats. We know it was a hoax, instead of being fully loaded, the boats were only half loaded. Someone third decided that targets in first class could not enter the lifeboats.

But not only the captain was a Jesuit, but his officers were as well, and at the time they were going to hit England, and the men who normally operate ocean liners were replaced by coadjutors were ready to board and took an oath to die for the Black Pope if they did. And so they accomplished the sinking of the Titanic. How is it possible for men to commit suicide as Captain Smith obviously did with some of the selected crew, and it can be said that these men died of their own will. They were completely stripped of their own personality and, on the orders of their commander, did as they were told. There is no

---

90. Full astern.

such thing as a disobedient Jesuit. This serves as a warning to all other people in authority – not only in our country (USA) but in England and Europe. "Mess with us and we will do to you what we did to all those people on the Titanic and thwart the investigation," he said. Because the subsequent Titanic investigation blamed Bruce Ismay – J.P. Morgan's right-hand man and Captain Walde of England's,[91] who were scapegoats because they could blame it on the people in power at the time, who cancelled their reservations. It's all about the fact that it was like the Warner Commission – the commission investigating the causes of the 9/11 attack in 2001: a whitewash and cover-up, and a concealment that is even more powerful than the murder itself.

After removing many leading opponents of the Central Bank, the Jesuits proceeded to pass the 16th Amendment to the U.S. Constitution and the Federal Reserve – both in 1913 – and opened the Federal Reserve Bank to finance their crusades. Without the Federal Reserve Bank, there is no war in Iraq.[92]

I admit that this all sounds like another sick conspiracy theory, and one directed against the current Pope Francis, who is a Jesuit. The Jesuits have been repeatedly accused of various shady dealings, which has earned them the nickname "commandos of the Catholic Church." Just think of the cult novel by Alexandre Dumas titled "Viscount de Bragelonne", where the Jesuits carry out a swap of the person of King Louis XIV for his brother Philip the Iron Mask, which was perfectly shown in the film 'The Man in the Iron Mask'.[93] Personally, I do not believe

---

[91]. It is probably about Captain **Stanley Lord** and the ship SS **Californian**, who was blamed for failing to help the survivors of the **Titanic**, and was rehabilitated a few years ago.

[92]. Bill Hughes, translated by Andy Choiński.

[93]. Dir. Randall Wallace (1998).

that it was the Jesuits who did this, although they obviously had the ability to do so.

The Jesuits are behind the annihilation of the Titanic, okay, so be it, but it's just that this operation was so complicated, because there were too many unknowns in it. The sheer number of kamikaze coadjutors who died a wet death as a result of it is questionable. Well, but maybe they were brainwashed to the point that their instinct for self-preservation disappeared, or maybe they were all "high" on drugs with well-known results? It is possible...

Next point: the action the author is talking about would have had to have been planned at least in 1908 or even earlier, before the plans for the Titanic were on the drawing boards. Well, even then its weaknesses should have been known, which could then have been exploited by sending the ship to the ice field. Why complicate things so much? – a small explosive charge near the boiler room was enough – the explosion rips the side of the ship under the waterline and the outboard water floods the boilers with the known result – a powerful explosion of steam empties the boiler room and widens the hole in the hull. Question: would this be enough to sink the colossus? It is difficult to answer. But it just happened to be manageable. Britannic went down from a weaker explosion of a German naval mine...

Another thing – some Jesuit made his way aboard the Titanic, took pictures and came down before the ship went out into the Atlantic. Titanic, indeed, left Dublin, passed to Liverpool, then to Southampton, from Southampton to Cherbourg and then to Queenstown/Cork from where it set course for N.Y. Now the thing is no longer determinable, but would have been possible. If one assumes that the crews were complicit with the bombers, the thing is quite possible! But whether this was the case, no one knows anymore, and if there were any traces left, they were meticulously erased and the documents destroyed or buried for great centuries in the archives of the Vatican or some Jesuit province.

So, to the question of who sank it: the Jesuits or competitors, I bet on the latter. Perhaps it was the competition from White Star Line that ensured Titanic encountered the Labrador-Greenland icefield, although I have no evidence of that.

To summarize: this kind of attack, or sabotage as one might call it, resembles solving a multi-step system of equations with many unknowns, where one must apply what is known as fuzzy logic, where unlike the axiom:

if $A = B \wedge B = C \Rightarrow A = C$

we have something like:

if $A = B \wedge B = C \Rightarrow C$ may, but does not have to $= A$

because we are dealing with people who, by their nature, are probabilistic beings and their actions cannot be predicted completely. The thing is possible, but it would be very difficult to execute and can only be considered as a theoretical possibility...

୧୨

Chapter 17
Impossible meetings

Of course, the Titanic tragedy has given way to literary and movie productions. We present two excerpts from fantasy novels by Daniel Laskowski, in which he describes the events leading up to the disaster and the moments just after it as seen from two perspectives: the two Mermaids a.k.a. Water People who were aboard it and the present-day sailors who happened to be in the same place and time. These are such variations on a subject, but ask yourself, Reader: couldn't such events have taken place on that fateful night of April 14/15, 1912?

***

The Mystery of Horheberis

(excerpts)

I stood beneath a sign reading Quai 11eme and looked at the immensity standing in the far roadstead. The mighty four-cabin liner, gleaming with the white of its superstructures and the black of its hull, stood in the thick, almost London-like haze like an unreal visitor from another world. Cherbourg bid us farewell in April's chilly fog and drizzle. In the mist enveloping the harbor, I could see its top lights and red, portside lights, and five rows of à giorno lit windows and portholes. It was almost 7 p.m. The fog was thickening...

We were waiting for the last tender that would take us to the transatlantic liner. Olive O'Connor and I – Amadea Wildbury-Harsholm. We were returning to America from Egypt, where we had accompanied the expedition of Lord George Herbert Carnarvon. We were draughtswomen whose duties included making drawings of artifacts, maps, sketches, architectural objects and, in a word, anything the scholars saw fit. Admittedly, there was the latest aid – photography, but our eyes and hands were as useful as the big boxes on tripods...

Our luggage was already on the ship, and we were waiting for one more special shipment from our expedition, which got lost somewhere. We had trouble with it ourselves – it was the mummy of some Egyptian princess, which was supposed to go with us to one of the museums of New York for further research. First it got lost somewhere on the ship "Amun Ra", on which we sailed from Luxor to Alexandria. Then it almost led to the disaster of the steamer "Olivier", on which we sailed to Marseille. Then there were problems with it when transported by rail to Paris and from Paris to Cherbourg. In Paris the crate got lost and we had to wait two days before it was found... Now there were some problems with it again at customs. If I were superstitious, I would say that she is a Jonah – a person who brings bad luck to all the ships she travels on...

Standing next to us were passengers from "Nomadic," a smaller ship that stood at the quay. I looked over as Mrs. and Mr. Astor nervously strolled around the quay. Next to them stood the unmoving Molly Brown. They were probably the last of the big ones – the Guggenheims and others had already embarked...

"Mademoisielles...?" I heard behind me.

We turned around as if on command. The French customs officer saluted politely.

"Yes?" I spoke up.

"Your doom has been found. They are just loading her," he smiled, "by the way, she will have interesting company."

"Ou, what kind of company?" Olive was interested.

"Also an old thing, only a little younger than yours. It's a la mauffé sculpture. Supposedly from the time of the Knights Templar, but who knows... I can tell it to you ladies as savants."

Olive smiled charmingly.

"Ladies forgive me," the customs officer said and saluted, "I wish you a pleasant journey," he said on the way out.

"Finally," I muttered, "we can finally go out to the quay."

And we went out, mixed in with the multicolored and multilingual crowd of emigrants heading for the Promised Land of Lincoln and Washington.

The Tender finally bounced off the berth and, finally hissing and tapping the steam engine, began to shorten the distance separating us from the snoozing colossus on the wave. I expected it to be big, but I hadn't seen something this huge before. I read from the advertising leaflet next to the ticket that only the RMS "Olympic" was bigger than it, but it was the most luxurious steamer the sea waves had carried. A floating palace. A dream of something unrealizable. A marvel of 20th century technology. After half an hour, the tender reached its black side, which bore large gold letters forming an inscription – the name of this floating colossus and its home port:

TITANIC
LIVERPOOL

Embarkation of passengers went smoothly and after a few minutes we found our cabin on deck D – second class. Our employer didn't make much of an effort, but we couldn't complain. It could have been just the two of us and we didn't have to explain to anyone what, how and why. Two women traveling alone aroused unhealthy sensations in the East and here – contrary to appearances – too.

"Well, finally," Olive sighed and flopped down on the comfortable bed. She took off her heavy coat and warm cap, and her copper hair flowed in graceful locks down her back and shoulders. "You know I've had enough of this whole trip…"

"Me too," I said, taking off my overcoat and hat, "it's only six days and you'll be strolling down Broadway."

After the hot sun of Egypt we were just cold. Admittedly, we were used to traveling, but the need to change clothes with the change of latitude was giving us a hard time… We hoped that in the States it would be warmer than in Europe – cloudy and snotty.

Suddenly the deck vibrated slightly under our feet, and then began to vibrate gently. I understood – the machinery moved all forward and the ship began to turn with its bow towards the high seas. It was April 10, eight o'clock in the evening Cherbourg time…

The next day the "Titanic" arrived at the quay of the port of Queenstown. We both stood on the observation deck looking at the green hills of Ireland visible in the distance. Olive had tears in her eyes.

"I feel like getting off here," she said.

"You're an Irishwoman, that's understandable," I said, "but you're an American too, and that's the third generation... You were born in the States."

"Yes, but something draws me here," she replied, "as if I instinctively know that my true homeland is here, not there..."

I put my arm around her, and now I was affected by her sad and nostalgic mood.

Suddenly something disturbed it. Almost tangibly I felt someone's gaze on me. I carefully turned my head and looked to the left, above Olive's head. On the higher deck, first class, stood a man, who stared at us with his penetrating eyes. Just him, because everyone else was looking in the direction of the port, from where the tender bringing the rest of the passengers to New York had just arrived. Mostly emigrants from Ireland. Impoverished, but with great hopes and ambitions...

And this guy was staring at us. I didn't like it. It could have just been some socialite who decided to pick up two lonely women. It could have been some Jack the Ripper who felt like murdering us. Finally, it could have been someone who had a taste for our cargo located in the ship's abysmal hold. With the discoveries of Carnarvon and Carter, the demand for antiquities in Europe and America increased and...

"Nonsense," I thought to myself, "why exactly would he attach himself to us? Out of two thousand passengers on this ship, he attached himself to us exactly. Nonsense..."

But this thought did not give me peace.

From the sea drew a chill and dampness.

"Let's go from here," I said, "I'm cold."

We returned to the cabin. I opened my notes and set about studying the inscriptions that were on the coffin of Princess Hor–heb–eris. The one that was now traveling with us to America. It was a strange name, because it didn't match either the ancient Egyptian language or Greek. Hebrew and Aramaic dropped out in the qualifying run – they were not used in the court of the Pharaoh of the 18th Dynasty…

"What are you going to do?" Olive asked.

"First of all, to determine who she was in the state. And an interesting thing, there is not a word about her in the inscriptions and papyri. It seems that she was…"

"Cursed?" Olive raised her eyebrows. "She actually has no ornaments, while her burial place was isolated from other family members. That would fit. In that world, in the fields of Osiris, she won't have a plug nickel…

In the evening, at dinner, I looked around for the mysterious stranger, but did not notice anyone who even resembled him. We were surrounded by people from the middle classes – in this respect the "Titanic" accurately reflected Edwardian society. We lived and ate on the D deck. I didn't think anyone from the upper decks would go down to the low–life. The fact that we happened to have a second–class cabin protected us from people from the high–society and the low–life. Could anyone threaten us from fellow passengers? I seriously doubted it, after all, who could possibly be picking on us? We didn't have much money, our clothes weren't worth much either, and I doubt anyone would be interested in our notes, sketches and photos. The only thing of any material value (or rather, historical or collectible value) was the malodorous mummy of Princess Horheberis, now in the hold on E deck.

We quietly ate the evening meal and contemplated how to spend the evening. The shores of Ireland had already disappeared into the darkness and the lights of ships and fishing boats clinging to the coastal waters flashed on the horizon. Around 10 p.m., the "Titanic" made a turn in a southwesterly direction and laid in a proper course toward America. We went to the cabin and lay down falling asleep immediately with a dead sleep.

During the night I had the feeling that there was someone in our cabin. I lay down without opening my eyes and clearly felt the presence of a third person. I listened, but apart from the sound of the machines and Olive's breathing, I heard nothing. I cautiously opened my eyes and swept the cabin with a quick glance. In the light drizzling here from the upper decks, I saw no one. I moved around.

"Amadea," I heard Olive whisper quietly, "are you sleeping?"

"No, not anymore," I answered in an equally whispered voice, "what happened?"

"Someone was here," she whispered. "I could clearly feel it."

I felt a spike of anxiety, but I didn't let it be known.

"Who was it?" I asked yawning widely. "I hope some handsome...?"

"N... no," she replied. "I don't know..."

Unbelievable, but Olive was chattering her teeth.

"I'm scared," she whispered. "It's scary here!"

Well, this is something new – Olive O'Connor is scared! The woman who killed a lion by packing a whole drum from her S. & W. in its head when it craved fresh human flesh is afraid of ghosts! That's something new!

"You must be joking," I muttered, "turn to the wall and try to sleep."

"I'm telling you, someone was here," Olivia sat on the bed and lit the lamp, "it was her."

I sat down on the bed and stuck my eyes into her.

"Who? Who her? What are you talking about woman?"

Olive hugged me, as if looking for support and defense.

"Sh... she..." she said overcoming the chattering, "Princess Horheberis..."

I'm getting cold.

"You are telling fairy tales," I said calmly, "she has already been dead for more than two and a half thousand years. She could not come here."

"And yet she was here," Olive slowly comes back to herself, "I felt her as I feel you now!"

I can believe her – she, being Irish, had this sixth and seventh sense... Irish–Scots can do much, much more than normal people, in whom civilization has killed the spirit of Nature and blunted the natural alertness of the wild animal. I have heard more than one strange story about the abilities of Iroshkos witches and clairvoyants.

I couldn't sleep until morning. The worst part was that I could not find any rational explanation for what was happening that night...

We spent the entire forenoon on the deck and took advantage of the pale – compared to Egypt – sunshine, which only warmed a little here. I looked around for a guy with an astringent gaze, but again I didn't see him. Maybe I just thought he was following us, or maybe I was just oversensitive...

And yet I saw him after lunch, when we went out to the walking deck again. Before I had time to say anything to Olive, he came up to us tipping his hat.

"The ladies are so lonely," he began, "it's begging to be changed."

"And how do you know that we are lonely?" I replied.

"You can see that right away!" he said.

"Are you so observant?" said back Olive. "By the way, I don't talk to strangers."

"How do you know if we don't have fatigants?" I asked.

He smiled.

"You can see that!" he exclaimed, "first of all, you don't wear any rings, and therefore no one was interested in you. Until today..."

We burst into laughter.

"That's nice!" said Olive, "and by the way, who are you our knight and protector?"

At this the man showered us with a hail of nice words and trivialities. I understood that the guy's name is Alexandre de Saint Claire is French or Swiss and that he is sailing to New York on business, which actually did not surprise me, because most of the upper decks sailed there and also on business.

"And dear ladies as I see it, you are engaged in ancient Egypt?"

"Yes, but we are not scholars but rather a sort of support staff for drawing, photography and so on."

"Oh... extraordinarily," he said, "and the ladies are familiar with it?"

"Yes, Lord Carnarvon also employs women."

"Who can draw and photograph?" he wondered. "I didn't think women were in charge of such things and in Egypt. Now I understand why the ladies have such sunburnt faces."

"You'd be surprised, the rest of the body as well," Olive said feistily.

"My ladies forgive me my curiosity, but how did you do it?"

"We sunbathed without clothes, I think it's obvious," I replied. "It's hard to work in such a harsh sun in such clothes, isn't it?"

We burst into laughter. Alexandre was clearly surprised and interested.

"Are you, ladies... suffragettes?"

I laughed lifting the hem of my skirt.

"Somehow I don't wear blue stockings," I replied, "only woolen knee socks. They are more comfortable and I don't have to wear that idiotic strips for stockings... And as for your question, the French call us les savantesses..." (...).

The awakening was sudden. I heard a voice calling my name. I got up and imposed my bathrobe on myself. At first I thought the voice was coming from outside, but I was wrong, outside there was nothing but dark water washed by the bow of the "Titanic". We must have had quite a ride, because the bow jibs were deep and foaming in the darkness of the moonless night.

Above the ocean the stars glittered icily. I stepped out into the corridor and heard my name again. I moved to follow the voice and started down to the E deck and then to one of the holds on the port side of the ship on the F deck.

And then it happened. Out of nowhere, a short man dressed in a White Star Line uniform materialized in front of me.

"What are you doing here?" He asked in a pleasant voice, "are you looking for something?"

"Someone called me here," I replied truthfully, "Did you call me by name?"

"Let's say it was me," he replied somewhat arrogantly and raised his head, and I felt an unpleasant thrill down my spine at the sight of his face...

His face was unexpectedly narrow. Black, curly hair fell sloppily out from under his cap. The underside of his face was covered with a goatee, and his complexion looked as if it had been burned by the sun for many years. Narrow lips and a hooked nose completed the rest. He giggled.

"I'm not beautiful, am I?"

"Honestly?" I replied somewhat annoyed, "you remind me of the devil from the stories of our grandmothers."

"Or maybe that's just who I am?" he said with open mockery in his voice.

"Maybe, but I won't give you my soul anyway," I replied, "Besides, you would be a bit surprised if you saw it..."

He smiled mischievously.

"I know, Little Mermaid, I know this perfectly well," he said with a sneer in his voice, "You and your friend will escape your fate, but many people will go with me to the Abyss..."

I felt a twitch of horror.

"What are you talking about?" I shouted.

"About what will happen in two days. And for a long time the people will talk about it in their tales..."

"What will happen?!" I shouted.

"You'll see... Just two more days!.. Two days..."

He moved down the corridor and vanished into thin air behind the bulkhead.

I screamed in terror and woke up.

Leaning over me was Olive. Her face expressed horror.

"What happened?" I asked.

"You tell me," Olive said, "You were tossing and screaming in your sleep."

I breathed a sigh of relief. It was just a nightmare. Although...

"I dreamt of the devil. He predicted some kind of disaster, in two days..."

"You see!" she exclaimed triumphantly. "You did not believe!"

"And what, you were also predicted that?" I asked with curiosity that superseded fear.

Olive looked at me with fear, and undying fear.

"Well... no..." she replied, "but I also have this feeling that something is going on."

Suddenly something dawned on me.

"Listen Olive," I said, "what does la mauffé mean?"

A grimace of puzzlement crossed her face.

"I don't know. Admittedly, I learned French, but I don't recall there being anything like that..."

"And yet this customs officer..." I said.

"What customs officer, what customs officer?" Olive blinked her eyes, "what are you...?"

At once the pebble jumped into its place of the puzzle.

"Olive, he said something about the Templars!"

"Yeah, he said, and so what?"

"They worshipped someone they called Baphomet."

Olive nodded her head.

"Actually, that's right," she admitted.

"And do you know what people outside the order called it?"

"La mauffé?"

"Exactly! And do you know what it means? In Old French as much as... the devil!"

Olive went pale.

"Does it mean that we have the devil on board?"

I nodded my head.

"And they wrote that even God can not sink this ship..." Olive muttered.

"We are in no danger, we are Mermaids and..."

"...and we manage to save ourselves, and the rest?"

"We can try to warn them, but what good will that do? They will consider us crazy and lock us in some punishment cell." (...)

First we toured C deck, where there was a vestibule dripping with gold and crystal, and then we went out to the observation deck, located above A deck. I looked around me. There were many men and women, some couples in love, and people reading books and newspapers on deck chairs, trying to catch some sun. The sea was smooth and calm.

And empty.

As far as the eye could see there was not a single smoke or sail. We were in the middle of the Atlantic. Suddenly my attention was caught by a petite woman sitting at a table on which playing cards lay. There was something strangely familiar and mysterious about her at the same time. I looked at her, and after a moment the woman raised her eyes and our gazes crossed. Driven by some force, I approached her.

"Did you...?" I began.

She smiled. There was something disturbing and attractive at the same time in the gaze of her black eyes.

"Do I know you?" I finally asked the question.

"My name is Madame Bellinsky and I am a fortune teller," she announced in a calm voice, "Do you want to know something about your future?"

"And I am..." I started, but Madame interrupted me.

"I know who you are," she replied, "sit down child."

She quickly shuffled the cards and handed them to me.

"Shuffle them to yourself, three times," she said.

I rearranged them.

She quickly spread the cards into four rows of seven in each row. They were ordinary playing cards from six upwards. She stared at the layout and raised her eyebrows slightly.

"And what do you see there, Madame?" I asked.

She looked at me with somewhat absent-minded eyes.

"What I can say is that this is the first successful hand of cards in several days."

"Ou, that's interesting," I replied, "and something more specific?"

I slipped two guineas into her hand.

"Well, look," she said, pointing to the lady of hearts, "that's you. Next to you is your friend," she pointed to the lady of diamonds, who was next to me.

"That's Olive," I replied, "and the third one?"

"Beware of this one," replied Madame, "there is a death and a mystery with her."

Who the hell was she talking about? – I wondered.

"Next to you dove great misfortune, but nothing will happen to you, I would say, you will come out of it with a defensive hand. It is close. Closer and closer, as with everyone. But you will get away with your life..."

At once her eyes became glassy. The voice thickened and tarnished, and after a while it shifted to a wheezing whisper.

"This lady... beware... it is someone great... great and cursed forever... she is... by your side... she can doom us all... there is evil by her side, great... great cosmic evil... beware of the black statue... beware... beware of yourself and your loved ones... it will be soon... soon HE will reveal his power... beware..."

At once her head flew back, and after a second her eyes looked conscious.

"But..." I started, but she did not let me finish.

"Go where you came from," she said firmly. "Go, and warn your friend."

She made a gesture with her hand, as if she was pushing me away. I got up from my chair and looked around. Olive and Sandy had disappeared from my sight. I looked at the table and went numb, Madame was not there...

"This is all some kind of paranoia!" I shouted in my spirit. "Where is she?"

I walked to the railing and looked at the water. Neither next to the ship, nor in the odkos or kilwater there was no one.

Only white ice cubes were dead floating on the dark blue water... (...)

[The next day] after lunch I sat down at a table with my papyri and delved into reading them. The first two were some paperwork with calculations of what who owed whom and why. Bills and business correspondence. I was puzzled as to what the princess needed these papers for, instead of verses from the "Book of the Dead." I was already about to put them away when my gaze came to rest on the verso of one of them. Some demotic writing was visible there, which I hadn't noticed.

Slowly syllabifying, I read it and felt the hair stand up on my head. On the pages were terrible curses cast by a certain Nefer–Nefer–Nefer–Nefer, the royal concubine on Princess Horheberis. Apparently, the whole burial process was quick, and they used by-the-book materials to cast the curse on the princess.

But why? – I thought – what did Horheberis do to the four-fold beautiful Nefer that the latter cast such a strong curse on her? Could it be hatred of the kind that Amneris had for Aida from the Verdi opera we saw in Cairo. Was it about the Pharaoh's favor? But Horheberis was his daughter, so...

"Excuse me, ma'am," I heard above me, "may I have a few words with you?"

I looked up and felt a spike of cold fear. This man had something amazing about him. He was maybe fifty years old. He was tall, at least six feet five inches tall. Black hair fell unruly out from under a black hat, the lines of which shaded his face. Deep-set black eyes pierced his gaze. The complexion was dark, as if burned by the sun of the tropics. The only colorful addition against the blackness of his clothes was a red scarf tied around his neck.

"Don't be afraid," he said softly, "I'm not as scary as I look."

And he smiled with the smile of a child. Joyful. Disarming.

"Allow me," he sat vis-à-vis me and his gaze swept over my papers.

"Why do you..." I started the question wanting to say why he accosted me, but he did not let me finish with a wave of his hand.

"You and I have similar interests, as I see," he said, "my name is, say, Smith. Which doesn't matter, because I travel incognito."

"Well, then I also see no reason to introduce myself to you," I burbled, "what do you want from me?"

He smiled again.

"I see that you are sitting over the hieroglyphs, aren't you?"

"Is that so," I replied, "so what? Do you read hieroglyphs?"

His face became serious, but his black eyes were cheerful.

"Yes. I use the Champollion method with good results."

I looked at him.

"Isn't it strange?" I asked, sending him the naive look of a teenager caught in an illicit game.

"What is strange?" He took a polite interest.

"The fact that on one ship meet at once people who are interested in ancient Egypt. And they are interested in ancient papyri at the same time."

Smith smiled radiantly.

"I will tell you," he said, "Egypt has become fashionable, but that is not all. Its magic has become fashionable. You are carrying the mummy of Princess Horheberis. You already know that she is cursed. And as I know life, you would like to know why – wouldn't you?"

I felt my eyebrows wander to my hairline. Smith, whoever he was, knew hieratic and demotic hieroglyphics, or he wouldn't have known what I knew. He must have read it now, looking at the papyri I had spread out on the table. Well, unless...

"Did you by any chance pay me a visit at the cabin two days ago?" I asked.

He laughed boisterously, but sincerely.

"No, gracious lady, for such visits I am already too old, which I regret immensely. On the other hand, what concerns me is that there are more of us here, and, as I hear from you, they are very interested in the mystery of Princess Horheberis."

"Well, perhaps you can enlighten me as to what the story is about?"

He tilted his head and sent me an amused look.

"Do you really not know it?"

"No, why should I" I replied, "but how do you know it?"

He nodded his head clearly amused.

"It's a longer story," he said.

"We have plenty of time," I replied, "I have the whole day to myself, and therefore I will be happy to listen to you."

"So let me start by saying that Princess Horheberis was one of the many daughters of the powerful Pharaoh Ahmos and Ahmes-Nefertari, who reigned in the years one thousand five hundred and fifty – one thousand five hundred and twenty-five before the birth of Christ," Smith began.

"As far as I know, Ahmos did not have a daughter by that name," I replied.

"Of course he had," Smith said with a slight rebuke in his voice, "but the memory of her, as you now know, has been erased."

"But why?"

"Haven't you read it?"

"Not yet. All I know is that she was cursed by, actually by everyone... Herheberis was a beautiful and power-hungry woman. However, she had no chance to obtain full power, that was reserved for men. She was to be married to one of the nomarchs of Upper Egypt. However, this union did not suit her ambitions and so she murdered her husband with the help of cobras, which she threw into his bedroom at night. This allowed her to take over the entire nom and slowly eliminate her husband's family."

"And it didn't get anyone's attention?" I asked in disbelief.

"As the nomarch's wife and princess, she stood beyond suspicion, and she had devised everything in such a way as to make it look like a normal accident: someone got poisoned by stale meat, someone stepped on a scorpion, the fortified bank of the Nile River collapsed under someone, someone fell into a crocodile pond..."

"And what next?"

"The princess returned to court and there met Elia, a priest of Set, who wanted to become a pharaoh and establish his own dynasty. Needless to say, what did this acquaintance mean? These two got on well, as if in a bark of poppy seeds. At first they both tried each other like swordsmen before dealing a blow, but when Elia confessed his intentions to Horheberis, they immediately joined forces. Pharaoh Ahmos' life was in danger."

"You mean his own daughter turned against him?" I asked in disbelief.

"That's exactly right. Horheberis desired what Queen Hatshepsut later succeeded in doing. She intended to achieve it with the help of the priest of Set, whom she would later betray anyway..."

"How do you know all this?" I asked, because I found this story very strange.

"We have our sources of knowledge," Smith said evasively.

"Well," I replied, "and what happened next?"

Smith lit a cigarette in a long cigar holder and was silent for a moment looking at the sunlit ocean.

"Then they both bemoaned the curse of Set on Pharaoh and his family. Of course, Pharaoh's counterintelligence finally gathered evidence against the princess and her lover. Of course, it was impossible to cause a scandal by openly bringing them to trial, so preventive and retributive measures were chosen, so to speak. A curse was cast on both lovers and their partisans. One night unknown perpetrators butchered Elia in the temple of Set, and the next day Princess Horheberis woke up in a bed sprinkled with an unusually heavy white powder that glowed slightly in the dark. And not forty days had passed when she joined her lover in the other world..."

"Was she poisoned?" I asked, "with what?"

"I'm afraid you won't know such a thing, dear savant," he said smiling, "it was radium oxide."

"Oxide of... what?" I asked amazed to the last limits, "after all, it was discovered only fourteen years ago!"

He looked at me with appreciation.

"I bow to your knowledge and... beauty," he said bowing his head playfully, "and what are the sources of your knowledge?"

"I have read about Madame Skłodowska's research probably or not in "Nature", and besides, she is a two-time Nobel Prize winner, so as a savant, as you deigned to call me, I must be up to date with this kind of news..."

He blew out a cloud of fragrant smoke and mused for a moment.

"And then it went on, as is normal in such cases. The priests of Amun or Ptah used this remedy on Pharaoh's orders, for there was a law against shedding royal blood, so she had to be killed so as not to cause bleeding wounds."

"And wasn't it enough to strangle her or simply hang her?"

"A simple fellah could be hanged or strangled, but not a person of royal lineage," Smith corrected, "besides, it was supposed to have an intimidating effect. And you should know that after her death Horheberis looked terrible. Her whole body was covered with ulcers, her hair and teeth had fallen out, her body was terribly skinny... Pharaoh wanted to show what punishment awaited someone who dared to raise his hand against his majesty, even if he was of royal lineage."

"But after all, she was embalmed," I objected.

"Yes, because that's what religion dictated. But as you can see, instead of verses from the Book of the Dead, here we have curses and terrible incantations. She was buried in a niche without anything of value except a metal mask on her face and without any assistance, and her grave was secured so that no human could get to it. Now I think you understand why?"

I nodded. Now it was all clear to me.

"Well, that's right. And now you understand why there is not a single inscription in her crypt. Not a single sign or the merest inscription containing her name."

"Were you there?" I asked a question that seemed a bit absurd, because we had never seen someone like that there.

He nodded his head.

"A little later than both of you," he said, "and that's why I followed you all the way to New York, because I would like to see her before..." he stopped, as if he bit his tongue.

"It can be done," I said with conviction, "I'll just tell the officer that I want to see our luggage and he will certainly agree. I'll arrange it even before we go ashore."

He shook his head.

"I would prefer today or tomorrow."

I raised my eyebrows. Interesting that everyone was in such a hurry, as if the world was going to end in two days (...).

The road reminded me of descending from Olympus to hell. We did not use the elevator and descended down the gangways. After several minutes of descending and wandering through corridors, we reached the mail hold, which was almost at the bow, already under the waterline. It contained a variety of packages, parcels and bundles, and even an automobile in which some boy was making out with a red–haired girl...

"Here it is," spoke up the volunteer, comparing the receipts with the list. "I don't suppose the you want to open it?" he said with some concern in his voice.

"Of course we want to," Smith replied, "and please don't disturb us."

We took the package with the coffin – fortunately not a large one – off the rack and proceeded to open it. Princess Horheberis lay in her simple wooden box just as she was buried almost three thousand years ago...

"Are you sure it's her?" He asked in a voice in which one could feel the tension.

He quickly reached into his pocket and brought out gloves made of thin but very strong rubber.

"Did you touch her, ladies, with your bare hand?" he asked me.

"No, we didn't even pack her, only people from Mr. Carter's team," I replied. "Why?"

"They are dead," he burbled, "and no one knows why."

"You must be joking, after all, it's impossible. There is no black magic, no curses and the like..." I resisted.

He looked at me briefly in the face.

"You are right," he replied, "indeed, there is none of that, but there are still bacteria, spores, viruses, rickettsiae... And radioactive powders."

"Ah, that's what you mean," I replied.

And just in case, I took a step back. Meanwhile, Smith took out the mummy, which was astonishingly small in comparison, and laid it on the plank.

"Princess Horheberis," he said, "we're about to find out what was at play here..."

He reached into his pocket and took out a small, silvery box the size of a large cigarette case, with several buttons and a small window in which numbers glowed white. I had never seen a similar device in my life. Smith pressed two buttons and placed the box on the mummy's chest. After a few seconds, the digits glowed orange.

"What does this mean?" I asked.

"Spores of fungi from the genus Aspergillus," he replied, "or more specifically Aspergillus flavus. Extremely toxic and causing fungal infections of the skin, lungs and producing aflatoxins, which are resistant to heat, so cooking and the sun's ultraviolet radiation do not kill them. Do you understand?"

"Are you a doctor?" I asked in amazement, because I did not expect what he said, and he said it with the absolute certainty of a knowledgeable man.

"Among other things," he answered evasively. "Now we will see alpha, beta and gamma radiation."

He flicked some kind of switch and the numbers on the box glowed again – this time green.

"Minimally," he said with a little surprise in his voice, "but on the other hand, the embalming process could wash the radioactive particles from her body..."

"Poisons?" I prompted him.

"It's impossible to detect, especially since back then they used alkaloids from plants and animal substances: cobra venom, scorpion venom, trumpet venom, or something like that. Undetectable after three thousand years... Okay, we close it and go from here. Disputes are transmitted by air."

We loaded Horheberis back into the coffin, and Smith closed its lid. When we were done, he summoned the ochre master, who led us out to the observation deck. I breathed a full sigh of relief.

Smith brought out a flat flask from his pocket and unscrewed the cap, which was a small glass. He poured some dark brown liquid from it and handed it to me.

"Drink it, but in a one gulp!" he said. "The taste of this is hideous, but it will help you."

"What is it?" I asked in amazement.

"Fungicide and disinfectant," he replied. "Come on!"

I drank.

The smell of this something was terrible, and the taste resembled gasoline mixed with Lysol. It must have contained a significant percentage of alcohol and something to prevent the vomiting reflex. It took my breath away for a moment.

"Oh mother," I groaned when I could finally breathe, "what a nasty thing!"

Smith drank his portion and squirmed.

"Now go to your place, change your clothes and bathe," he said this in a tone that allowed no objection. "Throw those clothes in the oven. Anyway, it doesn't matter anymore..." he added looking at his watch. (...)

"One more question," I said, "where do they produce such... such indicators with which you examined the Horheberis mummy."

I looked into his face, but he only smiled. He must have won his fortune, Smith, or whatever his name is, at poker.

"You won't believe me if I tell you anyway," he replied calmly, "so there's nothing to ask."

"But please tell me," I insisted.

He shrugged.

"Well, let it be," he said, "such things are produced in the XXV century, or more precisely in 2611. Do you believe me?"

"You are mocking me," I replied, "is that nice?"

"Well, you see," he replied, "it is as I said."

He looked at his watch again.

"Excuse me," he said, "but I'm already late. And you should do as I said. This is for the safety of you, your friend and her lover." (...)

I turned around and went to our cabin. As I walked I kept thinking about what had happened to me that afternoon. About Smith and his strange device. About Princess Horheberis' mischievous smile. About the strange remarks he threw into the conversation from time to time, which from a certain point of view were sinister. And yet we were in no danger. The sea was as calm as oil, the weather was beautiful... Admittedly, last night on the northwestern horizon we saw an ice-blink on the low clouds that lingered there, but so far, apart from small pieces of ice seen here and there on the calm water, there was nothing dangerous in sight... (...)

It was getting to eleven in the evening, and we were going to lie down. And then I noticed something peculiar. I had the feeling that I was waiting for something, that something was about to happen. And the worst thing was that this mood of anticipation was also given to Olive.

"Something is going to happen," I said, "I have a premonition of something that is going to happen and soon."

"Surprisingly, but me too," replied Olive. "You know what, let's go to the upper deck, maybe the view of the ocean will calm us down..."

"Maybe," I replied, taking my coat and hat.

We walked to the upper deck driven by some special anxiety. Despite the rather late hour, dancing and folk games were going on, we could hear music, people's laughter and conversations. In the corners we saw couples kissing. Yet something was already going on, which made us go out to the walking deck, where four huge chimneys stood... Three of them were belching smoke, and the fourth occasionally let out a cloud of steam.

We approached the railing, which was almost above the bridge. I swept my eyes over the horizon. It was strangely dark, despite the brilliant starlight blazing overhead. The ocean was smooth, and only the steady gust of air cut by our ship could be felt on our faces.

"We're probably doing about twenty knots," said Olive.

"Even twenty-one," I mumbled, looking at the bow odkos and the phosphorescent keelwater astern. In the light coming from the portholes and decks of the "Titanic" from time to time ice floes appeared. A frigid chill pulled from the water, and over the western horizon a brighter ice-blink could be seen in the sky.

At once I felt an icy grip on my heart.

"Oh mother, can you see what I see?" I heard Olive's voice.

Against the backdrop of the only slightly lighter sky, I saw a dark, black and bipedal shape.

"This is an iceberg..." I snapped out.

Almost at the same moment Smith stood next to us. He was looking at his watch.

"There!" He said without taking his eyes off the dial.

We heard the sound of the bell from the crow's nest and the cry of one of the watchmen.

"An iceberg ahead!"

I felt myself go numb with terror.

After a few seconds, the deck trembled, and astern the water fogged violently from the work of the machinery in reverse...

At once the ocean brightened. The sky remained dark, and the black shape ahead sharpened. Next to it floated smaller black spots. I looked at the deck – next to us stood some black figure. I could see Ollie's body through the thick coat and gown she was clad in, but Smith was dark. It was strange, but I could see in the darkness.

Why? – I thought in a panic.

I looked down and saw glowing human silhouettes spilling out onto the deck. I realized that they were sailors.

"Hold on," I heard Smith's voice, "we're about to hit it..."

The yawning cold and black shape approached slowly and moved away to the right at the same time. I realized that the helmsman gave all to the left, but it did not help much. After a few seconds, a wall of blackness sprouted up next to the starboard side, and the deck was again pierced by a jolt and a slight vibration passing into a distinct panting.

"It has happened," said Smith closing his chronometer, "Let the ladies go to the boat and bail out. "Titanic" will go down in two hours. And it's time for me..."

Slowly, he put his watch in his pocket and... disappeared. He literally vanished into thin air.

Olive screamed quietly.

The alarm siren wailed sharply.

"Don't shudder," I growled, "do you see what I see? Can you see in the dark?"

She nodded.

"Who was that?" She asked in a voice in which you could hear fear.

"I don't know," I replied, "but did you hear what he said?"

"We have to go to the boat..."

"Well, let's go!" I said and pulled her by the hand.

The ship stood. The black mass stopped moving relative to the ship, which meant that the "Titanic" was stopped. We went down to deck C. People somewhat irritated looked around looking out for crew members.

"We just have a problem, it's just a slight collision, nevertheless, please put on your life jackets and go to the lifeboats and life rafts," I heard the voice of one of the officers.

We had already run down to the E deck to go to the hold. In the perspective of the corridor, we saw an ever-growing puddle of water appear at the end of the corridor. The deck tilted forward. The ship was plunging forward.

I realized that the water had passed over the watertight bulkheads and overflowed onto the E deck, whose flooding would only be a matter of time. And a short one at that!

"Are we rescuing Horheberis?" Olive asked.

"And let her go to he..." I started, "I'd rather take our notes."

We turned back. People sensing danger gathered at the gangways and elevators. They were dressed in coats and jackets, over which they put life jackets.

"Ladies to the lifeboats," I heard the voice of some officer, probably Lowe.

Someone put life jackets on us and led us out onto the boat deck. The deck rocked again and the stern went higher up. A flare rose from the top deck and shone over the calm water. For a moment I couldn't see anything, because the flare blinded me thoroughly.

"Damn," I heard Olivia's voice, "don't look at it."

"I can see. It's blinding as hell. What do we do?" I asked.

"Let's get the hell out of here, that's clear."

"He, he, but where to? This water is not much warmer than ice..." I muttered. In the face of death, I began to have a gallows humor.

Olive leaned out through the railing. The ship plunged even further to the bow and the railing at the bow was already at water level...

Suddenly we felt a jolt and a deafening bang. A jet of dirty steam shot into the dark sky from the front chimney. The railing gave way and Olive and I flew into the dark water. I felt a powerful impact and the terrible, icy cold of the liquid surrounding me. Instinctively, I drew in a huge gulp of bitter-salty water and felt the choking weight of the liquid in my lungs.

"It's over..." I thought.

I wanted to scream, but I couldn't. Did I die? No. It was strange, but I couldn't feel the cold now and... I was breathing water! I looked around. Next to me I saw Olive, who was looking at me with a strange face. Besides, I could see perfectly in the surrounding darkness.

"Look!" She exclaimed, "we are Mermaids!"

It was obvious. Why hadn't we guessed that before? But there was no time to dwell on this problem now. Much more important things were happening.

We were about thirty feet underwater. I looked up – toward the surface. I could see in the darkness again. Above and beside us dangled the huge shape of a steamer, which was slowly sinking into the depths. Beside it we could see the silhouettes of people moving in the water. Their bodies under the influence of the cold quickly darkened and eventually took on the color of the surrounding water... I understood, these people were already dead. They were dying from the cold, which I did not feel at all despite the fact that my body was free of clothing.

Suddenly I felt Olive grab my hand and point to something in the depths.

Something was moving in the icy gloom, and that something was warmer than its surroundings because it glowed with a faint glow. A round, almost spindly shape floated slowly upward. Suddenly we heard a strange noise and the underwater ship stopped a few dozen yards away from us.

"Mr. Verne's submarine," I said.

"More like Admiral Holland's submarine," replied Olive, "but..."

Exactly, but... It was kind of strange. On the spindly hull you could see the superstructure, which was surrounded by a kind of basket made of metal bars. In front of the superstructure was something like a cannon... On the superstructure we saw black letters with a white border forming the U–25 inscription and a strange swastika broken to the left...

Suddenly my attention was caught by an upward movement. Four silhouettes broke away from the hull of the sinking ship and began to swim down – towards the strange underwater vessel. They had something in their hands that resembled a metal container. After that, accidents happened quickly. An elliptical hatch opened in the bow of the ship and people waving their fins entered it and disappeared inside with the container. After a few seconds we heard something like a swish and a noise, and the unknown ship sank into the dark abysses.

We exchanged astonished glances, and then slowly approached the ship. In its bow section there were several narrow crevices through which the water tore sharply. It was here that the "Titanic" impaled itself on an ice spur. Overcoming the strong current of the water, we looked at the crevices. The plates were not torn, as we feared, but dented inward and let go at the joints. So the hull was not open like a can of canned goods...

We drifted away as the hull again began to slide downward making an increasingly steep standoff accompanied by the bang and crackle of cracking bulkheads and decks, the roar of expanding air being pushed out of the compartments by the water. "Titanic" was sinking faster and faster caving in with its bow. From the holes in the hull some objects were spilling out, which slowly sank to the bottom and we lost sight of them. Suddenly the hull vibrated and we heard the monstrous crackle of cracking frames and longitudinals and the shriek of tearing sheet metal, and a moment later the roar of a powerful impact of the stern against the water. More debris sprinkled from the huge wound. The bow section made a swing that put the stern perpendicular to the water, and after a few seconds the final act of the drama began. The huge structure, accompanied by a rumble, dawn and crackle, bubbling with residual air and steam, finally plunged into the water and moved toward the bottom. At a depth of half a mile, the wreck disintegrated and disappeared from our sight...

Now only from the surface did the sound of screams and groans of dying people reach us, grotesquely distorted by the layers of water...

☙

Chapter 18
A Leap in Time?

And here are excerpts from the second story on the Titanic disaster, in which contemporary characters go back in Time and are powerless witnesses to the tragedy...

***

On this crystal night... (excerpts)

April 9, 8:00 p.m. GMT, London–Felixtowe

I had just come out of the bathroom and laid on the bed when my cell phone chirped. I turned up the dim light, reached over and turned on the phone. The wide screen displayed the contents of a text message:

Urgent. Please report to the port of Southampton – you take the position of chief on the NS "Californian Nugget" on April 7 – Poudeaux.

The first thing I did was to curse through clenched teeth. I had a vacation – the first vacation in three years, during which I took part in the Carribean Pearl affair, then we solved the mystery in Bermuda, and finally we did a little partan in Japan... I write we, because I was helped in all this by Janta – my wife, who is a Mermaid. Now we were finally going to spend our vacation in the mountains. Janta was to arrive from Japan, where the ruins of Daiichi–Fukushima still radiated and contaminated the ocean, which was, after all, her home. Tomorrow I was to pick her up at Heathrow, as she was flying in from Tokyo. Then we were to go to Scotland. The trip to the mountains, of course, came to nothing. Instead, I had to go to Southampton, and take this position – after all, our company, EuroTrash GmbH of Hamburg, was paying me to be ready for work, and I had to – like in the army – show up for every call.

"What am I going to tell Janta?" I thought about it and decided after a while that I would send her a text message, because I didn't know if she was already on the plane or still waiting at Narita...

I quickly tapped out a text message to her, then took out my duffel bag from the closet and started packing up.

April 10, 7:30 p.m. GMT, Southampton

Tender bounced off the berth of the ferry landing and headed for Southampton Water. We sailed having the lights of the city on both sides. Then it got dark on the port side – we passed Calshot Castle and turned left – into The Solent, where the anchorage of the Californian Nugget was located. This didn't surprise me – this was a nuclear–powered ship and as such would have caused protests from environmentalists and local residents. And that's why it was standing at anchor away from human eyes... There were massive forests on both sides of the strait, and that's why it didn't bother anyone. Simply put, no one saw it, and even if they did, it did not arouse any suspicion that it contained a cargo of several tons of radioactive plutonium...

The ship was darkened and apart from the position lights and a small lamp at the gangway, nothing illuminated it. In the darkness of an April evening, the ship drew a brighter shape against the cloudy sky and the glow of the lights of Yarmouth, Lymington and Milford on Sea. It was painted white and therefore slightly brighter than the darkness around us.

We reached the gangway. I stepped down onto the platform and the crewman handed me a bag.

"Have a good evening," he smiled in the semi-darkness, "we're on our way back."

"You too," I replied, "have fun."

The engine of the tendrer zapped sharply and the ship began to move away, and after a while disappeared into the darkness. I was left alone on the gangway. I was curious that no one came out to meet me. No gangway sailor, no watchman. No one. Not even a dog with a limp. A small motorboat was rocking by the gangway, with the words EuroTrash Co. Ltd. and the company's logo on the side.

"Interesting customs?" I thought.

I threw my bag over my shoulder and started climbing up the gangway. After a dozen steps I found myself on deck.

"Hallo out there!" I shouted into the darkness, "is anyone there?"

I heard a bolt slam and saw the hatch opening.

"Mr. Leshnevsky?" asked a female voice.

I confirmed.

"Welcome aboard," the hatch opened wider, and I glanced inside. "Sailor Ursula Dittmer," she introduced herself to me.

"Some German woman?" I thought. I took a closer look at her, she was dressed in a dark blue down coat and a cap with ear muffs, from under which light-colored hair fell over her shoulders. Her nylon-clad legs were clad in black boots. She was maybe twenty years old and had a futuristic H & K MP7 slung over her shoulder. I liked that less. Definitely.

"Oh it's that way?" I thought. The company began to appreciate the threat and simply rearmed us. After the Carribean Pearl story, someone in Hamburg and London learned the right lessons.

"And shouldn't you be outside?" I asked sympathetically.

She looked at me panicked.

"Sorry Mr. Chief, but it's so cold. It's cold from the water," she said with a tone of justification. "Ah, you are invited to the captain."

"Well, put on pants and winter boots. I give you my word that it will be warmer. And by the way, who is there?" I asked, "someone from the head of the company?"

"Director Poudeaux."

"OK, thank you," I replied, "where is my cabin?"

"Up the gangway and to the right," she smiled, "there is a sign on the door, you will hit it."

I picked up the bag and threw it over my shoulder again.

"Thank you. And have a nice watch," I said and stepped into the warm brightness of the ship.

In the cabin, I threw the bag on the berth and looked around. There was a standard duffel for a senior officer: a berth, a desk, an armchair, a table, two chairs and a wall-mounted closet. A forty-inch TV on the wall and a blue-ray player completed the equipment. The bare minimum of comfort. I threw the bag into the closet my jacket and cap flew to the berth. I'll unpack later, I decided. A briefing with the captain still awaited me. I wish I had asked the little one at the gangway who was in charge...

I left the cabin and headed for the upper deck, where the captain's quarters were located. The door to the saloon was open, there was a streak of harsh light coming from it and female and male voices.

"It promises to be interesting...?" I thought.

It seemed to me that the crew was a half-and-half female and male company. I quietly approached the open door and materialized in its space. I swept my gaze around the interior of the lounge. Other than Director Poudeaux, there was no one there that I knew.

I knocked on the doorframe. Six pairs of eyes looked at me.

"Good evening," I said.

Poudeaux rose from his chair.

"Ladies and gentlemen," he said solemnly, "here is your senior officer."

"Robert Leśniewski," I introduced myself without waiting for the director to growl and distort my name like any Frenchman or Englishman.

"That's right," Director Poudeaux shook my hand and at the same time pointed out the others to me. "This is your captain Birgit Thornsen, your first officer Della Roget, your machine chief Juta Hartmann and the purser Jean Marc Dairac."

I shook hands with all of them. The women were in their thirties, the purser was a dried-up fifty-year-old.

Poudeaux told us to sit down and began the briefing.

"Since we are here, let me finally introduce you to the company's instructions. We are leaving the port in just a quarter of an hour, after the briefing. You are going across the Atlantic via the northern route, along the orthodrome. At the height of Cape Race – as if to the mouth of the St. Lawrence. But you will not go to Canada, but to the States, specifically to Bar Harbor, Maine. And from there you will take a cargo to Europe, to Cherbourg to be exact. You will ask why exactly there? Well, you are to take a cargo of two and three-quarters kilograms of californium oxide from there. Therefore, the crew is armed and the operation is secret. Besides, there is a railroad coming to this rump, and californium two-five-one radiates so strongly that it must be encased in five hundred tons of lead and cooled. So you can understand for yourselves that this operation has the highest possible priority. Well, and one more thing – this cargo is worth – californium alone – one hundred and eighty million US dollars per gram! Please multiply this for yourself by two thousand..."

He fell silent for a moment giving us time to grasp the information we heard with our thoughts.

"And most importantly," he said at the end, "californium is an excellent material for atomic bombs. Two kilos is a critical mass. Just put together what you will be carrying and... boom! Also, please keep this in mind."

"Well, then, why wasn't the army taken to do this job?" I asked. "After all, playing with atoms is a job for them?"

Poudeaux took two stabs from an electronic cigarette.

"From the transportation of this filth is us. It was the military that approached us about this, because we are the only ones with specialized equipment for transporting such hot materials. And it goes on to CERN. It is theirs toy..."

8:30 p.m. GMT

"Chief, take the ship out to sea," said Birgit Thornsen.

"Aye, aye Ma'am," I replied and turned to the control panel.

"And don't be so servile," she added and I heard a smile in her voice. "I hate that American accent."

"Thanks, me either Ms. Captain," I replied turning on the dashboards, which were slowly glowing with indicator lights. "Shall we get started?"

She nodded her head.

"Machine! Small forward."

I snapped the contacts. Steam from the reactor's secondary circuit went to the turbines. The quiet sound of their operation reached us.

The control lights flashed green.

"Full power in five minutes," I said.

"We start in five minutes," replied Birgit. "We are starting the launch procedures."

Now we all looked at the clock. After five minutes, the green light of the reactor's primary cooling circuit went out. The green readiness lights of the power transfer systems and the orange lights of the reactor operation indicators were now burning on the desktop. Full readiness. I flipped the handle of the machine telegraph to the MAJOR THROW. Steam hit the turbine blades harder.

"There is a small forward," I replied. Birgit nodded again. She was tense, and her blue eyes stared into the darkness outside the window.

The deck vibrated underfoot. We set off. Behind the stern the water churned. The log reader – mechanical and satellite – lit up. Both began to show rising values. The ship was already on the move.

"By the channel or near Yarmouth?" I asked.

"Through The Solent," she replied. Again we looked at the dark water. On the radar we had only the ferry slowly gliding from Yarmouth to Lymington. The yellow flickering top light finally moved enough for us to pass without risking a collision.

"Half ahead," she said.

"Half ahead," I replied, moving the drive handle forward. Our gazes crossed on the log display screen.

"We have ten knots," I said, "gun it?"

"The reactor is still too cold," she muttered, "and so far that's enough."

The Californian Nugget drove slightly like a car. Only it was slower. The shore was slowly running backwards – a dark sheet of Channel waters spread out in front of us. The Isle of Wight stayed to the north.

"Rudder right twenty," she said, "and course S-SW. I'm going to sleep. Who has the first watch?"

"I. I have to figure it all out, since I'm here as Chief Officer."

"OK, chief, let you work it out. At six you will be changed by Mrs. Roget. And from tomorrow there will be a permanent watch schedule. Good night."

And she left, followed by Della.

I was left alone on the bridge. (...)

April 11, 06:00 a.m. GMT, English Channel

"Good morning and change Mr. Chief!" I heard the cheerful voice of Della Roget behind me. "And what, did you work it out all?"

"Good morning," I replied, turning away from the panels and control consoles, "and as for working out, I have not yet seen something that is so complicated in construction and simple in operation."

She smiled. She was really very pretty in her company uniform. Her dark hair flowed down her back tied in a ponytail. The deep gaze of intelligent green eyes. Small lips with pale pink full lips. Irish blood must have flowed in her, because she resembled the appearance of Celtic priestesses or Irish–Scot nuns... The white blouse, dark blue skirt lay perfectly on her shapely body. Few looked as feminine and sexy as this girl in this simple yet elegant outfit. Della was a Canadian from Ottawa and had sailed for the fifth or sixth year as a navigation officer.

"That's why this ship is manned by women," she said. "Two-thirds of the crew..." she added.

"...and the men are for the donkey work," I finished.

"I didn't mean it to sound like that," she said unusually kindly.

"I was joking," I replied, "I'm not in the mood today. There's a storm coming from the west, and it's a nasty one, if we go out into the ocean, it will rock us."

"Is there a warning?" she raised her eyebrows. "After all, just yesterday they announced nice weather."

"The low has moved from under Iceland to the southeast and quite quickly," I replied. "It is very deep, nine hundred and thirty in the eye of the cyclone. It's going to swing quite a bit – wind ten, wave something around that too..."

She nodded, and an amused grimace ran across her face.

"I'm not worried about it," she said and shrugged her shoulders charmingly. "In about forty-eight hours we will enter the zone of frontal storms. We'll handle it up somehow."

I also hoped so...

April 12, 6 p.m. AZOT, Atlantic

An April evening in the Atlantic was falling. Dark clouds were piling up in the northwest in a blackish pyramid, the tide was slowly rising. The deck rose and fell in an ever faster rhythm. The wave slowly but inexorably became more frequent and steeper.

"We are sailing into the mouth of the monster," I heard the voice of our captain behind me.

"It doesn't look too bad," I replied, showing the meteo-radar screen. "So far there is no precipitation and no lightning. And those clouds are far away too."

"OK, right, but since you can see them from such a distance, they have piled up at least fifty kilometers..."

We were silent for a while.

"Don't you think it's all so..." she searched for the right word for a moment, "...so strange?"

I raised my eyebrows slightly. This is something I didn't expect. I should rather be the one to ask the question.

"What strange?" I asked cautiously.

"This cruise," she replied.

"And is there something I don't know about?"

"More than one thing!" she snorted. It must have been on her mind, because at once she decided to tell someone.

"Meaning?" I asked another question.

"Look at the facts," she said in a hushed voice, as if she feared eavesdropping, "you had a leave of absence, you were brought down in exchange for Trygvessen. The crew, it's a conglomeration of men and women selected on a roundup of who could sail. We're sailing on a ship that's going on its first voyage, because apart from trials in the Irish Sea, it's never been to sea. In addition, it's a nuclear ship, not a motor ship or steamer. I guess this is some kind of experiment by the company, whether this ship is capable of being run by an inexperienced, out-of-tune crew, and on top of that it has some nightmarish, shenanigans mission for CERN to fulfill... Doesn't it seem strange to you?"

It seemed to me, and very much so. The explanation about the experimental cruise seem to hold up. It was possible.

"It is possible, Ms. Captain," I replied. "Perhaps your hypothesis about the experimental cruise has some basis..."

She turned abruptly to me.

"Robert, there is something very stinky about this. I haven't been cruising since yesterday and you know what it reminds me of?" She suspended her voice and looked at me questioningly.

I shook my head.

"Don't you know? Really???" she was genuinely amazed. "Even the timing is right!"

"What are you talking about?"

"April one thousand nine hundred and twelve..." she said quietly.

I understood.

"Captain, you are exaggerating a little," I said in a reassuring tone. "Our "Nugget" is not the "Titanic", and after all, at that time they were up against a powerful high and smooth ocean with an ice field and floating growlers. If we are threatened by anything, it's the ten ahead of us..." I pointed with a movement of my head to the piled up waves and ominous clouds above. Are we storming?

She sighed and nodded.

"May you be right," she muttered, extending her hand. "And by the way, we've started to address each other by first names. Call me Birgit."

"Robert, Bobik for friends," I shook her hand. She raised her eyebrows.

"Bo... bik? And what is that? Bob?"

I smiled.

"It's in Polish. That's what they called me at school and at home. It's a kind of... an inflection of the name Robert."

She shook my hand.

"OK, I understand," she said. "But we'll drink bruderszaft after the storm."

"Sure, as soon as we survive this carousel."

"We will survive," she replied, "I intend to be buried at my home in Skagen..."

April 14, 10:00 a.m. AST, Atlantic

I woke up with a headache. The pressure must have been low and I guess we were in the eye of the low, because it swung as if less and the wind quieted down. The sun was shining behind the porthole.

"Well, yes," I thought, "in a few hours it will start to swing again, but the wind will hit from the other side..."

I washed up and embraced, and then went down to the mess hall. Della Roget was there. She was standing almost in the middle and balancing the rocking of the ship with her hips. A coffee mug was fuming in her hands.

"Hi," I said. "How was the night?"

She croaked.

"It could sway less," she muttered, "and by the way, did you have an evening visit?"

"And yet!" I thought. Ursula was not lying.

"I had, that little Ursula, you know the blonde one," I said.

Della smiled and looked at me expectantly.

"And what was next?" She asked looking at me investigatively.

"Well, nothing," I replied in cold blood, "she started to rant something about being a robot, so I sent her to hell. Some idiocy..." I waved my hand.

I took a mug and poured myself coffee from the hanging loo. Della sighed.

"Bob, we have a problem," she said, "it was no idiocy. This is how it really is."

"If they are robots, I don't understand why they confided in us and why they tried to convince us that..."

"First Law of Robotics," Della got into my words. "A robot cannot do harm to a human being."

"Well, okay, but..."

"This is AI, artificial intelligence, and therefore they think like humans."

"Are you suggesting that they think like humans?"

She smiled.

"I know that..." she said with emphasis on the word "know".

The caffeine finally made my gray cells work.

"Good heavens!" I almost exclaimed, "you mean they intend to prevent us from this operation because of the cargo we will take with us from the States?"

She nodded.

"Two thousand seven hundred and fifty grams of dicalcium trioxide or $251Cf_2O_3$ is the material for a Hiroshima–type bomb. Or material for fuel cells. Or."

"Sure, only to make a bomb out of it you need metallic californium well and it would be the most expensive nuclear bomb in the world. This is about something else."

"But what?"

"Californ is an excellent source of neutrons and alpha particles, so maybe that's it?"

She nodded while looking through the porthole.

"Maybe..." she muttered. "Either way, I don't like it very much."

"Oh, I have one more question: did he want to make love to you?"

She laughed.

"Yes, but the funniest thing about it is that he didn't have anything to...!"

10:20 p.m. NDT, Atlantic

First, the sense of balance reacted. It sensed that something had changed and in the immediate environment. After a long moment, the brain, still stupefied by sleep, startled. The rocking ceased. The ship stood or moved on an even keel. The atomic drive worked silently, the drive transmission mechanisms were almost perfectly dampened. The Californian Nugget would be a very difficult target to target even for the sonars of an ultra-modern submarine. I rose and sat down on my berth. The remnant of the sleepy fog drifted away into the distance. I stood up and peeked through the porthole.

Outside was the pitch black of night. In the sky the stars shone crystal-clear. The water was smooth, like a table covered with a black tablecloth. The stars were reflected in the water as smooth as a pond. Everything looked so unreal like a theater decoration. Something didn't play, or reminded me, but I didn't know what yet. And suddenly what I had been subconsciously waiting for happened. The intercom signal sounded.

"Mr. Chief, I'm sorry if I woke you up," I heard the voice of Della Roget, "come to the bridge. I'm asking you... It's urgent."

In her voice I sensed astonishment.

And fear.

"Well I think it's urgent," I thought. Something unusual was happening. Della was scared of something, otherwise she wouldn't have called me but our captain. That is, she wanted to consult me first.

I dressed in a flash and took a puff from the cabinet. Then I quickly left the cabin and headed upstairs. As I walked, I looked at the ocean, which breathed an icy calm. There was something disturbing about it. Some undefined menace lurked among these unprecedentedly calm waters. That deep, tarry blackness of sky and water that was not illuminated by the silvery light of myriads of stars. I entered the bridge, Della was already waiting for me... She was anxious, her irritation was evident.

"What is going on?" I asked, embracing the situation with my eyes.

She handed me a mug of coffee. Its smell had a calming effect on me.

"Tell me what happened," I encouraged her.

"Something strange happened," she said, "first I noticed some light in the water. Then all of a sudden the storm calmed down and at the same time all the electronics on the bridge went down. Actually, the GPS, communications and all satellite Internet links went down. It all happened virtually simultaneously."

I took a huge sip of mocha and my breath was taken away.

"What did you add there?" I asked when I caught my breath.

"Fifty percent of the benefits of medicine," she replied with a slight smile, "we will need it."

"Cognac?" I asked disgusted, "probably not..."

She laughed despite the tension.

"For you Jackie Daniels," she replied in an innocent face. "I would never pour you cognac in my life..."

I breathed fire like a dragon. There must have been a hundred there. At least. But it was necessary to return to reality.

"What do you think about this?" With a movement of my head I pointed to the dashboard, "what could have happened?"

"Basically, the only thing that fell was that which has to do with satellites," she said. "It looks as if all navigation and communications satellites disappeared. But this is a small thing. After all, we were sailing in a storm. It was a ten. We had a low, almost nine hundred and thirty hectopascals, and now?"

I looked at the meteo data panel. The green digits were blazing and forming a number. I felt the overhang of the copra.

"And what do you think?" Della looked into my face satisfied with the reaction I manifested.

"Well no," I said bewildered, "I don't think that's possible, one thousand and thirty-eight? And how much was in the eye?"

I asked about the pressure in the eye of the atmospheric low, which until a few days ago was a tropical storm in the Bahamas and Bermuda.

"As far as I remember, it was seven hundred and fifty-nine...," she said uncertainly.

"Wave?"

"Almost nine, the wind also something around that..."

"And the temperature?" I asked, because something was dawning on me that this could be some kind of key to this riddle.

"It was plus twelve and plus ten, and now we have... Oh mother!" groaned Della with horror, "now we have minus two air and zero water!"

In fact, it was very strange. Admittedly, not far away ran the cold Labrador Current, but this would not give such a drastic change in air and water temperature. Something completely incomprehensible was happening.

"What about the light?" I asked, as I recalled its strange presence.

"It was in the water. I noticed it about two or three cables to starboard. Then it passed in front of the bow and changed direction to one hundred eighty degrees, straight south. And that's when…"

I nodded my head.

"The sea calmed down and the clouds disappeared from the sky?"

"That's exactly right," she confirmed. "And on top of that, all the navigation fell down and I basically don't know where we are."

10:25 p.m. NDT, Atlantic

"Give a little forward," I said. "Course two four five."

Her fingers ran across the computer keyboard. White and orange lights shone on the panels, and after a moment flashed green. The deck vibrated slightly underfoot.

"Did you look at what we have on the radar?" I asked.

She shook her head that she hadn't.

I looked at the meteoradar screen. It was clear, which was natural. There was no cloud within miles. The main radar was set to a range of thirty miles. To starboard at a distance of eight miles there was a ship of some sort going by. On the starboard side slightly behind was going something very large. The flash was sharp and clear.

"A cruise ship," I thought. "But why so fast?"

Behind it, in front of the bow, one could see a shimmering ribbon stretching for miles along and across.

"What's that?" I heard Della's voice behind my ear, who over my shoulder was looking at the monitor.

"The ice field," I replied, "is drifting south. And these brighter spots are icebergs, or rather growlers."

"But this is some iceberg at half past eleven?" Della pointed to a brighter flash in the southwest.

"Probably, but a small one," I waved my hand. "It is off our course."

"Do you know what puzzles me?" Della put down her cup. "The fact that I haven't seen a single plane here, and yet there should be a whole lot of them. From Europe to America and to Iceland…"

She was right. There was not a single plane in sight. It was very strange.

"Are we waking up Birgit?" She asked.

"And why should we? After all, nothing is happening, there is no direct or even indirect threat to the ship…" I shrugged.

"Well, yes, you are right," Della looked at the radar screen. The green dot on the port side was burning more and more intensely.

"What kind of ship is this?" she became interested.

"I don't know," I replied, "it doesn't have a transponder…"

"The other one doesn't either."

"Indeed, you are right," I replied.

This was also strange, because for several years all ships had transponders installed, as did aircraft. This was used to identify the vessels. This large cruise ship did not have this device, and that was strange. It shouldn't be like this... I decided to take a look at the ship on optical, it should be visible by now.

I reached for the binoculars and put them to my eyes. For a while I swept the horizon with my eyes. Della stood next to me with the other binoculars in her hand.

"Do you see anything?" She asked.

"No," I replied.

This was also strange. The radar indicated that the ship on the left should be visible, and in the meantime the horizon was pitch black, and in that bottomless blackness stars smoldered above it. Silvery and motionless.

"Amazing transparency of the air," said Della, "you can see all of them up to the sixth stellar magnitude and even below... Wait a minute!... I don't understand something here..."

"What?" I asked.

"Well, look. There is Mars, in the Gemini. Jupiter in Serpent or Scorpio. And Saturn on the border of Taurus and Aries."

"That is, either the alignment of the planets with respect to Earth has changed, which we rule out, or..."

"...the time has changed..." Della finished it in a whisper.

Fear lurked in her eyes.

"No way," I muttered, "empty threats, far away to the Bermuda Triangle…"

Suddenly a strange thought dawned on me. I pressed the intercom button to the engine room. Silence answered me.

"Who is in the machine?" I asked for formality, as I was reminded of the schedule. Herbert Smythe should be there.

"Herbert," replied Della.

"He does not answer," I replied. And anticipating Della's answer I added, "I'll go see what's going on there. It seems to me that we have another problem…"

11:30 p.m. NDT, Atlantic

We had another problem, because all the robots died. Not literally, but their "brains" were off, because the power supply itself was working. I remembered what Ursula had told me. The activation and control signal had disappeared, which caused them to shut down. That, at least, I understood. Either the robot control center went down, or the satellite transmitting the signal went down. But why? – For this I had no concept. I returned to the bridge.

"All the robots are dead," I made a throat–cutting gesture, "there is no guiding signal."

"This is what I might have expected…" she whispered, "are we waking up the captain?"

I shrugged.

"No way, there's nothing going on yet, let she get some sleep… And besides, we don't need the robots for now anyway, so we'll handle it."

We fell silent looking at the shrill black ocean and the sky full of stars.

"Well, I can finally see it," Della pointed in my direction to a speck of light visible on the horizon.

I reached for the binoculars and looked in the indicated direction. The spot of light turned into an elongated line of lights.

"A large craft, but..." Della moved the binoculars away from her eyes.

"But what?" I asked.

"Nothing, it looks strange... Like a large cunard steamer."

I shrugged.

"There aren't any like that anymore. Or at least they do not sail," I replied.

Della looked into my eyes.

"Well, and that one, there? A specter from the past?" she raised her eyebrows solemnly.

"Well, call them through the UKF," I suggested, "maybe they will speak up?"

"Do you think?"

"We can try, maybe they are on the intercept..." I shrugged.

The crazy night was going on, and if you had to have fun, it was good and to the end.

Della turned on the port UKF station. All we heard in the speaker was a sunny hum.

"Californian Nugget to ship going course two–seven–zero, over!"

Silence answered us. Della repeated the call several times, but to no avail.

"I think they're off," she muttered while turning off the device.

At that moment it was as if a flip–flop in my brain had been unlocked.

"Let's enter the data into the computer regarding the position of the planets and figure out when the configuration we have overhead took place, OK?"

She nodded wordlessly and began pasting the data into the navigation computer.

And I again watched the strange ship following a course of two hundred and seventy, directly to the west. And slowly a terrible suspicion grew in me... This ship... Those brightly lit decks, those four tall chimneys, from three of them billowed clouds of dark smoke obscuring the stars. I felt an unpleasant thrill... But it was absolutely unbelievable...

"Great heavens!" I heard behind me, "no, I think it's impossible!"

"What is impossible?" I turned to Della. On her face now I saw surprise and horror.

"Mr. Chief, this position of the planets and the moon was about the middle of April one thousand nine hundred and twelve...!"

I nodded my head. The terrible truth had finally reached me and found confirmation.

"You are right, Madam First," I replied in a completely calm voice, to which I tried to give a soothing sound, "we fell into a hole in time, as you suggested. So..."

I walked over to the main radar monitor and pointed my finger at the bright dots and dashes.

"...so," I picked up, "that ship to the north is the SS Californian, and that one is the RMS Titanic, and that dot, that's the iceberg it's going to run against... Well, and the ice barrier and Mt. Temple behind it, still five minutes away. We have only four miles to them now."

11:40 p.m. AST, Atlantic

We were silent looking into each other's eyes. Slowly the terrible truth was coming to her. Della was breathing spasmodically. She was terrified and did not hide it.

"Chief, what do we do? It will be necessary to warn these people!"

"It's not possible," I replied. "They are seven kilometers from us, but neither they have even a UKF, and we have at least an aldis."

"But we can swim up there, and..."

"We can't. If only because we can't change reality. It has already happened, and we can't get involved, do you understand? Our ship is the X-ship that was seen simultaneously from the sinking Titanic and from the Californian standing adrift!"

"But in five minutes..."

"I know," I replied, "in five minutes there will be a collision."

We looked into each other's eyes.

"We have to do something," she said, "we have to!"

I shook my head.

"We will not do anything, do you understand?"

"But why?" she exclaimed with pain in her voice, "why?"

"It's obvious," I replied calmly but emphatically, "IT HAS ALREADY HAPPENED. Look at it like a Cameron or Negulesco movie. Do you understand? WE CAN'T HELP THEM ANYMORE! And for now we are standing adrift. I have a feeling that what threw us into this hole in time will pull us out of it back to the 21st century..."

Della stomached the idea in silence. She didn't understand that any intervention by us would end up with something that no one could predict. The butterfly effect – each change in THIS Reality caused a sequence of changes that completely altered OUR Reality... Well, what if the Guggenheim and Astor had survived the disaster, and the Titanic had sailed all the way to New York? The consequences of that would have been incalculable.

"I wonder if there would have been a Great War?" she broke the silence. Slowly, she bucked up herself.

"Maybe yes, maybe no," I muttered, "I don't know. Perhaps the US would not have participated in this war, or maybe it would have participated from the very beginning..."

Our gazes crossed on the radiolocator screen.

11:45 p.m. NDT, Atlantic – N 41°46' – W 050°14'

We watched as the two bright spots – the larger and luminous one marking the Titanic and the darker and fuzzier one marking the growler slowly came together for a moment, and then separated again.

"It happened," I said quietly.

Three and a half miles away, a drama began to unfold over which we had no control. We could do nothing, just watch.

And it was terrible. I turned on the radio station and set it to self-tuning. I remembered that the Titanic's radio station was operating at three hundred and six hundred meters – five hundred and one thousand kilohertz, and after a while we heard the characteristic strong Morse beeping from the receiver.

– /-.-./--.-/-../ - CQD - pause and - /--/--./-.--/ – MGY. A call for help and the Titanic code.

"Why isn't it send an SOS?" asked Della looking through binoculars at the distant transatlantic.

"Wait," I replied, "Phillips and Bride will recall that there is an SOS signal in use."

We said nothing. Indeed, after a few minutes, the SOS and position flowed from the loudspeaker.

"Forty-one, forty-four north; fifty, twenty-four west," said Della, "after all, it's..."

"Yes, I know," I answered her, "Captain Smith gave Phillips the wrong position, and only after a few minutes corrected it. Oh, now..."

From the chirp of dots and dashes we read the new position.

"Forty-one, forty-six north and fifty-fourteen west," said Della.

Silence fell again.

April 15, 02:20 a.m. NDT, Atlantic

"It's over," said Della looking south through the binoculars. "The end. Damn it!"

I sighed. I felt despicable, but I couldn't change anything.

"Let's move from here," I said, "a little ahead, course two five zero."

Della entered the command into the navigation computer. So much for the fact that it had no radio connections to other external devices. The deck vibrated under our feet. I threw the Titanic one last look and...

"Madam first? Did you see that?"

Some greenish light was approaching us from the south. It was gliding under the black water and advancing in a north-northeast direction.

"That would be it," Della regained her resonance, "is it some kind of submarine?"

"It looks like it," I muttered.

"But in one thousand nine hundred and twelve and THAT big????"

In fact, this thing was going just below the surface of the water shining some kind of searchlight, while some two hundred meters behind it boiled water grinding with two propellers.

"Damn, it looks like a Red October, a Typhoon-class missile ship..."

"But it doesn't have a conning tower, or rather it does, like some U-boat, one with such a basket..."

She was right. When the ship entered our keelwater at once the light began to fade.

"It's sinking," she whispered. "And now what? Torpedo into the side?"

"Oh, probably not..." I said with absolute certainty. I already knew what was happening. "Better hold on!"

What followed was something terrible. At the same time, the stars disappeared and the sky showed clouds illuminated by the ghostly greenish light of the moon. The wind and the wave hit, the deck jerked beneath our feet, like a vicious horse. I looked at the GPS navigator screen – the position digits glowed a reassuring green. The radio sounded a cacophony of voices and signals. The radar screen was covered with concentric streaks of waves. Everything was back to normal – if a severe storm could be called any kind of normal...

The End

www.ingramcontent.com/pod-product-compliance
Lightning Source LLC
Chambersburg PA
CBHW032056230426
43662CB00035B/432